Understanding Copyright Law:
A Beginner's Guide

by
Linda A. Tancs

Oceana's Legal Almanac Series:
Law for the Layperson

Oceana®
NEW YORK

OXFORD
UNIVERSITY PRESS

*Oxford University Press, Inc., publishes works that further Oxford University's
objective of excellence in research, scholarship, and education.*

Copyright © 2009 by Linda A. Tancs
Published by Oxford University Press, Inc.
198 Madison Avenue, New York, New York 10016

Oxford is a registered trademark of Oxford University Press
Oceana is a registered trademark of Oxford University Press, Inc.

Library of Congress Cataloging-in-Publication Data

Tancs, Linda A.
    Understanding copyright law : a beginner's guide / by Linda A. Tancs.
        p. cm. — (Oceana's legal almanac series. Law for the layperson)
    Includes bibliographical references.
    ISBN 978-0-19-973022-3 ((hardback) : alk. paper)
    1. Copyright—United States. 2. Copyright. I. Title.
    KF2995.T365 2009
    346.7304'82—dc22   2009026296

Note to Readers:

This publication is designed to provide accurate and authoritative information in regard to
the subject matter covered. It is based upon sources believed to be accurate and reliable and
is intended to be current as of the time it was written. It is sold with the understanding that
the publisher is not engaged in rendering legal, accounting, or other professional services. If
legal advice or other expert assistance is required, the services of a competent professional
person should be sought. Also, to confirm that the information has not been affected or
changed by recent developments, traditional legal research techniques should be used, including checking primary sources where appropriate.

*(Based on the Declaration of Principles jointly adopted by a Committee of the
American Bar Association and a Committee of Publishers and Associations.)*

> You may order this or any other Oxford University Press publication
> by visiting the Oxford University Press website at www.oup.com

In memory of uncle Ron, my best writing instructor

-and-

In gratitude to my husband Barry for his constant
support and encouragement

Table of Contents

ABOUT THE AUTHOR

Linda A. Tancs has extensive experience as a transactional attorney in both corporate and private practice, concentrating in intellectual property, entertainment, information technology, e-commerce and general business matters. Ms. Tancs holds a Juris Doctor degree, with honors, from Seton Hall University School of Law in Newark, New Jersey, where she won first place for a meritorious paper on copyright law submitted in ASCAP's Nathan Burkan Memorial Competition. She is admitted to practice in several jurisdictions in the United States, as well as internationally.

Ms. Tancs managed the worldwide trademark portfolio of leading industrial and consumer products companies and regularly counseled in-house attorneys, executives and small business owners on trademark, trade dress, advertising, domain name issues and product packaging. Ms. Tancs is the author of *Understanding Trademark Law: A Beginner's Guide*, another legal almanac in the series.

Ms. Tancs has held leadership positions in bar associations, taught legal courses at two colleges and has authored several articles for legal periodicals and general interest magazines. She operates her own consulting practice in the field of brand identification and management and offers dispute resolution services in the nature of mediation. She is also certified as a coach in the fields of personal, executive and organizational coaching by New York University and works with both lawyers and non-lawyers to meet their personal and professional goals.

INTRODUCTION

This text explores the mechanics of registering, maintaining and enforcing copyrights. Copyright is a form of legal protection for literary, performance and visual arts-based works, among other things. In fiscal year 2007, the United States Copyright Office registered 526,378 claims to copyright. Copyright protection can be secured under the laws of many other nations as well. This book will emphasize the process for registering a copyright with the United States Copyright Office.

The reader will be introduced to the nature and functions of intellectual property law as it relates to copyright. Intellectual property law is an evolving body of law that seeks to create a fair balance between the privilege to enter markets and compete and the privilege to realize the full value of one's own goods and services without unfair competition. Through this book, the reader will gain an understanding of the types of property subject to copyright; how to protect and use copyrighted property; how to complete a copyright application; pre- and post-registration procedures; how to monetize copyright assets; infringement issues; and copyright in the digital age.

The appendices, together with the bibliography and recommended reading, provide readers of this almanac with relevant statutes and other information to further the reader's knowledge of the matters discussed in this book. The glossary contains a summary of key terms defined throughout the book.

The information presented in this book is intended for general information purposes only and does not constitute the provision of legal services or advice. If such services or advice are required, the assistance of an appropriate professional should be sought.

CHAPTER 1:
THE NATURE AND FUNCTION OF
A COPYRIGHT

THE HISTORY OF COPYRIGHT

Article 1, Section 8, Clause 8 of the United States Constitution autho-rizes Congress to "secur(e) for limited Times to Authors . . . the exclu-sive Right to their respective Writings. . . ." Pursuant to its constitutional authority, Congress passed the first copyright law in 1790, modeled after England's Statute of Anne. The new law secured for authors the exclusive right to exploit their works in the nature of maps, books and charts for both an original term and a renewal term of fourteen years. Since then, federal copyright law has undergone many revisions, such as an expansion of the scope of copyrightable property, the inclusion of the right to federal jurisdiction over claims of infringement, and an extension of the term of copyright. In particular, the Copyright Act has undergone two significant amendments through the enactment of the Copyright Act of 1909 (1909 Act) and the current law, the Copyright Act of 1976 (1976 Act). This text will focus on the provisions of the 1976 Act, and section references provided in this Almanac will relate to that act unless otherwise specified.

The 1909 Act was enacted at the behest of President Theodore Roosevelt, who recognized the need to modernize the law. The result was legisla-tion that: (i) increased the term of copyright for published works to an initial term of 28 years and a like renewal term; (ii) conferred common law (i.e., state law) protection on unpublished works; and (iii) required a copyright notice to prevent the work from entering the public domain— that is, to prevent it from losing copyright protection, thereby becoming available to everyone.

Although various revisions were made to the 1909 Act to keep up with changing technologies, the next major overhaul of copyright law occurred with the passage of the 1976 Act (effective as of January 1, 1978). Unlike the 1909 Act, the 1976 Act confers federal protection on both published and unpublished works and does not require the use of a copyright notice (discussed further in the section below entitled **Notice of Copyright**). The new law also specifies that copyright subsists in a work from the moment it is created, which is defined as its fixation in a tangible medium of expression, such as a writing for a literary work or a sound recording of music. The term of protection has been likewise modified to life *plus* 70 years for individual authors and 95 years or more for corporate and anonymous works. The duration of copyright will be discussed in more detail in the section below entitled **Duration of Copyright**.

In some instances, the provisions of both acts collide. For example, a work in its renewal term under the 1909 Act and subsisting as of January 1, 1978 under the 1976 Act (as originally enacted) was granted an additional renewal term of 19 years, yielding a total term of protection of 75 years. Similarly, a work still in its initial term on January 1, 1978 was granted a renewal term of 47 years rather than 28 years, provided that the copyright claimant filed for renewal of the initial term as required under the the 1909 Act. These additional terms were further enhanced by 20 years after passage of the Sonny Bono Copyright Extension Act of 1998, discussed further below.

Appendix 1, "Copyright Act of 1790," and Appendix 2, "Copyright Act of 1909," of this Almanac provide the text of the copyright law enacted in 1790 and 1909, respectively.

WHAT IS A COPYRIGHT?

The Constitution does not define the term *copyright*. Moreover, as noted above, the nature of copyrightable matter has changed legislatively from a published work under the 1909 Act to one that enjoys protection from the moment of its creation in a tangible way under current law. To the extent that *copyright* can be defined, section 102(a) of the 1976 Act sets forth two criteria for a work to enjoy federal copyright protection: the work must be original and it must be fixed.

Originality is often referred to as the touchstone of copyright. In fact, over a century ago, the U.S. Supreme Court decided that the Constitution's use of the word *authors* limited copyright to an author's original intellectual conceptions. Sometimes misunderstood, the concept of originality does not mean that the work must be commercially novel or unique or even that the work be more than a *de minimis* expression of creativity. Rather, it means that the work must simply be original *to its author*. As a result, several television networks can parlay the idea of a nanny giving child-rearing tips into a reality show without infringing each other's works. So long as an idea is independently arrived at by its author, the same concept may find multiple means of expression in multiple formats.

The format giving rise to copyrightable expression addresses the statutory requirement that the work be fixed in a tangible medium of expression. It must be tangible in the sense of a writing or a recording, for example. Also, according to section 102(a), the medium may exist now or come into existence in the future and should communicate the work directly or with the aid of a machine or device. The machine or device requirement expressly overrules an earlier decision of the Supreme Court made under the 1909 Act that would have invalidated works embodied in a medium requiring perception by a machine or other device (such as computer programs).

Not all works are capable of federal copyright protection. For instance, works that remain unfixed in a tangible medium of expression (such as an oral statement or account) are not subject to the 1976 Act and may therefore be protected under common law according to section 301 of the Act. Similarly, section 105 precludes copyright protection for any work of the U.S. Government although it is permitted to take ownership of copyrights through assignments, bequests or otherwise. The governmental preclusion as to outright ownership differs from other countries such as the United Kingdom, where government works (e.g., those produced by ministers and civil servants) are protected under Crown copyright. Furthermore, the Code of Federal Regulations (CFR), the federal rules implementing copyright registration and procedure, provides that, among other things, titles and other short phrases are not copyrightable.

Provided a work is eligible for protection and the originality and fixation requirements are met, several kinds of works qualify for protection under federal law. These include literary works, musical works, performing arts, visual arts, audiovisual works, sound recordings and architectural works, including derivative works and compilations of all the foregoing. This Almanac will address the registration requirements for literary works, visual arts, performing arts and sound recordings in Chapter 2, "The Application Process," of this Almanac.

Appendix 3, "Copyrightable Subject Matter," of this Almanac contains provisions from sections 102 and 103 of the 1976 Act covering copyrightable subject matter.

Appendix 4, "Material not Subject to Copyright," of this Almanac sets forth uncopyrightable subject matter as discussed in the CFR.

THE FUNCTION OF A COPYRIGHT

In the simplest sense, a copyright guarantees certain rights to its owner. Section 106 of the 1976 Act confers upon a copyright owner the exclusive right to exercise what is often referred to as a bundle of rights. These are the rights of reproduction, adaptation, distribution, public performance (including, in the case of sound recordings, the right to perform the copyrighted work publicly by means of a digital audio transmission) and public display. Each of these rights may be exercised by the copyright owner to the exclusion of all others unless a license is issued to a third party, and a right may be transferred in whole or in part. These rights, however, are not absolute. For example, under certain circumstances fair use may be made of a copyrighted work. The concept of fair use will be discussed in greater detail in Chapter 5, "Infringement Issues," of this Almanac in the section entitled **Defenses**. Each right, together with some select limitations, is discussed below.

The Right of Reproduction

The right of reproduction—a *copy right*—is the cornerstone of copyright ownership. Set forth in section 106(1), it confers upon the copyright owner the right to reproduce the copyrighted work in copies or phonorecords. The term *copies* is defined in section 101 as the material object in which a work is fixed by any method now known or later developed. Therefore, the owner's right of reproduction extends to any medium which may hereafter be devised. Phonorecords are likewise defined as material objects in which sounds are fixed in any manner now developed or otherwise. Phonorecords are more commonly known as cassette tapes, CDs or LPs.

Despite the broad scope of the reproduction right, section 108 provides limitations in favor of libraries or archives. Specifically, such institutions will not be deemed to be in violation of the copyright owner's right to reproduce the work in copies provided that: (i) only one copy of the work is reproduced at a time; (ii) there is no direct or indirect commercial advantage; (iii) its collections are open to the public or other researchers; and (iv) the reproduced work retains any copyright notice or, in the absence of a notice, contains a legend or warning concerning the potential copyright in the work. Another limitation on exclusive copy rights is found in section 117, which allows the owner of a copy of a computer program to make additional copies of the program for certain activities such as archiving, machine maintenance and repair and to aid in the operation of a machine. Limitations apply as well to phonorecords. Specifically, section 115 provides a framework for compulsory licensing, allowing individuals to reproduce phonorecords for the purpose of distributing them to the public for private use. Additionally, public broadcasting companies are granted rights in section 118 to reproduce copies or phonorecords of transmission programs.

The Right of Adaptation

Section 106(2) grants the copyright owner the right to prepare derivative works. Section 101 defines a derivative work as one that is based upon a pre-existing work and recasts, transforms or adapts that work. Examples of derivative works include motion picture adaptations, abridgments, translations, musical arrangements and art reproductions. The computer program provision set forth above in section 117 is a key limitation on the copyright owner's exclusive right of adaptation. Specifically enacted to address the needs of computer users, this provision was originally drafted in 1980 by a presidential commission, CONTU (National Commission on New Technological Uses of Copyrighted Works). Its provisions concerning computer maintenance and repair were subsequently added in 1998 by the Computer Maintenance Competition Assurance Act.

The Right of Distribution

A copyright owner has the right to control the first distribution of the material embodiment of a work to the public. According to section 106(3), distribution includes a sale or other transfer of ownership (even gratuitously), or a rental, lease or lending. The right of distribution is distinguishable from the right of reproduction because the distribution right relates solely to the transfer of possession of the copyrighted article and not to any copying of it. An important limitation to this right, however, is set forth in section 109. Known as the first sale doctrine, section 109(a) provides that, once a first sale has been made, the owner of a copy of a work or a phonorecord can sell or otherwise dispose of possession of that article without the authority of the copyright owner. In other words, such an action would not constitute copyright infringement. Accordingly, the owner of a book may sell or otherwise dispose of that article without violating the copyright owner's underlying rights. It is important to note that the doctrine applies in favor of *lawful owners* of copies or phonorecords (i.e., not pirated material). The doctrine, moreover, does not apply to situations where possession arises from rental, lease, loan or other activities not giving rise to a transfer of ownership. In these cases, any further distribution would be allowed only with consent of the copyright owner.

Despite the copyright owner's limitations on controlling secondary markets for works under the first sale doctrine, Congress has created exceptions to the doctrine from time to time in response to commercial considerations. For instance, under section 109(b), amended by the Record Rental Amendment Act of 1984, the lawful owner of a phonorecord (e.g., a record store merchant) is prohibited from renting it to third parties for direct or indirect commercial gain. The purpose of the act was to restrict record store buyers from renting phonorecords and recording the contents, thereby eliminating the need to purchase a phonorecord. This behavior had the obvious effect of displacing sales that would have accrued to the benefit of the copyright owner of the sound recording. A similar provision protecting computer programs is likewise found in section 109(b) by virtue of the Computer Software Rental Amendments Act of 1990. Another important restriction on the first sale doctrine is set forth in section 602, which protects the copyright owner against the illegal importation of goods.

The Right of Public Performance

Section 106(4) grants a copyright owner the right to publicly perform literary, musical, dramatic, choreographic and audiovisual works as well as pantomimes and motion pictures. Section 101 defines a public performance as one which takes place publicly or among the public at large or a transmission of a performance publicly or to the public at large by means of a device or process, regardless whether the transmission is received by all persons at the same place or at the same time. Moreover, performing a work is defined as a means to recite, render, play, dance or act it, including the display of images for motion pictures or other audiovisual works. Contrary to the 1909 Act, the current public performance right is not limited to performances for profit.

However, current law does provide many exemptions to the copyright holder's public performance right in favor of non-profit organizations and activities. For instance, section 110 exempts face-to-face teaching activities as well as instructional broadcasting so long as each activity takes place in non-profit institutions in a place devoted to teaching such as a classroom. However, the broadcasting, or transmission, exemption is limited to non-dramatic musical or literary works. Another exemption in section 111 gives common carriers (excluding cable systems) the right to pick up programs originated by others. As a result, a hotel, apartment house or similar establishment can make transmissions to guests in private lodgings. Other provisions, such as section 116, provide for a voluntary licensing arrangement between jukebox operators and copyright owners of non-dramatic musical works.

Perhaps not surprisingly, it can be cumbersome for the holder of a per-formance right related to musical works to protect and enforce those rights unaided. Unless an exemption applies, the performance of these works (such as live performances) represents a source of revenue for the copyright holder. To assist copyright owners in the administration of licenses and revenues for non-exempt public performances, perform-ing rights societies were founded. The oldest society, the American Society of Composers, Authors and Publishers (ASCAP), was founded in 1914. ASCAP, together with BMI (Broadcast Music, Inc.) and SESAC (so named originally for the Society of European Stage, Authors and Composers), represent songwriters and publishers and their right to be compensated for having their music performed in public. Among other things, they negotiate blanket licenses with the users of non-dramatic musical works so that they can legally play any song in the society's portfolio. Each of these performing rights societies also distributes col-lected fees among its members. Performing rights and collections for digital audio transmissions of sound recordings will be discussed in Chapter 6, "Internet Issues regarding Copyrights," of this Almanac in the section entitled **Digital Performance Right in Sound Recordings Act**.

The Right of Public Display

Like the performance right, the copyright owner's display right applies to *public* exhibitions. Section 106(5) grants copyright owners a right of public display for literary, musical, dramatic, choreographic, pictorial, graphic, or sculptural works as well as pantomimes and motion picture images. Section 101 defines *display* as the means used to show a copy of a work, either directly or by means of a film, slide, television image or any other device or process. In the case of a motion picture or other audiovisual work, a display constitutes the showing of individual images nonsequentially. The right of public display was not granted in earlier copyright acts.

The limitations set out in section 110 above apply equally to the right of public display. Moreover, section 109(c) provides the owner of a copy of a work the right to publicly display it where the copy is located with-out the consent of the copyright owner. This exemption further provides that if the work is displayed indirectly (i.e., by using a film projector), then only one image at a time can be displayed. Another exemption regarding the display right is found in section 113(c), which provides that if a work has been lawfully reproduced as a design for useful arti-cles, then the copyright owner cannot prevent the display of pictures or photos of such articles in connection with advertisements or commen-taries related to the display of the articles. By way of illustration, the designer of a car hood ornament could not, under section 113(c), prevent its display in a car advertisement.

Appendix 5, "Exclusive Rights in Copyrighted Works and Limitations," of this Almanac contains the statutory reference to the exclusive rights discussed above as well as the select limitations addressed herein.

NOTICE OF COPYRIGHT

Section 401(a) of the 1976 Act provides a copyright owner with the option of placing a notice of copyright on a published work. Although, as evidenced in the marketplace, most copyright owners elect to put notice of copyright on their works, the once mandatory nature of the notice requirement under the 1976 Act was abrogated with the passage of The Berne Convention Implementation Act of 1988 (the Berne Act). As a result of the Berne Act, the form of copyright notice commonly seen today was rendered optional as of March 1, 1989, the effective date of the law. The object of the act was to bring the United States into conformance with the laws of other nations wherein the lack of copyright notice does not result in a potential forfeiture of a work's copyright. Prior to implementation of the Berne Act, section 401(a) required that a notice of copyright be placed on all publicly distributed copies of a work. Unlike the 1909 Act (where a failure to provide the required notice resulted in automatic forfeiture of the copyright), the 1976 Act contained provisions to protect against forfeiture—provided that, among other things, the copyright owner published a small amount of copies without the notice or made a reasonable attempt to add the notice to previously distributed copies once the omission was discovered. Following Congress's amendment regarding the formalities of copyright notice, the United States became an adherent to the oldest multilateral copyright convention, the Berne Convention for the Protection of Literary and Artistic Works (known as the Berne Convention).

Despite the lack of formality required under the Berne Convention, section 401(b) prescribes the precise form of notice that must be used if a copyright owner elects to publish a work with notice of copyright. Such a notice consists of three elements: the copyright symbol or an acceptable variant, the year of first publication of the work, and the name of the copyright owner. With respect to the first element, it is acceptable to use the letter C in a circle, thus: ©, or the word "Copyright," or the abbreviation "Copr." With respect to phonorecords, the appropriate symbol is simply the letter P in a circle rather than the letter C. In some instances, the second element (the year of first publication) may be omitted, such as with the use of pictorial, graphic or sculptural works that are reproduced on stationery, jewelry, dolls, and toys. With respect to the last element, the copyright owner may be an individual or an entity. An individual may be referred to by a pen name if that name is widely recognized by the public as the name of the owner; initials may also be used. In addition to the above formalities, the notice is also required to be rendered conspicuously so as to give reasonable notice to third parties of the claim of copyright. Indeed, the evidentiary weight of a proper notice as to form and placement is substantial; it will cut off any defenses of a violator as to innocent infringement. Therefore, the notice is commonly used notwithstanding its optional nature.

Sometimes an additional form of notice, such as "All Rights Reserved," is used in conjunction with the formalities above. This notice is not required under the 1976 Act; rather, it is commonly used in response to a requirement of a property rights notice under another international convention to which the United States earlier adhered with various Latin American nations, the Buenos Aires Convention. This Convention has been largely superseded by the Berne Convention, which will be discussed in greater detail in Chapter 3, "International Considerations," of this Almanac.

Appendix 6, "Copyright Notice Requirements," of this Almanac contains the notice requirements set out in sections 401 and 402 of the 1976 Act.

DURATION OF COPYRIGHT

As mentioned earlier in this chapter, the duration of copyright under earlier copyright acts varied from a 14-year initial period and 14-year renewal term under the 1790 Act to a 28-year initial period and 28-year renewal term under the 1909 Act. For works created under the 1976 Act, there is no renewal term *per se*. The text below will discuss duration of copyright as it relates to: (i) works created on and after 1978 pursuant to section 302; (ii) special rules for certain sound recordings; and (iii) unfixed works. Moreover, unless a contrary rule applies, the copyright term in any work runs through the end of the calendar year in which it would otherwise expire.

When the 1976 Act was enacted, works by an individual author on or after January 1, 1978 were granted a copyright term consisting of the author's life plus 50 years. For joint works, the term was for the life of the surviving author, plus 50 years. Works for hire (discussed in more detail in Chapter 2, "The Application Process," of this Almanac in the section entitled **Identification of the Author and Nature of Authorship**), anonymous or pseudonymous works were granted a term of 75 years from publication or 100 years from creation, whichever is shorter. These terms were subsequently amended upon passage of the Sonny Bono Copyright Term Extension Act of 1998 (CTEA). So named for the late entertainer and former Congressman Sonny Bono, a supporter of copyright extension, CTEA increased the term of existing copyrights by 20 years. According to the Senate Report accompanying the legislation, the purpose of the act was to harmonize U.S. copyright law with that of the European Union, where copyright terms already extended past the life of the author to ensure that authors (and their heirs) had ample time to benefit fully from the exploitation of their works. As a result of CTEA, each of the terms referenced above is extended by 20 years to (i) life plus 70 years for authors and (ii) a term consisting of 95 years or 120 years for corporate, anonymous and pseudonymous works. In no event does CTEA grant copyright protection to works already in the public domain.

As set forth in section 102, sound recordings are protected by copyright. Specifically, the copyright law was amended in 1971 by way of The Sound Recording Amendment, Pub. L. No. 92-140, 85 Stat. 391 (1971), which granted copyright protection for unpublished and published sound recordings fixed on or after the law's effective date on February 15, 1972. For sound recordings fixed prior to that date, section 301(c) provides that state law will continue to address claims of infringement or other matters until February 15, 2067 (extended from 2047 by CTEA). Thereafter, federal law will preempt any right or remedy under the common law of any state for those earlier sound recordings. In other words, any common law copyright protection will be lost.

Dissimilarly, the owner of any work that does not meet the definition of copyrightable subject matter (i.e., a work that is not fixed in a tangible medium of expression) will continue to enjoy any rights or remedies under state law—that is, federal preemption thereof under section 301(a) will not apply. In effect, this provision grants a perpetual common law copyright to unfixed works.

Appendix 7, "Duration of Copyright," of this Almanac sets out the relevant provisions concerning duration of copyright, including information on pre-1978 works.

DISTINCTIONS AMONG COPYRIGHTS, PATENTS AND TRADEMARKS

Copyrights, patents (as well as trade secrets) and trademarks collectively form the foundation of jurisprudence known as intellectual property law. Notwithstanding their common heritage, each subject area uniquely protects the fruits of one's intellectual labors. Sometimes, however, the scope of copyright law is confused with other areas of intellectual property, and this section will address a few of the common misconceptions. For example, copyrights and trademarks are mistakenly treated interchangeably on occasion, as when a writer uses the © symbol after the title of an article. As noted earlier in this chapter, titles and other short phrases are not copyrightable. Phrases, slogans, titles and words are, however, potentially capable of functioning as trademarks if used in a manner that distinguishes one party's goods or services from those of another. Moreover, it does not follow that if something is copyrighted it is also trademarked. The distinction can perhaps be best understood by examining the popular character Mickey Mouse. As a work of graphic art, Mickey Mouse initially qualified for copyright protection decades ago. Over time, the character also became exclusively associated with The Walt Disney Company by the consuming public. Therefore, the character became a trademark as well; it represents for the public a distinct source (Disney) with which it is associated.

Unlike trademarks or copyrights, patents protect an underlying system or process that is of a novel, non-obvious and useful nature. As set forth earlier in this chapter, copyright is not awarded based on the novelty, imagination or usefulness of a work. Simply stated, copyright protects the expression of an idea; whereas, patent protects the underlying idea itself. This distinction is codified in section 102(b) of the 1976 Act, which states that copyright protection does not extend to any idea, procedure, process, system, method of operation, concept, principle, or discovery. Indeed, these classifications form the basis of the "useful arts" referred to in the foundation for patent protection under Article 1 of the Constitution.

CHAPTER 2:
THE APPLICATION PROCESS

ABOUT THE UNITED STATES COPYRIGHT OFFICE

The U.S. Copyright Office administers a national copyright system and is solely responsible for accepting applications and issuing registrations. Since 1870, copyright functions have been centralized in the Library of Congress (the national library of the United States); in 1897, the Copyright Office became an independent department within the Library of Congress, led by a Register of Copyrights. Located at 101 Independence Avenue, SE, Washington, D.C., the department's staff examines claims to copyright and issues (if the copyright is found to be registrable) certificates of copyright registration. In addition to the copyrightable subject matter set forth in Chapter 1, "The Nature and Function of a Copyright," of this Almanac, the Office examines claims to mask work protection filed under the Semiconductor Chip Protection Act of 1984 and claims in vessel hull designs filed under the 1998 Vessel Hull Design Protection Act. Among its other activities, the Copyright Office maintains for public inspection and searching all deposits, registrations and recordations, provides copyright policy advice to Congress, oversees deposits of copyrighted material with the Library of Congress and administers compulsory and statutory licenses.

BENEFITS OF COPYRIGHT REGISTRATION

As noted in Chapter 1, "The Nature and Function of a Copyright," of this Almanac, the 1976 Act does not require registration of copyright for federal protection to attach. Rather, copyright protection inheres in a work from the moment it is fixed in a tangible medium of expression. However, the benefits of securing a federal registration of copyrightable work are many. For example, section 410(c) provides that a certificate of registration made before or within five years after first publication of a work constitutes *prima facie* evidence of the validity of the copyright (i.e., the ownership thereof and required originality), an important facet in pursuing or defending litigation. Registration (or in some jurisdictions, evidence of a pending registration) is also required in many instances before a claim for infringement can be commenced. Moreover, without registration certain remedies such as statutory damages (i.e., a range of money damages set forth in the copyright law in section 504) and attorneys' fees may be foreclosed. Statutory damages and other remedies will be discussed in greater detail in Chapter 5, "Infringement Issues," of this Almanac, in the section entitled **Remedies**.

COPYRIGHT SEARCHES AND INFORMATION REQUESTS

The Copyright Office provides a wealth of information and reference services to the public. For general information, the public may visit the Copyright Public Information Office or call (202) 707-3000. Moreover, recorded information on copyright is available 24 hours a day, seven days a week, and information specialists are on duty to answer questions in person or by phone or e-mail from 8:30 a.m. to 5:00 p.m., Eastern Time, Monday through Friday, except federal holidays. Written inquiries for materials should be addressed to the Library of Congress, Copyright Office, Publication Section, LM-455, 101 Independence Avenue SE, Washington, DC 20559-6000. The Copyright Office Forms and Publications Hotline number, (202) 707-9100, is available 24 hours a day to accept requests for specific registration application forms and informational circulars published by the Copyright Office. Many of the informational circulars available from the Office will be discussed throughout this Almanac.

Furthermore, most of the information that the Copyright Office makes available on paper is also available for viewing and downloading from the Copyright Office website, located at http://www.copyright.gov. In particular, records may be searched under the "Search Records" tab. For a fee, the Copyright Office will conduct searches of its records and prepare a report based on the information requested.

Reference specialists and researchers may be especially interested in the Copyright Card Catalog. Housed in the James Madison Memorial Building, the catalog comprises an index to copyright registrations in the United States from 1870 through 1977. Records are available in varying formats, including book form, microfilm and electronically through the website. Researchers may also investigate the ownership of a copyright by examining the Assignment and Related Documents Index and the Copyright Office History Documents file and may obtain copies of original applications and documents for a fee.

More information on investigating copyrights and the copyright status of a work is available online by accessing both Circular 22 and Circular 23 on the website or by calling the hotline. Appendix 8, "Search Request Form," of this Almanac contains the Copyright Office's Search Request Form for fee-based search assistance.

A GENERAL OVERVIEW OF THE COPYRIGHT APPLICATION PROCESS

The Copyright Office strongly encourages eligible applicants to file all required forms electronically, using eCO. The system can be accessed from the Copyright Office website by clicking on "Electronic Copyright Office." The advantages of filing with eCO include a lower filing fee ($35 as of this writing), faster processing time, and the ability to upload certain samples of copyrightable subject matter directly to the Copyright Office. New users of eCO must first register their name, address, e-mail address, user identification and password with the Copyright Office. Currently, eCO accepts basic registrations for the works covered in this Almanac, including any single work, a collection of unpublished works by the same author and owned by the same claimant, or multiple published works contained in the same unit of publication and owned by the same claimant, such as a CD song collection.

Another filing option is to use Form CO, also available from the Copyright Office website through the eCO portal. Form CO is a bar-coded version of the original paper application forms that can be mailed to the Copyright Office. The bar-code scanning technology allows the Copyright Office to process CO forms faster than those applications made on the original forms without the technology. Nonetheless, applicants must complete the form on a computer, download the form and mail it, together with the required samples of copyrightable matter, to the Copyright Office with a higher fee ($50 on or after August 1, 2009, as of this writing).

Likewise, applicants using the Copyright Office's original paper forms (which are available by mail by contacting the agency) must mail all required materials to the Office. The fee for original paper filings is $65, effective on or after August 1, 2009, as of this writing.

Here are four steps in the copyright application process to use as a reference guide for a filing under the 1976 Act:

1. A copyright submission consists of the copyright application, a deposit of the work (to be discussed in greater detail in the section below entitled **Deposit**), and the required fee. In limited instances, a work may be pre-registered without a deposit, which does not constitute an application for registration. Pre-registration will be

discussed in greater detail in the section below entitled **Types of Applications Generally**.

2. Based on the subject matter of the copyright application, it will be forwarded to an examiner in the Copyright Office who handles applications of that kind. The Copyright Office consists of several examining sections (e.g., literary, performing arts and visual arts) collectively known as the Registration and Recordation Program, and each division is comprised of specialists trained in the nuances of examining applications in their area of expertise. The examiner will review the application for compliance with the 1976 Act. For instance, if a literary work is submitted, an examiner in the literary unit of the Copyright Office will review the submission to ensure that (i) the application is properly completed, (ii) the deposit reflects the work noted in the application, and (iii) the correct fee has been tendered. Also, the examiner will decide whether the work is of a kind entitled to copyright protection in the first instance and, if so, whether it is fixed in a tangible medium of expression and has the required *de minimis* degree of originality to warrant copyright protection.

3. If the examiner refuses registration of the subject matter, a communication giving the examiner's conclusions will be sent to the correspondent listed in the application. This procedure will be discussed in greater detail in the section below entitled **Office Actions**.

4. If the application is not refused, or any objections to it are resolved, then the application will be approved for registration. A certificate of registration will then be issued in a matter of months. The certificate will be discussed in more detail in the section below entitled **Certificate of Registration**.

This Almanac will address the procedure for registering literary works, visual arts, performing arts and sound recordings. Appendix 9, "Form TX for the Registration of a Literary Work," Appendix 10, "Form VA for the Registration of Visual Arts," Appendix 11, "Form PA for the Registration of Performing Arts," and Appendix 12, "Form SR for the Registration of a Sound Recording," of this Almanac provide the reader with the forms for filing these applications via mail, together with their instructions. Appendix 13, "Continuation Sheet for Application Forms," of this Almanac provides a continuation sheet for paper filings, consisting of additional space within which to provide information relevant to the claim for registration, if required. The information requested in these forms can be used as a guide for filing electronically.

Appendix 14, "Form CO," of this Almanac contains Form CO in blank form for informational purposes, together with instructions. However, readers are reminded to complete Form CO online; do not print out a blank form and then complete it as the required bar code will not appear on the document.

ELEMENTS OF A COPYRIGHT APPLICATION

Copyright application forms are substantially similar. With respect to the types of copyrightable matter to be discussed in this Almanac, all of them except sound recordings can be registered using either a short-form or a long-form application if filed via mail. Sound recordings are registrable using the long form. In other cases, the complexity of the claim will dictate the form to be used, and both forms are provided in Appendices 9 through 11 of this Almanac for works other than sound recordings. The contents of an application discussed herein (also found in section 409 of the 1976 Act) are based on the more comprehensive long form as that is the format used by the Copyright Office in its online registration system. Those contents are as follows:

(1) The title of the work, including any previous titles;

(2) The author(s) and the nature of the authorship;

(3) The year of creation of the work and, if published, the date and nation of first publication;

(4) The copyright claimant;

(5) Previous registrations, if any;

(6) Claim limitations, if any;

(7) The correspondence contact;

(8) A certification made by the author or other claimant, or a rights owner, or authorized representative;

(9) The address for return of the registration certificate;

(10) A deposit in the nature of the material in which copyright is claimed; and

(11) The nonrefundable filing fee or indication of the deposit account to be charged.

Each of these elements is discussed below.

The Title of the Work

Each work should be given a title for purposes of indexing and identifying the work at the Copyright Office. If there is a title on the work (such as the title of a book), then the complete title should be used. Otherwise, an identifying phrase should be used as the title or else state that the work is "untitled." If the work was previously known by another title, that title should also be indicated. Furthermore, if the work was published as part of a larger work (such as an anthology or other compilation), then the title of that larger work should be listed.

Generally, only one titled work may be filed per application, and this Almanac addresses such filings. In some instances, however, a group of works may qualify for a single registration. For example, Form GR/CP (available online or by calling the hotline) is an adjunct application to be used for a group of contributions to periodicals in addition to the filing of an underlying application for a literary work, performing arts work, or visual arts work. Also, Form SE/Group provides for the registration of two or more issues of a serial published at intervals of one week or longer under the same continuing title. Serials include periodicals, newspapers, magazines, bulletins, journals and similar works. More information on serial group registrations is available online by accessing Circular 62b on the website or by calling the hotline.

Identification of the Author and Nature of Authorship

An author may be an individual, joint parties, a company or even a minor if the law of the minor's domicile permits it. In any event, the author of a work is its creator, unless the work is a work made for hire. "Work made for hire" is defined in section 101 of the 1976 Act as either (i) a work prepared by an employee within the scope of his or her employment or (ii) a work falling within one of nine specific categories of commissioned works, provided that a written agreement as to the work's status as a work made for hire is made between the creator of the work and the one at whose instance the work is being commissioned. These nine categories are enumerated as: (i) a contribution to a collective work; (ii) part of a motion picture or other audiovisual work; (iii) a translation; (iv) a supplementary work; (v) a compilation; (vi) instructional text; (vii) a test; (viii) answer material for a test; or (ix) an atlas. The employer, or commissioner, of the work made for hire is the author of it. Corporate owners should be identified by giving the fullest form of the corporate or organizational name.

In the case of individual or joint authors, the name(s), citizenship and domicile should be indicated on the application. In some cases, however, the author's contribution to a work may be anonymous or pseudonymous. In either event, the author may be identified as "anonymous." A pseudonymous author may also be identified using the pseudonym or using the author's real name followed by the pseudonym. It is also permissible to identify an anonymous author at a subsequent time.

The 1976 Act provides, however, that the duration of a copyright in an anonymous or pseudonymous work will be affected by the disclosure of the author's identity. Specifically, section 302(c) amends the copyright term from 95 years from first publication or 120 years from creation (whichever expires first) to a term of life of the author plus 70 years based on the life of the author(s) whose identity is ultimately revealed. Therefore, any potential issues related to disclosure should be carefully addressed.

Other issues can arise from joint authorship. Section 101 specifically defines a "joint work" as one prepared by two or more authors with the intention that their contributions be merged into inseparable or interdependent parts of a unitary whole. The unitary wholeness of the resulting work creates a tenancy in common among the authors, meaning that each co-owner may use or license the work, subject to a duty not to transfer the work and to account to the other owner(s) for any profits. The existence of joint authorship, however, is not always easy to determine. For example, the question whether the authors intended to create a joint work poses an evidentiary burden in the event of a dispute. Further, the statute does not define the nature or scope of an inseparable or interdependent part. Consequently, some courts have interpreted this provision to mean that each author must contribute a separately copyrightable contribution to the work or else it is not considered to be jointly owned.

The nature of an author's contribution to the work is also required to be delineated in the application. In addition to naming the work as one made for hire, anonymous, or pseudonymous, the nature of the material created by the author in which copyright is claimed must be further described. Examples of descriptions in Form CO include *text*, *music*, *lyrics*, *sound recordings* and *2-dimensional artwork*. The examples in the form are instructive for use with paper filings although the nature of authorship is not limited to the descriptions found online. Other forms of authorship include choreography, translations and dramatizations.

Appendix 15, "Definitions Related to Authorship," of this Almanac contains the statutory definitions related to authorship discussed in this section.

Year of Creation and Date and Nation of Publication

For registration purposes, the year in which a work is created is the year in which a completed version of the work submitted for registration was fixed. If the work will be amended at a later date, the subsisting registration may be subject to correction in limited instances by way of a supplemental registration. Supplemental registrations will be covered in more detail in the section below entitled **Supplementary Copyright Registration**. Of course, not all completed works are necessarily published, and there is no requirement that a work be published to be registrable. *Publication* is defined in section 101 as a public distribution, or offering for distribution, of a work by sale, rental, lease or lending. If a work has been published, the year of creation will in no event be later than the year of first publication.

Moreover, in the event that a work has been published, the complete date (i.e., month, day and year) should be given, together with the nation of first publication. The United States can be designated the nation of first publication: (i) for works first published therein; (ii) for works first published simultaneously in the United States and another country; or (iii) for works published in the United States within 30 days following publication in a country that is not party to an international copyright treaty such as the Berne Convention.

Although not mandatory, online filers have the option of providing an ISBN number for eligible works. An ISBN, or International Standard Book Number, is a unique numerical identifying code assigned to books and book-like products of publishers. Only an entity qualified by the International ISBN Agency can issue ISBN numbers. In the United States, the company responsible for the issuance and administration of ISBNs is Bowker (http://www.bowker.com). ISBNs are particularly useful for cataloging works and tracking sales through the use of bar code technology; an ISBN is a prerequisite to obtaining a bar code label. An ISBN should also be distinguished from an ISSN (International Standard Serial Number), which is a numerical code assigned to serial publications. Like the ISBN, an ISSN is a unique identifier. Similar to the ISBN system, an international center also administers the application of the codes and qualifies certain agencies around the world to coordinate the assignment of ISSNs locally. In the United States, the ISSN Publisher Liaison Section (formerly known as the National Serials Data Program) within the Library of Congress registers ISSNs for serials published in the United States. More information on ISSNs can be obtained from the website located at http://www.loc.gov/issn.

The Copyright Claimant

The author of the work or other person or entity to whom ownership is transferred is the copyright claimant. The requirements of this section of the application are straightforward. The name and address of the individual or institutional author(s) must be indicated. If the claimant is a transferee, then the nature of the transfer must also be indicated. Form CO allows applicants to indicate in particular whether a transfer was made by written agreement (e.g., an assignment of copyright) or bequest. Nonetheless, other transfer scenarios may apply and should be noted as applicable.

Previous Registrations

The requirement to disclose earlier registrations of a submitted work is intended to address whether there is any basis for a new registration. Generally, a version of a work that is substantially similar to a previously registered work is not registrable unless (i) the new work is a first-published edition of a previously registered unpublished work, or (ii) the earlier registration identifies someone other than the author as the copyright claimant, and the author now seeks registration. Previous registrations must be disclosed by year and registration number.

Claim Limitations

A limitation of copyright claim pertains to the identification of: (i) any previously registered or published works upon which the copyright claim is based; (ii) public domain material; or (iii) material not owned by the claimant. The purpose of this section of the application is to exclude such pre-existing material from the scope of the current matter comprising the copyright claim. Examples of new works that incorporate pre-existing matter include a new arrangement of a song in the public domain, a revised version of a previously-published book, an English translation of a foreign novel, or a movie based on a screenplay. In more general terms, the limitation of claims section addresses derivative works or compilations.

Derivative works and compilations are both defined in section 101. As mentioned in Chapter 1, "The Nature and Function of a Copyright," of this Almanac, a derivative work is one that is derived, or based upon, a pre-existing work in a form that can be recast, transformed or adapted. In other words, it must differ meaningfully from the underlying work. It is important to note that a pre-existing work that is not in the public domain must be licensed for use as part of a derivative work to avoid infringement. Contrary to derivative works, copyright in a compilation inheres in the originality of selection, coordination or arrangement of pre-existing materials or data rather than in a transformation of the underlying material. Similar to derivative works, however, a claim related to a compilation does not extend to the underlying materials, i.e., the material that has been compiled. If any such material is likewise original to the author, however, it should be noted. The term *compilation* includes collective works, which are defined in section 101 as anthologies, encyclopedias and other works in which a number of independent contributions are assembled into a collective whole.

Correspondence Contact

The application must specify a name and correspondence address to which communications may be sent regarding the application. If an applicant chooses to retain counsel for the filing process, the correspondence contact may be an attorney. The correspondent may also be the author, the claimant or a rights and permissions contact. The rights and permissions contact is the person with whom contact should be made to request permission to use the work. The completion of a rights and permissions section of an online or paper application is optional.

Certification

The copyright application must be signed and dated to be accepted. A proper signatory to the application is: (i) the author; (ii) the copyright claimant, if other than the author; (iii) an owner of exclusive rights (to be discussed in more detail in Chapter 4, "Monetizing Copyrights," of this Almanac in the section entitled **Special Licensing Considerations**); or (iv) the authorized agent of any of the foregoing. The signatory will certify under penalty of perjury that the information contained in the application is correct to the best of the signatory's knowledge.

Return Address

The return address indicates the person to whom the registration certificate, if issued, should be mailed. The information should be completed legibly on documents filed via mail as it will appear in a window envelope.

Deposit

Section 408(b) of the 1976 Act prescribes the nature of the material to accompany an application, known as the deposit for copyright registration. With few exceptions, the deposit to accompany an application must include one of the following elements, as applicable: (i) one complete copy or phonorecord of an unpublished work; (ii) two complete copies or phonorecords of the best edition of a work published in the United States; (iii) one complete copy or phonorecord of a work first published outside the United States; or (iv) one complete copy or phonorecord of the best edition related to a contribution to a collective work. Section 101 defines *best edition* as the edition published in the United States that the Library of Congress deems most suitable for its purposes. The Library of Congress has taken additional steps to define its best edition requirements in a statement entitled *Best Edition of Published Copyrighted Works for the Collections of the Library of Congress*. The statement can be reviewed in its entirety by accessing Circular 7b from the Copyright Office. Generally, the Library of Congress considers the highest quality of a work to be the best edition (e.g., the hard bound edition, rather than the soft bound edition, of a book).

Although the deposit requirement discussed above only applies in the event that an application for copyright registration is made, this deposit requirement must be distinguished from the mandatory deposit of copies or phonorecords for the Library of Congress. Section 407 sets forth a mandatory requirement that works published in the United States be deposited with the Library of Congress within three months following publication. The purpose of this deposit requirement is to enrich the national archives. In many instances, copyright registration of published works is used as a means to satisfy the mandatory deposit requirements. In fact, to satisfy requirements for both mandatory deposit and copyright deposit, the Register of Copyrights should receive a completed copyright application, the fee, and the required number of mandatory deposit copies. Generally, the mandatory deposit must consist of two complete copies or phonorecords of the best edition of the work. Specific requirements are set forth in the CFR regarding such works as sound recordings, motion pictures, and CD-ROMs. If the required deposit is not made, the Register of Copyrights may make a written demand for the required deposit at any time after publication, and fines may be imposed for refusal to comply.

Appendix 16, "Copyright Deposit Requirements," and Appendix 17, "Mandatory Deposit Requirements," of this Almanac contain statutory and regulatory references to the copyright deposit and mandatory deposit requirements, respectively.

Filing Fees

A current fee schedule for all Copyright Office filings is located at http://www.copyright.gov/docs/fees.html. As of this writing, a fee increase is due to take effect on or about August 1, 2009. Those intending to process at least 12 transactions per year with the Copyright Office are eligible to open a deposit account, make advance deposits into the account and charge copyright fees against the balance in the account in lieu of sending payments with each transaction. Information on opening a deposit account can be found in Circular 5. In other cases, based on the mode of service, the Copyright Office accepts credit cards, electronic transfers of funds, currency or checks and other drafts made payable to the Register of Copyrights.

TYPES OF APPLICATIONS GENERALLY

In the first instance, a copyright claimant must decide upon the nature of the application to be filed. This text focuses on an application to be filed online or via mail as discussed above; the specific applications related to literary works, visual arts, performing arts and sound recordings are discussed in detail below. However, in some instances, an application for pre-registration of a work is available. Pre-registration is not a substitute for registration. Therefore, a work qualifying for pre-registration should ultimately be registered in the traditional manner if registration is sought.

Pre-registration is provided for in section 408(f) of the 1976 Act and was enacted pursuant to the provisions of The Artists' Rights and Theft Prevention Act of 2005 (the ART Act). The ART Act provides for, among other things, a pre-release registration process for unpublished works in danger of being infringed before their official release date, such as motion pictures. An application for pre-registration, which can only be made online through eCO using Form PRE, consists of two elements: the application and the filing fee. Pursuant to the statute, the Copyright Office has the authority to determine the types of works that would most benefit from pre-registration. Accordingly, the eligible works as of this writing are as follows: (i) motion pictures; (ii) sound recordings; (iii) musical compositions; (iv) literary works in book form; (v) computer programs, including video games; and (vi) advertising or marketing photographs. In each case, the work must be in process—that is, already created and fixed in some form—and the claimant must have a reasonable expectation that the work will be commercially distributed. In many respects, the content of a pre-registration application is the same as a traditional application and requires identification of the title of the work, the author(s), the claimant and the nature of the work. In lieu of the deposit requirement, however, the work must be described in sufficient detail, together with the date that creation commenced, the anticipated date of completion and the anticipated date of commencement of commercial distribution. The owner of a pre-registered work is entitled to bring an infringement action before the authorized commercial distribution of a work and before full registration thereof. Nonetheless, to preserve the benefits of pre-registration, full registration must be effectuated within one month after the copyright owner becomes aware of infringement and no later than three months after first publication, or else a court must dismiss an action for copyright infringement that occurred before or within the first two months after first publication. It should be noted as well that pre-registration does not guarantee a finding that the work will be deemed registrable by the Copyright Office when a full application is made.

Appendix 18, "Pre-registration," of this Almanac contains the statutory and regulatory references regarding the pre-registration process.

LITERARY WORKS

Literary works are defined in section 101 as works expressed not only in words but also in numbers, verbal or numerical symbols or other indicia. Accordingly, the class of works eligible for filing in this category is diverse, including fiction, nonfiction, poetry, textbooks, reference works, directories, catalogs, advertising copy, compilations and computer programs. For paper filers, Form TX (set forth in Appendix 9, "Form TX for the Registration of a Literary Work," of this Almanac) is the vehicle for registration of literary works. This section will highlight issues of particular interest related to computer programs as well as automated databases and online works.

The term *computer program* is defined in section 101 as a set of statements or instructions used in a computer that bring about a certain result. Copyright protection, then, extends to all of the copyrightable expression embodied in the computer program. Consistent with section 102(b), however, such protection would not extend to the ideas, algorithms, systems, methods, concepts or layouts. Of particular concern to copyright claimants in computer programs is the protection of trade secrets in those programs in light of the deposit rules. Methods of preserving trade secrecy, discussed in Circular 61, provide for deposit of the work in one of the four following ways: (i) the first and last 25 pages of source code with portions containing trade secrets blocked out; or (ii) the first and last 10 pages of source code alone with nothing blocked out; or (iii) the first and last 25 pages of object code plus any 10 or more consecutive pages of source code, with no blocked-out portions; or (iv) for programs 50 pages or less in length, the entire source code with trade secret portions blocked out. For computer programs without trade secrets, the first 25 and last 25 pages of source code are generally provided, unless the total work does not exceed 50 pages. In that case, a visually perceptible copy of the entire source code should be deposited.

In some instances, an applicant may be unable or unwilling to make the required deposit and, in lieu thereof, may submit only an object code version of the work with a statement that the work contains copyrightable authorship. The practice of the Copyright Office is to accept registration of such a work under its "rule of doubt," theorizing that a court might find the work copyrightable. The rule of doubt, therefore, does not provide the claimant with a conclusive determination by the Copyright Office that the work constitutes copyrightable authorship.

The above deposit requirements should be distinguished from the mandatory deposit rules. Under those rules, the submission of a published computer program that is not copy protected requires the deposit of one complete copy of the best edition; if the work is copy protected, two copies of the best edition are required. Like the Copyright Office deposit requirement, the Library of Congress deposit requirement provides recourse to an applicant who is unwilling or unable to make the required deposit by way of a petition for special relief from the deposit rules. A grant of special relief from the rules is an extraordinary remedy and may be terminated at any time on notice to the claimant.

Another issue concerning registration of computer programs involves the use of commercially available authoring tools (e.g., Lotus) in their creation. Such tools are referred to as add-on computer programs. There is no statutory definition for an add-on program, but it is generally understood that the protectable authorship of a work using an add-on tool is the set of new instructions authored by the claimant. This new material (identified as, for example, "new programming text") would be indicated as the nature of authorship and the new material created in the work in spaces 2 and 6b, respectively, on long-form TX.

Unlike computer programs, automated databases and online works are not defined in the Copyright Act. Moreover, sometimes a frequently updated online work may constitute an automated database. Circulars 65 and 66 address copyright registration for automated databases and online works, respectively. Circular 65 defines an automated database as a body of facts, data or other information assembled into an organized format for computer use. Generally, databases are treated as compilations; therefore, they are copyrightable provided that the factual compilation represents original authorship. The deposit requirement generally consists of one copy of identifying portions of the work, reproduced on paper or in microform. Specific deposit requirements vary depending whether the work is a single-file, multiple-file or revised database. Also, Copyright Office deposit submissions are eligible for special relief requests. Notably, automated databases available only online in the United States are exempt from the mandatory deposit rule.

Online works, unlike computer programs and automated databases, may consist of matter other than a literary work. Therefore, the form to be used should correspond to the type of authorship being registered. Moreover, the Copyright Office regulations do not specifically address the deposit requirements for online works accessible over the Internet, such as those accessed, transmitted or distributed via FTP (file transfer protocol). Pending the establishment of regulations for online works, the current deposit requirement consists of one of the following options: (i) a computer disk labeled with the title of the work and the author and containing the entire work, together with a representative portion of the work in a tangible format that can be examined by the Copyright Office or (ii) a reproduction of the entire work regardless of the length without a computer disk. If a work is published via hard copy as well as online, then the regular deposit rules for copies of a work apply instead of the online requirements. In any event, filers using eCO have the option to upload their deposits to the Copyright Office website provided that the file (or multiple files, as the case may be) is not too large.

Appendix 19, "Definitions Related to Literary Works," of this Almanac contains the statutory definitions related to literary works. Readers should consult the applicable portions of Appendix 16, "Copyright Deposit Requirements," and Appendix 17, "Mandatory Deposit Requirements," of this Almanac for a thorough review of Copyright Office and mandatory deposit rules regarding all forms of literary works.

VISUAL ART

The general scope of visual art eligible for registration is set forth in the definition of pictorial, graphic and sculptural works in section 101, which includes two-dimensional and three-dimensional works of fine, graphic and applied art, reproductions, maps, globes, charts, models and technical drawings. An exhaustive list of works is found in Circular 40. Eligible works include useful articles and works of artistic craftsmanship provided that the mechanical or utilitarian aspects of the work can be physically distinguished from features of copyrightable authorship. Therefore, a carving on the back of a chair or a design on flatware could be copyrightable independently of the utilitarian nature of the chair or flatware itself so long as the artistic aspects of the work do not fuse with the functional attributes. For paper filers, Form VA (set forth in Appendix 10, "Form VA for the Registration of Visual Arts," of this Almanac) should be used to apply for registration of visual art. The specifications of identifying material required to be submitted with an application are detailed in Circular 40a. Generally, the deposit for a two-dimensional work requires prints, transparencies, photocopies, drawings or similar depictions. For pictorial and graphic works, specifically, the deposit materials must reproduce the actual colors of the work. Not surprisingly, three-dimensional sculptural works and many works of applied art (i.e., the application of design to objects of function and everyday use such as ceramics, jewelry, textiles and furniture) are exempt from deposit.

The Visual Artists Rights Act of 1990 (VARA) protects another class of visual art specifically defined in section 101 as "a work of visual art"—namely, paintings, drawings, prints, sculpture and photographs in numbered limited editions of 200 or fewer copies. The nature of these works includes murals, canvas works, castings, carvings, models, lithographs, serigraphs and etchings. Simply put, VARA provides that an author of a work of visual art enjoys rights of attribution and integrity with respect to that work. These rights are collectively known as moral rights—that is, a natural right of an artist that exists separate from the copyright and represents an artist's personal stake in a work. The concept of moral rights has been long recognized by other countries (most famously in France), particularly those adhering to the Berne Convention. The right of attribution is the artist's right to be credited with authorship of a work and to prevent attribution for a work not of the artist's creation. The right of integrity, on the other hand, is the right to prevent mutilation of a work in such a manner that the artist's honor or reputation would be impaired. In some instances, these rights may overlap. For instance, an artist whose work has been impaired will likely exercise the right to be released from attribution for the work. Notably, as a natural or personal right of the artist, these rights belong to the artist regardless whether he or she is also the copyright claimant. Thus the rights cannot be transferred but can be waived in a signed writing. VARA also has specific provisions requiring notice to the artist before a work of visual art incorporated into a building can be removed from that building.

Although arguably sweeping on its face, VARA does have its limitations. For example, it does not apply to works that degrade due to the passage of time or that change as a result of conservation efforts. Also, it does not apply to works that are exhibited publicly, including their lighting or placement, unless such an activity modifies the work in a grossly negligent manner. Furthermore, VARA excludes from its coverage such items as motion pictures, books, advertising, periodicals, merchandising items or non-copyrightable matter. Another significant limitation is the exclusion of works made for hire from the ambit of a work of visual art. The issue whether a work is excluded from coverage under VARA (particularly whether it qualifies as a work made for hire) is frequently litigated. Under section 501, a violation of VARA is an infringement and triggers such remedies as monetary damages, costs, attorneys' fees and injunctive relief. A violation of VARA does not trigger criminal liability, however.

Appendix 20, "Definitions Related to Visual Art," of this Almanac contains the statutory definitions related to visual art under VARA and otherwise. Readers should consult the applicable portions of Appendix 16, "Copyright Deposit Requirements," and Appendix 17, "Mandatory Deposit

Requirements," of this Almanac for a thorough review of Copyright Office and mandatory deposit rules related to visual art.

Appendix 21, "Visual Artists Rights Act of 1990," of this Almanac contains the text of VARA as set forth in section 106A of the 1976 Act.

PERFORMING ARTS

The term *performing arts* is not explicitly defined in the 1976 Act. However, Form PA (set forth in Appendix 11, "Form PA for the Registration of Performing Arts, of this Almanac) provides that works of the performing arts include dramatic works (including music), pantomimes and choreographic works, motion pictures and other audiovisual works, and musical works, including accompanying words. Quite obviously, these works are those that are prepared for the purpose of being performed before an audience or indirectly performed by means of a device or process. For paper filers, Form PA serves as a vehicle for the protection of works by playwrights, composers, lyricists, book writers of musicals, choreographers and other creative artists. This section will focus on copyright registration for musical compositions.

Guidelines for registration of musical compositions are set forth in Circular 50, which provides that these works include original compositions as well as original arrangements of earlier compositions—in other words, derivative works. Copyright in a musical work includes the right of the owner to make a sound recording. However, sound recordings and musical works are separate works. Sound recordings will be discussed in the section below entitled **Sound Recordings**.

The author of a musical composition such as a song is the composer or song writer. The nature of the authorship is the music or music and lyrics, as the case may be. Owners of musical compositions should note, in particular, the deposit requirements for both unpublished and published works. For unpublished works, one complete copy of the lead sheet or sheet music, disk or tape (as applicable) should be submitted with the application. For published works, the deposit requirement is generally two copies of the best edition of the work, and Circular 50 specifies a hierarchy of items deemed to be the best edition for deposit purposes. For instance, for vocal music with orchestral accompaniment or instrumental music, a full score is preferable to a conductor's score. For unaccompanied music, an open score is preferable to a closed score. Moreover, for phonorecord deposits, a compact digital disc is preferred over a vinyl disc. In circumstances where a musical composition is published only in a motion picture soundtrack, the deposit requirement is met if it consists of a reproduction of the musical work and a sheet containing the title of the motion picture and any copyright credits for the music. Similarly, single contributions to a collective work (such as a hymn for a hymnal), works published only in phonorecord format or works that are only available by rental, lease or lending require only a single deposit with the Copyright Office.

Another issue facing the owner(s) of a musical composition is whether a collection of works can be registered with only one form, as illustrated by two or more individuals contributing lyrics and music to songs. For unpublished collections, if the copyright owner is the same for all songs or at least one author is common to all the songs, then the collection can be registered with one application. For published collections, one application will suffice if the copyright claimant owns all of the compositions.

Readers should consult the applicable portions of Appendix 16, "Copyright Deposit Requirements," and Appendix 17, "Mandatory Deposit Requirements," of this Almanac for a thorough review of Copyright Office and mandatory deposit rules regarding all works of performing arts.

SOUND RECORDINGS

A sound recording is defined in section 101 of the 1976 Act as a work resulting from the fixation of a series of sounds; in other words, it is a captured performance of an aggregate of sounds arising from such things as music, drama or lectures. A sound recording should be distinguished from a phonorecord, the physical embodiment of the underlying recording. Federal protection of sound recordings is of recent vintage. In fact, sound recordings fixed prior to February 15, 1972 were protected under state or common law. When the 1976 Act was enacted, those sound recordings fixed as of the above date were granted federal protection. Pursuant to section 301, sound recordings fixed prior to February 15, 1972 will continue to be protected at common law until February 15, 2067. Thereafter, none of those recordings will be subject to copyright.

As noted above in **Performing Arts**, registration of a sound recording should be distinguished from registration of the underlying musical composition. Each has a separate copyright, which may be held by separate parties. Circular 56a explains that, if the same author owns the underlying composition and the sound recording (as would be the case if an artist writes and performs his own music, for example), then paper filers can file a single application using Form SR (set forth in Appendix 12, "Form SR for the Registration of a Sound Recording," of this Almanac). However, in many instances, a musical artist will work with a record company; generally, the record company will acquire sole copyright to the sound recordings embodying the musician's performance through a work for hire arrangement. Absent such an event, the author is the performer or record producer (or both), and the nature of the authorship is referred to as "sound recording/performance." For deposit purposes, the best edition of a sound recording is a compact disc, followed in descending order by a vinyl disc, tape, cartridge or cassette. Generally, unless the work is unpublished or published first outside the United States, two complete phonorecords must be deposited.

Appendix 22, "Definitions Related to Sound Recordings," of this Almanac contains the statutory definitions related to sound recordings.

PRE-REGISTRATION ADMINISTRATIVE ACTION

Office Actions

In some cases, an examiner at the Copyright Office may send a letter to an applicant concerning a procedural or substantive matter related to an application. This communication is commonly referred to as an office action, also referred to as an official action. Sometimes, this communication may constitute a refusal to register the copyright claim. Section 410(b) of the 1976 Act provides a statutory basis for the right of an examiner to refuse registration of a copyright and to communicate those reasons to the applicant; likewise, the procedural steps and right to appeal related to reconsideration are set forth in the CFR. Some reasons a work might be refused registration are that the work: (i) is not original to the author; (ii) constitutes an uncopyrightable idea, concept or form; (iii) consists entirely of a useful article; or (iv) is a compilation of facts lacking originality in their selection, coordination or arrangement.

A finding that a work lacks originality to its author may arise because an examiner determines that the claim is simply a copy of another work that is not in the public domain, such as a note-by-note copy of a popular melody. Alternatively, an examiner may find that a work is partially composed of pre-existing material and therefore is not entirely original. Such a finding would occur, for instance, if an applicant claiming copyright in a computer program uses an add-on program to create the claimed work, as discussed above in the section entitled **Literary Works**. In such a case, an examiner may require the claimant to revise the application to note the derivative nature of the applicant's claimed work, provided that the applicant's portion of the work contains some degree of originality.

Furthermore, a work that is not subject to copyright will be refused registration regardless of how original it may appear. As set out in

Chapter 1, "The Nature and Function of a Copyright," and Appendix 4, "Material not Subject to Copyright," of this Almanac, some works are not subject to copyright protection, including short phrases, single words, blank forms or formats and familiar shapes, symbols or designs. A singular idea, process or concept may be eligible for patent protection instead.

Likewise, artistic features embodied in useful articles may fuse with the functional or utilitarian aspects of those articles, resulting in a denial of copyright. Obviously, this determination is highly subjective, and many courts have reversed an earlier determination of the Copyright Office that the artistic features of a work are not conceptually separable from its functionality. In particular, one well-known case held that two belt buckles bearing sculptured designs cast in precious metals and principally used for decoration were copyrightable notwithstanding their utilitarian function. In some cases, depending on the nature of the utilitarian function served by the article, it may be possible to register the technical drawing(s) as visual art.

Another famous case set the foundation for determining whether a compilation of facts evidences enough creativity to merit copyright protection. In *Feist Publications, Inc. v. Rural Telephone Service*, the U.S. Supreme Court determined that, where the assembly of uncopyrightable facts is at issue, such a compilation must represent some degree of creativity in the selection, arrangement or coordination of those facts to support a copyright claim. As a result of this important case, compilation copyright is no longer granted on the basis of the effort—or "sweat of the brow"—involved in the collection of facts or data, as was the decision among many courts hearing cases regarding refusal of copyright.

If an examiner refuses registration (particularly with respect to any of the issues discussed above), then an applicant may make a request for reconsideration to the Registration and Recordation Program within three months following the date on the notice of refusal. If the applicant's arguments are unpersuasive and the refusal is continued, the applicant may elect to file a second argument with the Copyright Office Review Board within three months following the date of the second notice continuing the examiner's refusal. If the application is still refused, the decision is appealable to the United States District Court for the District of Columbia.

Not all communications from an examiner are an outright refusal to register the claim to copyright. In the event that an examiner invites a reply from an applicant related to the sufficiency of the application (particularly with regard to an issue that is subject to easy correction, such as substituting another type of form for the registration of the material submitted), the Copyright Office generally allows the applicant 120 days from the date of the examiner's letter to reply, unless a different period of time is stated in the letter. The consequence of failing to reply to any such letter is that the case file will be closed. To reapply for registration after a case file is closed, an applicant must submit a new registration package.

Appendix 23, "Refusal of Registration," of this Almanac contains the statutory and regulatory references related to office actions refusing registration.

REGISTRATION AND POST-REGISTRATION

This section covers the certificate of registration of copyright and will highlight three issues following successful registration: (i) supplementary registration; (ii) copyright renewals for certain works; and (iii) cancellation of completed registrations.

Certificate of Registration

If an application is deemed to be in condition for issuance of a registration, then the Register of Copyrights will issue a Certificate of Registration under seal of the Copyright Office in a number of months (depending on office staffing at the time) to the mailing address identified in the application. The certificate will detail the work's registration number, its examiner's initials, the date the application and deposit(s) were received and its effective date. Pursuant to section 410(d) of the 1976 Act, the effective date of the registration will relate back to the date that the completed application was received at the Copyright Office if the submission was later determined to be in condition for registration as of that date. As an original document, a registration certificate should be kept in a safe place along with other valuable papers. Additional copies of a registration certificate (including certified copies) are available by writing to the Copyright Office.

Supplementary Copyright Registration

Section 408(d) of the 1976 Act provides that a supplemental registration may be made by the author, claimant or exclusive licensee of a work to correct or amplify information given in the basic registration. Circular 8 indicates the nature of permitted corrections or amplifications, such as the addition of authors or claimants, address corrections or a change in title of the work. Note, however, that supplemental registrations are not appropriate to change the content of a work in a material way.

In such an event, depending on the nature of the changes made, a new application may be warranted. An application for supplemental registration must be made by mail using Form CA. In addition to the form, the filer must submit a photocopy of each side of the certificate being amended as well as the supplementary filing fee. If the application is accepted for registration, the filing will be assigned a new registration number and will co-exist with the basic registration as part of the official record of the work.

Appendix 24, "Form CA for the Correction of a Registration," of this Almanac contains Form CA and its instructions.

Renewals

Not all subsisting copyrights require renewal. After all, under the 1976 Act, copyrights coming into existence on or after the effective date of the act enjoy long periods of protection during which renewal is not required, as discussed in detail in Chapter 1, "The Nature and Function of a Copyright," of this Almanac. Furthermore, for those works in existence as of the enactment of the 1976 Act and subject to a renewal term (in particular, those originally copyrighted between January 1, 1964 and December 31, 1977), renewal registration became optional as a result of The Copyright Renewal Act of 1992. That legislation, together with CTEA, automatically extended the term of protection for works in the above time period to 95 years. Despite the automatic extension of copyright, renewal of these works is encouraged. Circular 15 explains, for instance, that a renewal certificate will not issue for these extended works unless a renewal application is filed. The renewal certificate, constituting *prima facie* evidence of the validity of the copyright during the renewed and extended term, creates for the registrant a public record to protect against claims of innocent infringement and to facilitate claims of ownership if the owner chooses to license the work. It is instructive to note that copyrights secured before January 1, 1964 required renewal prior to the expiration of their 28ᵗʰ year of copyright or else copyright would be lost; under the renewal act, works between 1964 and 1977 can be renewed, if so elected, at any time during the renewed and extended term.

Section 304 of the 1976 Act governs who may claim renewal of copyright. Generally, the right lies with the author, if living. If the author is deceased, then the claimants are as follows: (i) the surviving spouse and/or children; (ii) if none, then the executor(s) under a will; or (iii) if none of the above circumstances applies, then the next of kin of the author. In some instances, however, only the owner of the copyright may claim its renewal, as in the case of a posthumous work, a composite work, the work of a corporate body, or a work made for hire. Renewals must be filed via mail using Form RE.

Appendix 25, "Renewal Terms," of this Almanac contains references from section 304 of the 1976 Act concerning renewals and renewal terms.

Appendix 26, "Form RE for the Renewal of Copyright," of this Almanac contains Form RE together with its instructions.

Cancellation of Completed Registrations

In some cases, the Copyright Office will cancel a registration at its own instance. For example, if a check sent in payment of a fee for registration is returned for insufficient funds following the issuance of the registration, the Copyright Office will cancel the registration. A registration may also be cancelled if the Copyright Office ultimately determines that the subject matter is not copyrightable or that the deposit is not sufficient to support the registration, provided that the applicant has failed to cure the defect on 30 days' notice. It should be noted that the Copyright Office does not offer a tribunal for cancellation of a copyright at the instance of a third party who wishes to challenge a registration.

Appendix 27, "Cancellation of Registration," of this Almanac contains the Copyright Office's regulations regarding cancellations.

CHAPTER 3:
INTERNATIONAL CONSIDERATIONS

INTERNATIONAL CONSIDERATIONS GENERALLY

Most countries offer some form of copyright protection, and claimants seeking to protect their works outside their home jurisdiction will need to consult the laws of nations of interest to determine the extent of protection accorded to foreign authors. In other words, there is no single mechanism to protect a copyrighted work at once throughout the world. However, various international conventions, or treaties, afford their adherents the opportunity to manage copyright relations with dozens of countries, thus allowing for protection of many foreign works under the terms of that particular treaty. The United States is a signatory to many of the leading treaties affecting copyright. This text will provide general information on the Berne Convention, the WIPO Copyright Treaty, the WIPO Performances and Phonograms Treaty and TRIPS.

Appendix 28, "Contracting Parties to Treaties," of this Almanac provides a list of adherents to each of the above-referenced treaties as of this writing.

THE BERNE CONVENTION

The United States officially became the 80th nation to join the Berne Convention as of March 1, 1989. The treaty is so named due to its original signing in Berne, Switzerland, on September 9, 1886. Since then, the convention's terms have undergone various revisions; however, as between any two member nations, the latest version adopted by each country represents the controlling text within that country. The Berne Convention is administered by the World Intellectual Property Organization (WIPO), an agency of the United Nations responsible for the development of laws and regulations that advance the harmonization of intellectual property laws worldwide.

The Berne Convention espouses three guiding principles: (i) works originating from or first published in a member nation must be given the same protection in each of the other member nations as those nations grant to the works of their own nationals; (ii) such protection must not be conditional upon compliance with any formality (such as the placement of a notice of copyright on a work); and (iii) such protection is independent of the existence of protection in the country of origin of the work, but if a work ceases to be protected in its country of origin (e.g., the term of copyright has ended), then protection may be denied elsewhere once protection in the country of origin ceases. In addition to these principles, adherents to the Berne Convention recognize an author's moral rights in a work (discussed in Chapter 2, "The Application Process," of this Almanac in the section entitled **Visual Art**). Moreover, similar to the bundle of rights granted to a copyright owner under the 1976 Act, the Berne Convention requires its member nations to recognize, with certain limitations, a bundle of rights including: (i) translation rights; (ii) the right to make adaptations and arrangements of a work; (iii) public performance rights; (iv) broadcast rights; (v) reproduction rights; and (vi) the right to use a work as a basis for an audiovisual work and the right to reproduce, distribute, perform in public or communicate to the public that audiovisual work.

Section 104 of the 1976 Act provides a series of rules for unpublished and published foreign authors seeking like treatment for their works as granted to authors in the United States. For instance, under subsection (a), unpublished works are protected regardless of the domicile of the author. As for published works, subsection (b) will protect them so long as: (i) at least one author is a U.S. national or domiciliary or a member of a treaty party; (ii) the work is first incorporated or contained within a structure that is located in the nation of a treaty party; (iii) the work is first published within a treaty party; (iv) the work is protected by means of a presidential proclamation or first published by the United Nations or a related agency; or (v) in the case of a sound recording, the work was first fixed in a nation that is a treaty party. In some instances, a work first published in a non-treaty country may be protected under the principles of the Berne Convention if its publication takes place within a signatory country no later than 30 days following its first publication elsewhere.

WIPO COPYRIGHT TREATY

The WIPO Copyright Treaty, in force as of March 6, 2002, emerged from the WIPO Diplomatic Conference on December 20, 1996 and is considered a special agreement under article 20 of the Berne Convention. Two salient features of the treaty are its specific inclusion of computer programs and databases as copyrightable subject matter and its aim to protect copyright in transmissions over the Internet. Indeed, when the Berne Convention was last amended in the 1970s, information and communication technologies known today could not have been anticipated. As a result, article 8 of the WIPO Copyright Treaty provides authors with the exclusive right to authorize the communication of their works to the public by wire or wireless means, covering in particular on-demand, interactive communication through the Internet. Signatories to the treaty are required to adopt measures to enforce the rights of authors to control Internet submissions, including providing authors with remedies for a third party's circumvention of any technology designed to control or limit such transmissions (such as encryption). Notably, an Agreed Statement issued by WIPO with respect to article 8 specifies that the provision of server space, communication connections or facilities for transmissions is not by itself a circumventing, or infringing, activity. Furthermore, member nations are allowed the opportunity to create their own exceptions and limitations regarding appropriate activity in a digital network environment. Notwithstanding this freedom, the treaty does not permit its signatories to devise rights management systems that would impede the free movement of goods or enjoyment of rights.

WIPO PERFORMANCES AND PHONOGRAMS TREATY

The Performances and Phonograms Treaty, a sister treaty to the WIPO Copyright Treaty in force as of May 20, 2002, is intended to protect musicians and the recording industry from unauthorized use of copyrighted works arising from the Internet and other digital technology. The treaty enumerates rights for both fixed and unfixed (i.e., live) performances. For fixed performances, the treaty grants performers and producers four exclusive rights: the right of reproduction, the right of distribution, the right of rental, and the right to make the performance available in a chosen medium. For unfixed performances, three rights are granted to performers: the right of broadcasting (except in the case of rebroadcasting), the right of communication to the public (except where the performance is a broadcast performance), and the right to fix the work in a tangible medium of expression. Performers are also accorded moral rights—that is, the right to claim a performance and the right to reject an adaptation that would adversely affect the performer's reputation.

TRIPS

Unlike the Berne Convention and the WIPO treaties, TRIPS (Agreement on Trade-Related Aspects of Intellectual Property Rights) is not administered by WIPO. Instead, the body administering the treaty is the World

Trade Organization (WTO), an international organization dealing with the rules of trade between nations. TRIPS is Annex 1C of 18 agreements contained in the Marrakesh Agreement Establishing the World Trade Organization, signed in Marrakesh, Morocco on April 15, 1994.

WIPO and TRIPS co-exist as a means to bring global harmonization to copyright issues. As a result, in some ways their standards are quite similar. For instance, both promote the Berne Convention as a baseline for protection of intellectual property rights. However, TRIPS is substantively broader than the Berne Convention because it protects software, databases and sound recordings. It also provides rental rights for computer programs and cinematography. It also differs from the Berne Convention by failing to protect moral rights. Procedurally, TRIPS provides a unique dispute settlement process to which all members must adhere, consisting of a consultation, followed by a panel adjudication by three or five arbitrators and an appeals process. Although the treaties may seemingly be in conflict, TRIPS is applicable to copyright issues that are "trade-related." In fact, the preamble to the TRIPS Agreement delineates its mission to ensure, among other things, that measures and procedures are in place to enforce intellectual property rights in a way that does not impede international trade.

CHAPTER 4:
MONETIZING COPYRIGHTS

A GENERAL OVERVIEW

Like other forms of intellectual property such as trademarks and patents, copyrights are assets capable of producing value for their owners. Consider, for example, the tremendous licensing income realized from copyrights owned by Microsoft and The Walt Disney Company. In the record industry, many composers assign all or a portion of their copyrights to a music publisher, who, in turn, seeks opportunities to exploit the work and share any resulting income with the composer. The divisibility of copyright—that is, the ability to transfer or subdivide any of the bundle of rights discussed in Chapter 1, "The Nature and Function of a Copyright," of this Almanac—presents a copyright owner with significant opportunity for economic enhancement of a copyright portfolio. A transfer of rights is not always absolute, however; in many instances, rights may be recaptured. This chapter will address the following issues incidental to licensing and monetization: (i) transfers of copyright and recordation; (ii) termination of transfer; and (iii) special licensing considerations involving compulsory licensing, exclusivity, international licensing and orphan works. The chapter will conclude with a discussion regarding the ongoing need to police a copyright to protect its economic viability.

TRANSFERS OF COPYRIGHT AND RECORDATION

Section 101 of the 1976 Act defines a transfer as a separation of interest in a copyright. According to section 201(d), this separation can take effect in whole or in part (i.e., the owner's bundle of rights is divisible) and by any means of conveyance, such as by mortgaging an interest in the copyright, bequeathing it, or selling it. The transfer of an underlying copyright in a work should be distinguished, however, from the material object embodying it. Section 202 provides, for instance, that the transfer of an object does not transfer the underlying copyright in it. Accordingly, the sale of a book does not grant to the purchaser any interest in its copyright. Conversely, a grant of copyright does not transfer title to the object in which it is embodied unless otherwise agreed.

A document that transfers copyright ownership may be recorded in the Copyright Office. The execution of transfer documents and their recordal are specified in sections 204 and 205, respectively. Section 204 dictates that most transfers (except for non-exclusive licensing arrangements or transfers occurring by operation of law, i.e., automatically without the need for some affirmative action) must be in writing and signed by the transferor (or an authorized agent). Although not required, an acknowledgment or notarization of the transfer is *prima facie* evidence of the execution of the document—in other words, the acknowledgment establishes the fact of the document's execution unless contrary evidence can be provided. Moreover, a transfer that is exclusive should be distinguished from a non-exclusive transfer. Simply put, an exclusive transfer (e.g., a license to distribute a work that is exclusive to one party) is defined in section 101 as a transfer of copyright ownership; a non-exclusive arrangement (e.g., a transfer of an adaptation right to several parties) is not. Therefore, a non-exclusive agreement need not be in writing under section 204 to be valid.

Recordal of transfers is not mandated by the 1976 Act, but a valid recordal does put third parties on notice of the rights being claimed by virtue of the transfer. As set forth in section 205, such notice can be particularly effective in addressing conflicting claims between parties having an interest in some or all of a copyrighted property. Moreover, this optional recordal process applies not only to transfers as defined in section 101 but also to any other transaction affecting a copyright, such as the grant of a non-exclusive license to a third party or the grant of a security interest in a copyright to a lender. Although the Copyright Office does not prescribe any particular form to evidence a transfer or a recordal, the Office does provide a Document Cover Sheet to submit along with the documentation being recorded. Generally, a submission will be acceptable for recording provided that the documentation: (i) contains an actual signature(s) or an attestation that the document is a true copy of an original; (ii) is complete and does not contain references to other documents not made a part of the document being recorded; and (iii) is capable of being scanned. The Copyright Office will send the submitter a certificate of recordation for each valid submission. Further information regarding recordals is set forth in Circular 12.

Appendix 29, "Transfers and Recordal," of this Almanac contains statutory references to transfers and recordal.

Appendix 30, "Document Cover Sheet for Recordal," of this Almanac sets forth the Copyright Office's Document Cover Sheet for recordals.

TERMINATION OF TRANSFER

A termination, or recapture, of a copyright grant is a reversion of rights to the transferor (or other designee allowed under the law), allowing the grantor or designee to regain control of a work and its economic potential. In some cases, the termination of transfer may be negotiated as part of the transaction, as when a musician agrees to transfer a copyright to a music publisher but retains a right of reversion if the composition is not commercially exploited within a set period of time. Barring a contractual arrangement, sections 203 and 304(c) of the 1976 Act govern the process for terminating a grant of a copyright transfer or a license. In some instances, a copyright owner may be able to exercise a right of termination under section 304(d) due to the increase in length of copyright terms under CTEA. This section will focus on a comparison of the termination rights under sections 203 and 304(c).

Although sections 203 and 304(c) accomplish the same goal, they each deal with grants executed during a specific time frame by certain defined grantors. Specifically, section 304(c) deals with grants executed *before* January 1, 1978 by an author or the beneficiary of a renewal term; section 203, on the other hand, only applies to grants executed by an author *after* January 1, 1978. Furthermore, the time periods after which a termination may be exercised differ widely. Under section 203, a grant may be terminated after 35 years; whereas, under section 304(c), a grant may be terminated after 56 years or on January 1, 1978, whichever is later. However, the right to terminate is not absolute. For example, copyright grants in works made for hire cannot be terminated. In other cases, an otherwise valid termination right can be foiled if the opportunity to terminate is not taken at the appropriate time or the termination notice is invalid.

The CFR prescribes the exact form of notice required for an effective termination of transfer. Regardless whether the notice is sent pursuant to section 203 or 304(c), it must include a clear identification of the following: (i) the statutory section under which the notice is being sent; (ii) the name and address of each grantee (or appropriate successor) whose rights are being terminated; (iii) a reasonable identification of the grant being terminated; (iv) a listing and description of the person(s) exercising the termination right; and (v) the effective date of termination.

An effective termination must also be signed and served on the parties against whom it will take effect. Like transfers, termination notices can be recorded at the Copyright Office.

Appendix 31, "Termination of Transfer," of this Almanac sets forth the statutory and regulatory requirements for a termination of transfer.

SPECIAL LICENSING CONSIDERATIONS

As mentioned above, a copyright owner's licensing of the exclusive rights granted by law can reap economic rewards. In many instances, licensing arrangements are entered into voluntarily between or among the parties. However, in some cases, if an agreement cannot be made, licensing is mandatory and represents an exception to the copyright owner's otherwise exclusive right to control the exploitation of a work. Section 115 of the 1976 Act addresses this form of licensing, known as a compulsory license, an excerpt of which is found in Appendix 5, "Exclusive Rights in Copyrighted Works and Limitations," of this Almanac. Pursuant to section 115, the copyright owner of a non-dramatic musical work (i.e., not a cast album for a musical) that has been recorded and distributed is required to issue a license to a third party desiring to make and distribute phonorecords of the work to the public for private use. Circular 73 addresses this form of licensing, indicating that its genesis arose out of a concern that the copyright owners of phonorecords would exercise a monopoly over their use, which would prevent others from exercising the opportunity to make and release their own musical arrangement of the work for the public's enrichment. In other words, the compulsory license gives third parties the right to record and release their own version of the same song. The intended user of such a license must notify the copyright owner of an intention to exercise the license by filing a notice of intention with the owner or with the Copyright Office if the owner cannot be determined. The license fee payable to a copyright owner under a compulsory license is set and revised from time to time by a Copyright Royalty Board comprised of three copyright royalty judges. As of this writing, the current rate is 9.1 cents per song or 1.75 cents per minute of playing time or fraction thereof, whichever is greater.

Obviously, a compulsory license is not exclusive to any one party. An exclusive license is one in which the licensor grants a single licensee the exclusive right and license to use a copyrighted work for the purpose(s) set forth in the agreement. Therefore, a copyright owner should carefully consider a grant of exclusivity and its scope in determining whether the deal is likely to yield the desired economic result.

Another potential impact on the economic viability of a copyright arises from the opportunity to license a work internationally. Undoubtedly, the licensing and collection of revenue from the commercialization of a work worldwide is a daunting task for a copyright owner. Resources exist, however, to manage this activity. One organization specializing in such international coordination is the International Federation of Reproduction Rights Organisations, a consortium of organizations around the world assisting copyright owners with the development and administration of international rights management systems. In the United States, the Copyright Clearance Center (CCC) is a member organization offering international rights negotiation services and repatriation of earnings from worldwide transactions. As the name implies, CCC also offers compliance services to potential users of copyrighted material by issuing them licenses to the works of its participating publishers to protect against claims of unauthorized use, or infringement.

A particular challenge for a potential licensee in any of the scenarios discussed above is the identification of the copyright owner from whom a license should be obtained. Indeed, in some instances, a copyright owner cannot be discerned despite a diligent search; works falling into this scenario are known as orphan works. The lost revenue opportunity arising from the lack of use of orphan works for fear of infringement liability has been documented by the Copyright Office and raised before Congress, which introduced orphan works legislation in 2008 (and earlier) in an attempt to address the issue. If passed, such legislation would insulate users of copyrighted material from liability for infringement in cases where the material was used only after an exhaustive good faith search of copyright records did not reveal a party to whom rights permission could be addressed. The law would require the attachment of a special orphan-rights symbol to the work to further encourage the discovery of a proper copyright claimant and, if one should arise, the legislation would require reasonable compensation to the owner of the work.

POLICING A COPYRIGHT

In addition to addressing potential sources of revenue to enhance the economic vitality of copyrighted works, it is equally important that copyright owners engage resources to monitor the use of their copyrights for instances of infringement that undermine the owner's market for the work. As noted above, organizations such as CCC act on behalf of their members in facilitating the licensing of third parties to reproduce works. Another organization, the Business Software Alliance (BSA), is a nonprofit trade association devoted to protecting the software copyrights of its members. In most cases, BSA approaches a company alleged to have used illegal copies of a software program on the advice of a third party who notifies the organization of the alleged infringing use. BSA normally requests that the targeted organization perform a self audit of the number of copies of a software program that it is licensed to use. If the audit reveals a number greater than that for which the company is licensed, BSA typically requests restitution, including fines and penalties. BSA boasts among its members such industry leaders as IBM, Apple, Dell, HP and Symantec.

Other vulnerabilities concerning the licensing of a copyright can be addressed at the corporate level by instituting a team approach to copyright protection. A team approach to copyright enforcement can encompass several initiatives. First, employees need to be educated about copyrights to understand their importance. Educational efforts can take many forms, such as seminars for marketing personnel with internal or external speakers, newsletters, intranets and the dissemination of books and other pre-existing materials. Another educational tool is a policy and procedures document discussing the basic principles of copyright law, including the rights of a copyright owner and remedies for infringement of those rights. This document, or manual, may also include a summary of the company's existing copyrights, an identification of those responsible for enforcement, and a list of third parties authorized to use the copyrights. Additionally, employees should be encouraged to make scouting a part of the job and instructed on the collection of evidence showing an infringing use of copyrighted material, whether encountered in business or in private life. If an employee cannot collect the evidence initially, then a report should be submitted indicating a description of the infringing article and the time and place where it was seen. Employees should also be instructed to report any suspected incidences of infringement immediately so that the ability to obtain an injunction or calculate damages is uncompromised.

Finally, whether the copyright owner is an individual or a corporation, good record keeping and maintenance is essential to support and enforce claims of copyright ownership. Accordingly, appropriate actions include notations regarding the status of a work as a work for hire or joint work, registration of works to preserve statutory damages, and recordals of transfers and terminations to maintain the chain of title.

CHAPTER 5:
INFRINGEMENT ISSUES

A GENERAL OVERVIEW

The rights accorded under federal copyright law attach to a work from the moment of fixation, giving a claimant the right to bring a dispute regarding infringement of a copyright in a federal, rather than state, forum. Conversely, infringement actions involving works that remain unfixed and thus subject to state or common law are appropriately brought in a state court. This chapter will address federal suits for infringement.

Copyright infringement litigation is not an inexpensive process. Accordingly, before commencing any court case, aggrieved copyright owners contemplating litigation should assess their position relative to the defending party. This assessment will entail the consideration of several elements such as: (i) the registered or unregistered status of the copied work and its validity as copyrightable matter; (ii) the similarities of the works at issue; (iii) the nature of the copying; (iv) previous disputes between the parties; (v) licensing potential or other possible synergies; and (vi) the desired outcome of the dispute. Once the relevant information is obtained on the activity giving rise to the dispute, a copyright owner should consider the appropriate measures to take to inform the defendant of the conduct giving rise to the complaint. In some cases, a letter explaining the consequences of the complained-of conduct with a demand to quit the alleged infringing activity, known as a cease and desist letter—or a demand letter—may suffice in lieu of litigation. For example, the Recording Industry Association of America routinely sends letters to online music retailers who allow users to sample recordings from copyrighted phonorecords, educating them as to the consequences of duplicating, digitally performing or distributing copyrighted sound recordings without the copyright owner's permission.

Such letters may be particularly useful for ending the activity of innocent infringers, many of whom simply harbor misconceptions regarding the application of copyright law to their alleged conduct. Arguably, no other area of intellectual property law is subject to as many mistaken notions about what does or does not constitute infringement as copyright law. For example, many users of copyrighted material mistakenly believe that copying is justified if the material does not contain a copyright notice. Of course, since the adherence of the United States to the Berne Convention, the copyright notice is optional. Therefore, the user of material without a copyright notice should not presume that the material is in the public domain and thus freely available for use. Another oft-heard belief regarding copyright is that a work is not infringed unless the entire work is used. Although a certain amount of use of a work may sometimes not be regarded as infringement but rather as a fair use (discussed further below in the section entitled **Defenses**), the viability of a fair use defense varies widely and must be considered in conjunction with the nature and extent of the copyright owner's exclusive rights. Furthermore, a consideration of these same rights should undermine a common belief that a work is not infringed so long as attribution is given to the source or the notion that works can be freely copied online. In fact, according to the Citizen Media Law Project, copyright infringement suits directed at online publishers such as bloggers are rising.

This chapter will discuss: (i) procedural and substantive aspects of a proceeding for infringement; (ii) contributory infringement and vicarious liability; (iii) defenses and remedies; (iv) criminal laws related to infringement; (v) piracy prevention; and (vi) insurance.

INFRINGEMENT PROCEEDINGS

Section 501(a) of the 1976 Act provides that an infringer is anyone who: (i) violates the exclusive bundle of rights of the copyright owner (discussed in Chapter 1, "The Nature and Function of a Copyright," of this Almanac); (ii) imports copies or phonorecords into the United States in violation of section 602; or (iii) violates an author's rights of attribution or integrity under VARA. This section will deal with a civil claim under scenario (i) above, which must be brought within three years following accrual of the claim.

In the first instance, a work allegedly infringed must be copyrightable. Accordingly, mere facts or those lacking originality in their compilation in some manner are not capable of being infringed. Likewise, those items listed in Chapter 1, "The Nature and Function of a Copyright," of this Almanac as being incapable of copyright protection (such as a word, short phrases or slogans) are not appropriate subject matter for a copyright suit. If the subject matter threshold is met, then the plaintiff must further prove ownership of the copyright at issue. Under section 501(b), either the legal or beneficial owner of an exclusive right in a work has the right to sue for infringement. Therefore, the copyright claimant or an exclusive licensee of one or more of the owner's rights may bring suit. Conversely, the holder of a non-exclusive right has no authority to bring a suit.

The validity of the copyright is also essential. As set forth in section 410(c), a certificate of registration made within five years after first publication of a work is *prima facie* evidence of the validity of the copyright and of the facts stated in the certificate. Of course, registration is generally optional, but its benefit in litigation as to proof of ownership and validity should not be underestimated. Moreover, section 411 expressly states that (except for VARA claims) registration of a work is a prerequisite for an infringement action. In some cases, however, a work submitted for registration is refused (as discussed in the section entitled **Office Actions** in Chapter 2, "The Application Process," of this Almanac) or the registration is still in process. As for the former scenario, section 411(a) provides that a plaintiff may bring an infringement suit on a failed registration provided that the Copyright Office is given notice of the proceeding so that the Register of Copyrights may decide whether to enter an appearance in the litigation for the purpose of addressing the issue of registrability. As for the latter case, the ability of a court to hear a claim based on a work in the process of registration is subject to varying interpretation. In fact, there is a split of authority among the federal courts whether an infringement suit can be brought following an application for copyright registration but before the registration certificate has been issued. Indeed, some courts require proof of actual registration before a suit can be filed; others only require proof of filing. Prospective plaintiffs are advised to check the governing rule in their jurisdiction prior to instituting suit.

Once the complaining party completes the necessary statutory and procedural prerequisites for establishing suit, then copying must be proved. Evidence of copying is largely circumstantial and illustrates two elements: (i) the infringing work is substantially similar to the copyrighted work and (ii) the defendant had access to the allegedly infringed work. The substantial similarity standard will obviously vary from case to case. The test is whether an ordinary observer comparing the works would determine that a copying took place. Without access to the infringed work, however, a substantially similar work may, in fact, have been independently created. Therefore, a plaintiff must show that the defendant had some reasonable opportunity to view or copy the work.

CONTRIBUTORY INFRINGEMENT AND VICARIOUS LIABILITY

The principles of contributory infringement and vicarious liability are not found in copyright legislation. Instead, the parameters of these companion claims for redress of infringement have been crafted over many years of court decisions. Contributory infringement liability attaches if the offending party had knowledge of the infringement and contributed to it in some way. For instance, several years ago an advertising agency was found liable for contributory infringement when ten words from a competitor's commercial were used in the ad produced by the agency for its own client. Understandably, the requirement that a party *knowingly* participate in the infringing activity has given rise to much debate and litigation, including a famous 2005 United States Supreme Court decision known as the *Grokster* case. In that case, the Court held that Grokster, Ltd. and other defendants providing peer-to-peer file exchange services of copyrighted films and music had induced infringement by end users of those services and were therefore secondarily liable to the plaintiffs. Accordingly, a defendant's act of inducing infringement (e.g., by providing the technological means to make it happen) is essentially an indication of knowledge of the infringing behavior.

Unlike contributory infringement, vicarious liability can attach regardless whether the defendant had any knowledge of the infringing activity. Vicarious liability arises when the defendant supervises the infringing conduct and has an economic interest in its outcome. In the advertising example above, the agency could be vicariously liable for supervising the development of the commercial.

DEFENSES

Defendants in civil infringement proceedings may avail themselves of any number of defenses to their conduct. For example, a defendant may assert that the case is barred as a result of the three-year statute of limitations or that the work is in the public domain. Another defense, copyright misuse, alleges that the plaintiff has acted outside the scope of the copyright or otherwise violated its terms. Misuse may apply when a plaintiff applies for copyright in a claimed original work that is, in fact, a derivative work or when a software licensor attempts to control ownership of developments or improvements that are outside the scope of the license agreement. Furthermore, section 302(e) of the 1976 Act sets forth that anyone obtaining a certified report from the Copyright Office after the earlier of 95 years following first publication or 120 years following creation of a work indicating no evidence of an author then living or a death less than 70 years before is entitled to the benefit of a presumption that the author has been dead for at least 70 years. Reliance on this presumption is a complete defense to any action for infringement. Moreover, where the copyright owner's right of distribution is alleged to have been infringed, the first sale doctrine (with some exceptions as noted in Chapter 1, "The Nature and Function of a Copyright," of this Almanac) may provide a defense to infringement provided that the defendant can provide proof that the copies in question are lawfully owned by the defendant and capable of being transferred.

Of all the defenses, fair use is a particularly notable and frequently invoked affirmative defense in which the defendant carries the burden of proof. This defense, applicable to both published and unpublished works, is set out at section 107 of the 1976 Act. This section explicitly states that a fair use of work for purposes such as criticism, comment, news reporting, teaching, scholarship or research is not an infringement. However, determining whether a use made for any of the purposes above is a "fair use" draws contentious debate, and the success of this defense is highly dependent on the facts and circumstances of each particular case.

Section 107 sets forth four factors that must be examined and weighed in particular to assess whether a use is fair. The first factor is the purpose and character of the use. Purposes include the above-mentioned activities related to comment, criticism, news reporting, teaching and the like. Other purposes explored in cases include parody and satire. The character of the use includes an analysis whether it is used commercially, not for profit or privately. In many instances, courts generally uphold use of a work for one of the commonly recognized purposes above as a fair use under the first factor unless the activity undermines the economic value of the copyrighted work. Thus a commercial use tends to weigh against a finding of fair use as does a large-scale verbatim copying of a work that does little to make productive use of the underlying work. The second factor of the fair use test is the nature of the copyrighted work being taken for an alleged fair use. A finding of fair use on this factor is more likely if the work is functional—that is, factual, historic or scientific—rather than creative. The third factor examines the amount and substantiality of the portion used in relation to the work as a whole. In other words, the quantitative and qualitative aspects of the appropriation are relevant. Generally, a wholesale copying of a work does not promote the finding of a fair use, particularly if any such taking absorbs the essence of the work. The last factor addresses the economic impact of the use on the copyrighted work. Clearly, if the use creates an adverse impact or replaces the need for the original work as opposed to fulfilling or creating a demand for it, then a finding of fair use on this factor is not likely.

REMEDIES

Various remedies are available to an aggrieved copyright owner, but fundamentally, injunctive relief (provided for in section 502 of the 1976 Act) is a desired outcome for any litigation. Injunctive relief usually includes a request for a temporary restraining order during the conduct of the litigation and a permanent order following a favorable decision on the case, barring any further infringing use of the copyrighted work. A plaintiff should note that injunctive relief is enforceable throughout the United States. Additional remedies include potential impoundment by the court of allegedly infringing articles and destruction of such articles if infringement is proved. A court also has discretion to award the prevailing party with costs of suit, which in some instances may include reasonable attorneys' fees.

Of course, a significant remedy sought by plaintiffs is the recovery of damages and profits. Section 504 provides plaintiffs with the ability to choose the nature of damages to be recovered from an infringer. Specifically, at any time up to final judgment, a plaintiff may choose to recover either: (i) actual damages together with profits of the defendant, or (ii) statutory damages. Either choice may be potentially problematic, however. For instance, in many cases a plaintiff may have difficulty proving actual damages or the amount may be negligible, and the establishment of profits requires the plaintiff to prove the defendant's gross revenue. Furthermore, profits can only be awarded so long as the amount is not duplicative of the award for actual damages. As a result of these difficulties, most plaintiffs opt for statutory damages if they qualify. As of this writing, statutory damages are set at an amount no less than $750 and no more than $30,000 per infringed work. However, if the infringement is proved to be willful, then the court may consider a larger ceiling of damages up to $150,000. Conversely, if the defendant is proved to have been an innocent infringer, the court may reduce the award to as little as $200. A defendant may be deemed an innocent infringer if the evidence proves that the defendant was not aware and had no reason to believe that his or her acts constituted an infringement of copyright, as might be the case in the event of a defendant's good faith belief that a work was orphaned as discussed in Chapter 4, "Monetizing Copyrights," of this Almanac. In other cases specifically involving libraries, archives, nonprofit educational institutions and public broadcasting entities, the court may elect to reduce an award of statutory damages if the party had a reasonable belief that use of the work constituted a fair use.

In addition to the potential for a reduction in statutory damages given the above examples, a plaintiff may also be precluded from choosing these damages if the allegedly infringed work was not registered in a timely manner. An election of statutory damages can only be made: (i) in the case of unpublished works, for infringements occurring after registration; and (ii) in the case of published works, for infringements occurring after first publication only if registration was made within three months following that publication. Notably, section 412 sets forth three instances in which statutory damages will not be jeopardized: (i) for actions related to attribution and integrity under VARA; (ii) for actions involving works in which registration is made within three months following the first transmission (in the case of a work consisting of sounds, images, or both, in which the first fixation is made simultaneously with its transmission); and (iii) for works pre-registered before the commencement of the infringement and having an effective date of registration not later than the earlier of (i) three months after the first publication of the work or (ii) one month after the copyright owner learned of the infringement.

CRIMINAL PENALTIES

Copyright infringement is subject to criminal as well as civil proceedings. Section 507 of the 1976 Act provides that a criminal proceeding must be commenced by a prosecutor within five years after the cause of action arose. Criminal infringement is defined in section 506 as that which is willful and done for any one of the following three reasons: (i) for the purpose of commercial advantage or private financial gain; (ii) for reproduction or distribution of copyrighted works in any 180-day period with a total retail value exceeding $1000; or (iii) for making unauthorized pre-release versions of works available via computer. Upon conviction, infringing articles are forfeited and destroyed. Section 506 also provides for fines related to fraudulent copyright notices, fraudulent removal of copyright notices, and fraudulent copyright applications.

Punishment for first, as well as subsequent offenses related to criminal infringement, is provided for in Title 18 of the United States Code at section 2319 and can include fines, imprisonment or both. Other criminal provisions relating to copyright infringement are found in Title 18 of the United States Code at section 2318. Section 2318 punishes trafficking in counterfeit labels for phonorecords, motion pictures or other audiovisual works. Punishment may include fines up to $250,000 and/or imprisonment up to five years. The effects of trafficking as well as preventative measures are discussed immediately below.

PIRACY

The impact of piracy and counterfeiting worldwide is staggering. For instance, a report commissioned by the Business Software Alliance indicated that software piracy resulted in a loss of $34 billion worldwide in 2005 alone. However, the problem is not limited to software. In fact, reports indicate that global trade in pirated and counterfeited goods costs U.S. businesses over $250 billion each year. Under the 1976 Act, section 602 grants copyright owners the right to bring infringement proceedings against those who engage in the importation of unauthorized copies of a work, which are subject to seizure and forfeiture. Furthermore, newer legislation such as the PRO-IP Act of 2008 dramatically increases damages for domestic piracy. Other measures available to copyright owners to address the economic consequences of piracy include recordation of copyrights with U.S. Customs and, on a global scale, use of the rights enforcement services offered by other countries.

U.S. Customs & Border Protection (CBP), a bureau of the Department of Homeland Security, maintains a copyright recordation system to assist in the global effort to prevent the importation of goods that infringe copyrights. CBP officers monitor imports at over 300 U.S. ports of entry to prevent the importation of counterfeited and pirated goods and can detain suspicious properties for five days upon reasonable suspicion. Filings with the CBP can be effectuated online using the Intellectual Property Rights e-Recordation (IPRR) system, located at https://apps.cbp.gov/e-recordations. Filings will require the submission of a certified copy of each copyright registration sought to be protected (available for a fee from the Copyright Office) along with copies of supporting documents. Electronic filings of these materials reduce the time from filing to enforcement by field personnel.

Other countries participating in enforcement strategies include the European Union. Specifically, customs recordation and seizure of pirated goods are available on a national or multi-national basis under EU legislation known as "Council Regulation (EC) No 1383/2003 concerning customs action against goods suspected of infringing certain intellectual property rights and the measures to be taken against goods found to have infringed such rights." For information on other anti-counterfeiting and piracy initiatives, copyright owners may wish to consult the intellectual property compliance and enforcement initiatives of the World Customs Organization (http://www.wcoomd.org), an inter-governmental organization exclusively focused on customs matters.

INSURANCE

Copyright litigation can reach into the hundreds of thousands of dollars. As a result, a prudent copyright owner should consider obtaining insurance coverage for intellectual property disputes. Coverage can include defense and indemnification for damages and legal expenses incurred with respect to alleged infringement of a third party's rights. Traditionally, the insurer's duty, if any, to defend or indemnify was covered under an "advertising injury" endorsement of an insured's comprehensive general liability (CGL) policy. However, insurers are increasingly limiting or excluding coverage for infringement claims under these endorsements.

In recent years, a new type of policy known as a "cyber policy" has emerged. As the name implies, these policies address cyber risks such as those arising from a security breach that compromises the storage of sensitive information. However, this coverage is not limited to computer-related loss or failure; many policies explicitly cover infringement claims and can be crafted to suit the buyer's needs. As a result, the insured now have greater opportunities to find adequate cover against copyright-related disputes.

CHAPTER 6:
INTERNET ISSUES REGARDING
COPYRIGHTS

COPYRIGHT IN THE DIGITAL AGE

Virtual worlds and digital transmissions provided via the Internet pose challenges for copyright owners. To be sure, users of copyrighted material sometimes fail to appreciate that information available over the Internet is no less protected by copyright law than material available via other means. For example, shopkeepers in a virtual world (i.e., an Internet-based community) have sued fellow virtual merchants in bricks-and-mortar courtrooms for copyright infringement of their online products. Furthermore, in a high-profile case, Google began digitizing vast libraries of books without the permission of book publishers and authors. In a recent settlement of the dispute, Google agreed, among other things, to make abstracts of in-print works available as part of its book search function only with the permission of publishers and authors. Against the challenges of new media and emerging technologies, various digital acts have emerged in an attempt to balance the rights of copyright owners with those desiring to use their copyrighted works. This chapter will address digital copyright from both a national and international perspective and will cover the U.S. enactment of the Digital Performance Right in Sound Recordings Act and the Digital Millennium Copyright Act as well as the European Union's Copyright Directive of 2001.

Digital Performance Right in Sound Recordings Act

The Digital Performance Right in Sound Recordings Act of 1995 (DPRA) created section 106(6) of the 1976 Act, which grants the copyright owner of a sound recording a limited public performance right regarding digital audio transmissions. Specifically, the law grants a sound recording copyright owner the exclusive right to control interactive digital performances of sound recordings, regardless whether the interactive service is fee based. Section 114(j)(7) describes an interactive service as one that enables a member of the public to receive a transmission of a sound recording, such as an online music retailer who provides customers with the ability to make or download copies of digital music files. DPRA provides a cause of action for infringement against online music providers who deliver a phonorecord by digital transmission of a sound recording without the permission of the sound recording's copyright owner. In simple terms, the act makes clear that music in digital form is no less of a sound recording than sound recordings embodied in the form of CDs, cassettes or vinyl. To assist copyright owners in the administration of licenses and revenues for digital performances, the Copyright Office has designated Sound Exchange (http://www.soundexchange.com) as the organization responsible for collecting and distributing performing rights fees to copyright owners. Sound Exchange works in a manner similar to that of ASCAP, BMI and SESAC discussed in Chapter 1, "The Nature and Function of a Copyright," of this Almanac, in the section entitled **The Right of Public Performance.**

Independent of license fees to be paid for the public performance of sound recordings under section 106(6), legislation introduced in Congress as of this writing would further amend subsection (6) to apply generally to audio transmissions rather than specifically to digital audio transmissions. This amendment, proposed in a recent draft of The Performance Rights Act (a bill in the House of Representatives—H.R. 848—recently sent to the Senate), would close a loophole in the 1976 Act which exempts AM and FM broadcasters from paying royalties for their use of music. The exemption does not apply to satellite radio, cable radio and Internet webcasts, nor does it apply to terrestrial broadcasters in other countries.

The Digital Millennium Copyright Act

In General

Enacted by Congress in 1998, The Digital Millennium Copyright Act (DMCA) was originally intended to implement the WIPO Copyright Treaty and Performances and Phonograms Treaty following U.S. adherence to their terms. In particular, DMCA enacts measures to meet the treaties' requirement that member nations provide enforcement against the unlawful circumvention of technological measures designed to prevent copying of online works. In broader terms, DMCA seeks to address the promotion of e-commerce (i.e., doing business on the Internet) while protecting the rights of copyright holders and therefore, its provisions are important for anyone doing business on the Internet.

DMCA is a sweeping piece of legislation. Among other things, it adds a new chapter (Chapter 12) to the 1976 Act and amends various other provisions to comport with its terms, provides protection for the backup and copying of computer programs in the course of maintenance, and provides a new intellectual property right in the design of boat hulls. This chapter will highlight the following features of DMCA: (i) the anti-circumvention provisions; (ii) limitations on liability, or "safe harbors," for certain Internet activities; and (iii) notice requirements for copyright holders for certain claimed infringements.

Appendix 32, "Provisions of the Digital Millennium Copyright Act," of this Almanac sets forth key provisions of DMCA as discussed below.

Anti-Circumvention under DMCA

Sections 1201(a) and (b) of the 1976 Act set out the anti-circumvention provisions of DMCA. Subsection (a) sets forth the general prohibition against circumventing a technological measure designed to control access to a work. Such technological measures include password protection and encryption of data. Subsection (b) delineates the various activities that may give rise to circumvention liability, such as importing, manufacturing, selling publicly, knowingly marketing or otherwise trafficking in any technology, product, service, part or component that is designed or principally operated for the purpose of circumvention. Like other cases of infringement, remedies for a violation of these provisions include injunctive relief, attorneys' fees, and an election of actual or statutory damages. Statutory damages are awarded for each instance of circumvention in an amount no less than $200 and no more than $2500 per infringement. Notably, circumvention is punishable criminally as well. Specifically, section 1204 provides harsh penalties for willful acts of circumvention designed for commercial or private financial gain. First offenders may be fined up to $500,000 and/or imprisoned up to five years; subsequent offenders may be fined up to $1,000,000 and/or imprisoned up to ten years.

Similar to exemptions on the copyright holder's bundle of exclusive rights, various exceptions to the stringent anti-circumvention rules have been promulgated in the public interest. These exceptions include activities related to law enforcement, parental controls on the viewing of material by children, library and educational services, encryption research, certain reverse engineering activities and security testing.

Moreover, from time to time the Register of Copyrights considers whether certain classes of works should be exempt from the general prohibition against circumvention under section 1201(a). In fact, DMCA mandates that the Copyright Office undertake public hearings every three years to determine whether there are certain classes of works whose use will be impaired unless the anti-circumvention provisions are not given effect. The last public hearings took place in 2006. As a result of those proceedings, the following six classes of works (codified in section 201.40 of CFR) were deemed exempt from the anti-circumvention prohibition for the period from November 27, 2006 through October 27, 2009: (i) audiovisual works for educational use in the classroom by media studies or film professors, when circumvention is required to produce compilations for instructive use; (ii) computer programs and video games distributed in formats that have become obsolete and that require the original media or hardware as a condition of access, when circumvention is accomplished for the purpose of preservation or archival reproduction of published digital works by a library or archive; (iii) computer programs protected by obsolete dongles that prevent access due to malfunction or damage; (iv) literary works distributed in e-book format when all existing e-book editions of the work contain access controls that prevent the enabling either of the book's read-aloud function or of screen readers that render the text into a specialized format; (v) computer programs in the form of firmware that enable wireless connections, when circumvention is accomplished for the sole purpose of lawfully connecting to a wireless telephone communication network; and (vi) sound recordings and associated audiovisual works distributed in compact disc format with access controls, when circumvention is accomplished solely for the purpose of good faith testing, investigating, or correcting security flaws or vulnerabilities.

As of this writing, the most recent hearings for proceedings required in 2009 took place in Palo Alto, California and Washington, D.C. in May 2009. Readers should consult the Copyright Office website for the results of those hearings. Once a determination of protected classes of works is again made, any non-infringing use of those works will not be subject to the general anti-circumvention prohibition for the ensuing three-year period.

Limitations on Liability

The limitations on liability or safe harbor provisions of DMCA abrogate liability for copyright infringement by online service providers who meet certain acceptable conditions of Internet activity. Set forth in section 512 of the 1976 Act, these activities include: (i) transitory digital network communications; (ii) system caching; (iii) the use of information location tools such as hypertext links; and (iv) the storage of information at the direction of a user. Notwithstanding a service provider's failure to meet the conditions of safe harbor, it is instructive to note that a copyright plaintiff must still prove that the provider committed infringement before liability will attach.

Of all the activities noted above, perhaps the best known safe harbor relates to (iv) above, set forth in section 512(c). Specifically, this limitation on liability applies to a scenario wherein a service provider provides storage on its system at the request of a user, such as eBay's placement of an auction site at the request of a seller. In some instances, a copyright owner may allege that the stored material infringes a copyright, and a service provider, taking no action other than allowing the storage of the alleged infringing material, will not want to be held liable for infringement. In such a case, the general conditions of safe harbor for a service provider (e.g., eBay) require that it: (i) not have actual knowledge that the stored material is infringing; (ii) not be aware of any facts or circumstances making it apparent that the material is infringing; and (iii) expeditiously remove any material found to be infringing, particularly after notice of the copyright owner. If the service provider exercises control over the activity giving rise to the claim for infringement, the provider must also not benefit financially from the infringing activity itself. In addition to the above parameters, the provider must designate an agent for the receipt of notice from a copyright owner that an infringing activity is taking place by reason of the provider's storage of material on its system or network. The Copyright Office maintains a directory of all such agents, which may be accessed at http://www.copyright.gov/onlinesp/list.

Appendix 33, "Designation of Agent Forms," of this Almanac contains the Copyright Office's suggested form for designating an agent or amending an existing designation, as the case may be.

DMCA Notice Requirements for Copyright Holders

Section 512(c)(3) provides the framework for an effective notice by or on behalf of a copyright owner (or an exclusive licensee) to a designated agent as referenced above. Specifically, the notice must be in writing and contain the following elements: (i) the copyright holder or authorized agent's signature, which can be rendered in pen and ink or electronically (e.g., /john doe/); (ii) identification of the infringed work; (iii) identification of the allegedly infringing material along with information that will assist the service provider in locating it; (iv) contact information of the complainant; (v) a statement that the complainant has a good faith belief that the material has not been authorized for use by the alleged infringer; and (vi) a statement that the information is accurate and, under penalty of perjury, that the complainant is, or is authorized to act on behalf of, the copyright owner.

In many respects, the notice (frequently referred to as a "takedown notice") resembles a demand letter as discussed in Chapter 5, "Infringement Issues," of this Almanac. Unlike a general demand letter, however, strict adherence to the statutory requirements is encouraged. Failure to substantially comply may result in the notice being ineffective to prove that the service provider obtained knowledge of the infringing activity and neglected to act expeditiously in its removal. With regard to removal, it should be noted that a service provider generally has no liability to the alleged infringer for a good faith removal or disabling of contents identified in the takedown notice.

EU Copyright Directive

Frequently referred to as the European equivalent of DMCA, the European Union's Copyright Directive of 2001 (Directive 2001/29/EC, which can be accessed from the European Union law portal at http://eur-lex.europa.eu/LexUriServ/LexUriServ.do?uri=CELEX:32001L0029: EN:HTML) came into force in June 2001. Like its U.S. counterpart, it was enacted to conform with the provisions of the WIPO treaties, to which the European Union is also a party. In general terms, it likewise seeks to strike a balance between the interests of copyright holders and users of their content in a networked environment. Furthermore, it imposes on EU member nations certain obligations with respect to technological measures. Specifically, it provides that member nations enact a general prohibition against circumvention of technological measures as well as protect against activities such as the manufacture, importation, distribution or possession of goods or services that are marketed or used to circumvent technological measures. Similar to DMCA, anti-circumvention measures are described as encryption, scrambling or other transformation of a work or a copy control mechanism designed to protect the work. The EU Directive also contains a series of limitations on the rights of a copyright owner, most notably that a transient or incidental copying as part of a network transmission is a legal use. Accordingly, Internet service providers are not liable for the data they transmit. Unlike DMCA, the EU legislation leaves many critical details concerning sanctions and remedies to the member states. However, like DMCA, any enforcement action available to a copyright holder must include injunctive relief and damages.

APPENDIX 1:
COPYRIGHT ACT OF 1790

COPYRIGHT ACT OF 1790

1 Statutes At Large, 124

An Act for the encouragement of learning, by securing the copies of maps, Charts, And books, to the authors and proprietors of such copies, during the times therein mentioned.

Section 1. *Be it enacted by the Senate and House of Representatives of the United States of America in Congress assembled,* That from and after the passing of this act, the author and authors of any map, chart, book or books already printed within these United States, being a citizen or citizens thereof, or resident within the same, his or their executors, administrators or assigns, who halt or have not transferred to any other person the copyright of such map, chart, book or books, share or shares thereof; and any other person or persons, being a citizen or citizens of these United States, or residents therein, his or their executors, administrators or assigns, who halt or have purchased or legally acquired the copyright of any such map, chart, book or books, in order to print, reprint, publish or vend the same, shall have the sole right and liberty of printing, reprinting, publishing and vending such map, chart, book or books, for the term of fourteen years from the recording the title thereof in the clerk's office, as is herein after directed: And that the author and authors of any map, chart, book or books already made and composed, and not printed or published, or that shall hereafter be made and composed, being a citizen or citizens of these United States, or resident therein, and his or their executors, administrators or assigns, shall have the sole right and liberty of printing, reprinting, publishing and vending such map, chart, book or books, for the like term of fourteen years from the time of recording the title thereof in the clerk's office as aforesaid. And if, at the expiration of the said term, the author or authors, or any of them, be living, and a citizen or citizens of these United States, or resident therein, the same exclusive right shall be continued to him or them, his or their executors, administrators or assigns, for the further term of fourteen years; *Provided*, He or they shall cause the title thereof to be a second time recorded and published in the same manner as is herein after directed, and that within six months before the expiration of the first term of fourteen years aforesaid.

Sec. 2 *And be it further enacted,* That if any other person or persons, from and after the recording the title of any map, chart, book or books, and publishing the same as aforesaid, and within the times limited and granted by this act, shall print, reprint, publish, or import, or cause to be printed, reprinted, published, or imported from any foreign Kingdom or State, any copy or copies of such map, chart, book or books, without the consent of the author or proprietor thereof, first had and obtained in writing, signed in the presence of two or more credible witnesses; or knowing the same to be so printed, reprinted, or imported, shall publish, sell, or expose to sale, or cause to be published, sold or exposed to sale, any copy of such map, chart, book or books, without such consent first had and obtained in writing as aforesaid, then such offender or offenders shall forfeit all and every sheet and sheets, being part of the same, or either of them, to the author or proprietor of such map, chart, book or books, who shall forthwith destroy the same: And every such offender and offenders shall also forfeit and pay the sum of fifty cents for every sheet which shall be found in his or their possession, either printed or printing, published, imported or exposed to sale, contrary to the true intent and meaning of this act, the one moiety thereof to the author or proprietor of such map, chart, book or books, who shall sue for the same, and the other moiety thereof to and for the use of the United States, to be recovered by action of debt in any court of record in the United States, wherein the same is cognizable. *Provided always,* That such action be commenced within one year after the cause of action shall arise, and not afterwards.

Sec. 3 *And be it further enacted,* That no person shall be entitled to the benefit of this act, in cases where any map, chart, book or books, hath or have been already printed and published, unless he shall first deposit, and in all other cases, unless he shall before publication deposit a printed copy of the title of such map. chart, book or books, in the clerk's office of the district court where the author or proprietor shall reside: And the clerk of such court is hereby directed and required to record the same forthwith, in a book to be kept by him for that purpose, in the words following, (giving a copy thereof to the said author or proprietor, under the seal of the court, if he shall require the same)."District of to wit: *Be it remembered,* that on the day of in the year of the indepen-dence of the United States of America, A. B. of the said district, hath deposited in this office the title of a map, chart, book or books, (as the case may be) the right whereof he claims as author or proprietor. (as the case may be) in the words following to wit: [here insert the title] in conformity to the act of the Congress of the United States, intitled ' An act for the encouragement of learning, by securing the copies of maps, chart, and book, to the authors and proprietors of such copies, during the time therein mentioned.' C. D. clerk of the district of." For which the said clerk shall be entitled to receive sixty cents from the said author or proprietor, and sixty cents for every copy under seal actually given to such author or proprietor as aforesaid. And such author or proprietor shall, within two months from the date thereof cause a copy of the said record to be published in one or more of the newpapers printed in the United States, for the space of four weeks.

Sec. 4 *And be it further enacted,* That the author or proprietor of any such map, chart, book or books, shall, within six months after the publishing thereof, deliver, or cause to be delivered to the Secretary of State a copy of the same, to be preserved.

Sec. 5 *And be it further enacted,* That nothing in this act shall be construed to extend to prohibit the importation or vending, Reprinting or publishing within the United States, of any map, chart, book or books, written, printed, or published by any person not a citizen of the United States, in foreign parts or places without the jurisdiction of the United States.

Sec. 6 *And be it further enacted,* That any person or persons who shall print or publish and manuscript, without the consent and approbation of the author or proprietor thereof, first had and obtained as aforesaid, (if such author or proprietor be a citizen of or resident in these United States) shall be liable to suffer and pay to the said author or proprietor all damages occasioned by such injury, to be recovered by a special action on the case founded upon this act, in any court having cognizance thereof.

Sec. 7 *And be it further enacted,* That if any person or persons shall be sued or prosecuted for any matter, act or thing done under or by virtue of this act, he or they may plead the general issue, and give the special matter in evidence.

Approved, May 31, 1790

APPENDIX 2:
THE COPYRIGHT ACT OF 1909

AN ACT TO AMEND AND CONSOLIDATE THE ACTS RESPECTING COPYRIGHT.

Be it enacted by the Senate and House of Representatives of the United States of America in Congress assembled, That any person entitled thereto, upon complying with the provisions of this Act, shall have the exclu-
5 sive right:

(a) To print, reprint, publish, copy, and vend the copyrighted work; <small>Exclusive right to print, publish and vend.</small>

(b) To translate the copyrighted work into other languages or dialects, or make any other version thereof, if it <small>Exclusive right to translate, dramatize, arrange and adapt, etc.</small>
10 be a literary work; to dramatize it if it be a nondramatic work; to convert it into a novel or other nondramatic work if it be a drama; to arrange or adapt it if it be a musical work; to complete, execute, and finish it if it be a model or design for a work of art;

15 (c) To deliver or authorize the delivery of the copyrighted work in public for profit if it be a lecture, sermon, address, or similar production; <small>Exclusive right to deliver lectures, sermons, etc.</small>

(d) To perform or represent the copyrighted work publicly if it be a drama or, if it be a dramatic work and <small>To represent dramatic works, or make record, or exhibit or perform, etc.</small>
20 not reproduced in copies for sale, to vend any manuscript or any record whatsoever thereof; to make or to procure the making of any transcription or record thereof by or from which, in whole or in part, it may in any manner or by any method be exhibited, performed, represented,
25 produced, or reproduced; and to exhibit, perform, represent, produce, or reproduce it in any manner or by any method whatsoever;

COPYRIGHT LAW OF THE UNITED STATES.

To perform music and make arrangement, setting, or record. (e) To perform the copyrighted work publicly for profit if it be a musical composition and for the purpose of public performance for profit; and for the purposes set forth in subsection (a) hereof, to make any arrangement or setting of it or of the melody of it in any system 5 of notation or any form of record in which the thought of an author may be recorded and from which it may be **Act not retroactive.** read or reproduced: *Provided,* That the provisions of this Act, so far as they secure copyright controlling the parts of instruments serving to reproduce mechanically the 10 musical work, shall include only compositions published **Music by foreign author.** and copyrighted after this Act goes into effect, and shall not include the works of a foreign author or composer unless the foreign state or nation of which such author or composer is a citizen or subject grants, either by treaty, 15 convention, agreement, or law, to citizens of the United States similar rights: *And provided further, and as a condition of extending the copyright control to such me-* **Control of mechanical musical reproduction.** *chanical reproductions,* That whenever the owner of a musical copyright has used or permitted or knowingly 20 acquiesced in the use of the copyrighted work upon the parts of instruments serving to reproduce mechanically the musical work, any other person may make similar use of the copyrighted work upon the payment to the copy- **Royalty for use of music on records, etc.** right proprietor of a royalty of two cents on each such 25 part manufactured, to be paid by the manufacturer thereof; and the copyright proprietor may require, and if so the manufacturer shall furnish, a report under oath on the twentieth day of each month on the number of parts of instruments manufactured during the previous month 30 serving to reproduce mechanically said musical work, and royalties shall be due on the parts manufactured during any month upon the twentieth of the next succeeding month. The payment of the royalty provided for by this section shall free the articles or devices for which such 35 royalty has been paid from further contribution to the copyright except in case of public performance for profit: **Notice of use of music on records.** *And provided further,* That it shall be the duty of the copyright owner, if he uses the musical composition himself for the manufacture of parts of instruments serving 40 **License to use music on records.** to reproduce mechanically the musical work, or licenses others to do so, to file notice thereof, accompanied by a

recording fee, in the copyright office, and any failure to
file such notice shall be a complete defense to any suit,
action, or proceeding for any infringement of such copyright.

5 In case of the failure of such manufacturer to pay to *Failure to pay royalties.*
the copyright proprietor within thirty days after demand
in writing the full sum of royalties due at said rate at the
date of such demand the court may award taxable costs to
the plaintiff and a reasonable counsel fee, and the court
10 may, in its discretion, enter judgment therein for any
sum in addition over the amount found to be due as
royalty in accordance with the terms of this Act, not
exceeding three times such amount.

The reproduction or rendition of a musical composition *Reproduction of music on coin-operated machines.*
15 by or upon coin-operated machines shall not be deemed a
public performance for profit unless a fee is charged for
admission to the place where such reproduction or rendition occurs.

SEC. 2. That nothing in this Act shall be construed to *Right at common law or in equity.*
20 annul or limit the right of the author or proprietor of an
unpublished work, at common law or in equity, to prevent
the copying, publication, or use of such unpublished work
without his consent, and to obtain damages therefor.

SEC. 3. That the copyright provided by this Act shall *Component parts of copyrightable work.*
25 protect all the copyrightable component parts of the
work copyrighted, and all matter therein in which copyright is already subsisting, but without extending the
duration or scope of such copyright. The copyright upon *Composite works or periodicals.*
composite works or periodicals shall give to the pro-
30 prietor thereof all the rights in respect thereto which
he would have if each part were individually copyrighted
under this Act.

SEC. 4. That the works for which copyright may be *Works protected.*
secured under this Act shall include all the writings of
35 an author.

SEC. 5. That the application for registration shall spec- *Classification of copyright works.*
ify to which of the following classes the work in which
copyright is claimed belongs:

(a) Books, including composite and cyclopædic works, *Books, composite, cyclopædic works; directories, gazetteers, etc.*
40 directories, gazetteers, and other compilations;
(b) Periodicals, including newspapers;

COPYRIGHT LAW OF THE UNITED STATES.

(c) Lectures, sermons, addresses, prepared for oral delivery;

(d) Dramatic or dramatico-musical compositions;

(e) Musical compositions;

(f) Maps;   5

(g) Works of art; models or designs for works of art;

(h) Reproductions of a work of art;

(i) Drawings or plastic works of a scientific or technical character;

(j) Photographs;   10

(k) Prints and pictorial illustrations:

Classification does not limit copyright. *Provided, nevertheless,* That the above specifications shall not be held to limit the subject-matter of copyright as defined in section four of this Act, nor shall any error in classification invalidate or impair the copyright protection secured under this Act. 15

Compilations, abridgements, dramatizations, translations, new editions. SEC. 6. That compilations or abridgements, adaptations, arrangements, dramatizations, translations, or other versions of works in the public domain, or of copyrighted works when produced with the consent of the 20 proprietor of the copyright in such work, or works republished with new matter, shall be regarded as new works subject to copyright under the provisions of this Act; but the publication of any such new works shall not affect

Subsisting copyright not affected. the force or validity of any subsisting copyright upon 25 the matter employed or any part thereof, or be construed to imply an exclusive right to such use of the original works, or to secure or extend copyright in such original works.

Not subject-matter of copyright: works in public domain; government publications. SEC. 7. That no copyright shall subsist in the original 30 text of any work which is in the public domain, or in any work which was published in this country or any foreign country prior to the going into effect of this Act and has not been already copyrighted in the United States, or in any publication of the United States Government, or any 35 reprint, in whole or in part, thereof: *Provided, however,* That the publication or republication by the Government, either separately or in a public document, of any material in which copyright is subsisting shall not be taken to cause any abridgement or annulment of the copyright or 40 to authorize any use or appropriation of such copyright material without the consent of the copyright proprietor.

SEC. 8. That the author or proprietor of any work made Copyright to author or proprietor for terms specified in Act. the subject of copyright by this Act, or his executors, administrators, or assigns, shall have copyright for such work under the conditions and for the terms specified in
5 this Act: *Provided, however,* That the copyright secured by this Act shall extend to the work of an author or proprietor who is a citizen or subject of a foreign state or Foreign authors who may secure copyright protection. nation, only:

(a) When an alien author or proprietor shall be domi- Alien authors domiciled in U. S.
10 ciled within the United States at the time of the first publication of his work; or

(b) When the foreign state or nation of which such Authors, when citizens of countries granting reciprocal rights. author or proprietor is a citizen or subject grants, either by treaty, convention, agreement, or law, to citizens of
15 the United States the benefit of copyright on substantially the same basis as to its own citizens, or copyright protection substantially equal to the protection secured to such foreign author under this Act or by treaty; or when such foreign state or nation is a party to an international International agreement.
20 agreement which provides for reciprocity in the granting of copyright, by the terms of which agreement the United States may, at its pleasure, become a party thereto.

The existence of the reciprocal conditions aforesaid Presidential proclamation. shall be determined by the President of the United States,
25 by proclamation made from time to time, as the purposes of this Act may require.

SEC. 9. That any person entitled thereto by this Act Publication with notice initiates copyright. may secure copyright for his work by publication thereof with the notice of copyright required by this Act; and
30 such notice shall be affixed to each copy thereof published or offered for sale in the United States by authority of the copyright proprietor, except in the case of books seeking ad interim protection under section twenty-one of this Act.

35 SEC. 10. That such person may obtain registration of Registration of copyright. his claim to copyright by complying with the provisions of this Act, including the deposit of copies, and upon such compliance the register of copyrights shall issue to him the certificate provided for in section fifty-five of this Act. Copyright certificate.

40 SEC. 11. That copyright may also be had of the works Copyright protection of unpublished works; lectures, dramas, music, etc. of an author of which copies are not reproduced for sale, by the deposit, with claim of copyright, of one complete

COPYRIGHT LAW OF THE UNITED STATES.

copy of such work if it be a lecture or similar production or a dramatic or musical composition; of a photographic print if the work be a photograph; or of a photograph or other identifying reproduction thereof if it be a work **Deposit of copies after publication.** of art or a plastic work or drawing. But the privilege 5 of registration of copyright secured hereunder shall not exempt the copyright proprietor from the deposit of copies under sections twelve and thirteen of this Act where the work is later reproduced in copies for sale.

Two complete copies of best edition. Sec. 12. That after copyright has been secured by pub- 10 lication of the work with the notice of copyright as provided in section nine of this Act, there shall be promptly deposited in the copyright office or in the mail addressed to the register of copyrights, Washington, District of Columbia, two complete copies of the best edition thereof 15 then published, which copies, if the work be a book or periodical, shall have been produced in accordance with the manufacturing provisions specified in section fifteen **Periodical contributions.** of this Act; or if such work be a contribution to a periodical, for which contribution special registration is re- 20 quested, one copy of the issue or issues containing such **Work not reproduced in copies for sale.** contribution; or if the work is not reproduced in copies for sale, there shall be deposited the copy, print, photograph, or other identifying reproduction provided by section eleven of this Act, such copies or copy, print, 25 photograph, or other reproduction to be accompanied in **No action for infringement until deposit of copies.** each case by a claim of copyright. No action or proceeding shall be maintained for infringement of copyright in any work until the provisions of this Act with respect to the deposit of copies and registration of such work shall 30 have been complied with.

Failure to deposit copies. Sec. 13. That should the copies called for by section twelve of this Act not be promptly deposited as herein **Register of copyrights may demand copies.** provided, the register of copyrights may at any time after the publication of the work, upon actual notice, require 35 the proprietor of the copyright to deposit them, and after **Failure to deposit on demand.** the said demand shall have been made, in default of the deposit of copies of the work within three months from any part of the United States, except an outlying territorial possession of the United States, or within six 40 months from any outlying territorial possession of the

ACT OF MARCH 4, 1909 (IN EFFECT JULY 1, 1909).

United States, or from any foreign country, the proprietor of the copyright shall be liable to a fine of one hundred dollars and to pay to the Library of Congress twice the amount of the retail price of the best edition of the
5 work, and the copyright shall become void. *Fine $100 and retail price of 2 copies, best edition. Forfeiture of copyright.*

SEC. 14. That the postmaster to whom are delivered the articles deposited as provided in sections eleven and twelve of this Act shall, if requested, give a receipt therefor and shall mail them to their destination without cost
10 to the copyright claimant. *Postmaster's receipt.*

SEC. 15. That of the printed book or periodical specified in section five, subsections (a) and (b) of this Act, except the original text of a book of foreign origin in a language or languages other than English, the text of all
15 copies accorded protection under this Act, except as below provided, shall be printed from type set within the limits of the United States, either by hand or by the aid of any kind of typesetting machine, or from plates made within the limits of the United States from type set therein, or,
20 if the text be produced by lithographic process, or photo-engraving process, then by a process wholly performed within the limits of the United States, and the printing of the text and binding of the said book shall be performed within the limits of the United States; which
25 requirements shall extend also to the illustrations within a book consisting of printed text and illustrations produced by lithographic process, or photo-engraving process, and also to separate lithographs or photo-engravings, except where in either case the subjects represented are
30 located in a foreign country and illustrate a scientific work or reproduce a work of art; but they shall not apply to works in raised characters for the use of the blind, or to books of foreign origin in a language or languages other than English, or to books published abroad in the
35 English language seeking ad interim protection under this Act. *Printed from type set within the United States. Book in foreign language excepted. Lithographic or photo-engraving process. Printing and binding of the book. Illustrations in a book. Separate lithographs and photo-engravings. Books for blind excepted. Books in foreign languages excepted.*

SEC. 16. That in the case of the book the copies so deposited shall be accompanied by an affidavit, under the official seal of any officer authorized to administer oaths
40 within the United States, duly made by the person claiming copyright or by his duly authorized agent or repre- *Affidavit of American manufacture.*

sentative residing in the United States, or by the printer who has printed the book, setting forth that the copies deposited have been printed from type set within the limits of the United States or from plates made within the limits of the United States from type set therein; or, 5 if the text be produced by lithographic process, or photo-engraving process, that such process was wholly performed within the limits of the United States, and that the printing of the text and binding of the said book have also been performed within the limits of the United 10 States. Such affidavit shall state also the place where and the estabhshment or establishments in which such type was set or plates were made or lithographic process, or photo-engraving process or printing and binding were performed and the date of the completion of the printing 15 of the book or the date of publication.

Printing and binding of the book.

Establishment where printing was done.

Date of publication.

SEC. 17. That any person who, for the purpose of obtaining registration of a claim to copyright, shall knowingly make a false affidavit as to his having complied with the above conditions shall be deemed guilty of a 20 misdemeanor, and upon conviction thereof shall be punished by a fine of not more than one thousand dollars, and all of his rights and privileges under said copyright shall thereafter be forfeited.

False affidavit, a misdemeanor: fine, $1,000 and forfeiture of copyright.

SEC. 18. That the notice of copyright required by sec- 25 tion nine of this Act shall consist either of the word "Copyright" or the abbreviation "Copr.", accompanied by the name of the copyright proprietor, and if the work be a printed literary, musical, or dramatic work, the notice shall include also the year in which the copyright 30 was secured by publication. In the case, however, of copies of works specified in subsections (f) to (k), inclusive, of section five of this Act, the notice may consist of the letter C inclosed within a circle, thus: Ⓒ, accompanied by the initials, monogram, mark, or symbol of the 35 copyright proprietor: *Provided*, That on some accessible portion of such copies or of the margin, back, permanent base, or pedestal, or of the substance on which such copies shall be mounted, his name shall appear. But in the case of works in which copyright is subsisting when this Act 40 shall go into effect, the notice of copyright may be either

Notice of copyright.

Notice on maps, copies of works of art, photographs, and prints.

Notice on accessible portion.

Notice on existing copyright works.

ACT OF MARCH 4, 1909 (IN EFFECT JULY 1, 1909).

in one of the forms prescribed herein or in one of those [See pages 47, 48.] prescribed by the Act of June eighteenth, eighteen hundred and seventy-four.

SEC. 19. That the notice of copyright shall be applied, [Notice of copyright on book.]
5 in the case of a book or other printed publication, upon its title-page or the page immediately following, or if a periodical either upon the title-page or upon the first [On periodical.] page of text of each separate number or under the title heading, or if a musical work either upon its title-page
10 or the first page of music: *Provided*, That one notice of [One notice in each volume or periodical.] copyright in each volume or in each number of a newspaper or periodical published shall suffice.

SEC. 20. That where the copyright proprietor has [Omission of notice by accident or mistake.] sought to comply with the provisions of this Act with
15 respect to notice, the omission by accident or mistake of the prescribed notice from a particular copy or copies shall not invalidate the copyright or prevent recovery for infringement against any person who, after actual notice of the copyright, begins an undertaking to infringe
20 it, but shall prevent the recovery of damages against an innocent infringer who has been misled by the omission of [Innocent infringement.] the notice; and in a suit for infringement no permanent injunction shall be had unless the copyright proprietor shall reimburse to the innocent infringer his reasonable
25 outlay innocently incurred if the court, in its discretion, shall so direct.

SEC. 21. That in the case of a book published abroad in [Book published abroad in the English language.] the English language before publication in this country, the deposit in the copyright office, not later than thirty
30 days after its publication abroad, of one complete copy of the foreign edition, with a request for the reservation of the copyright and a statement of the name and nationality of the author and of the copyright proprietor and of the date of publication of the said book, shall secure to
35 the author or proprietor an ad interim copyright, which [Ad interim copyright for 30 days.] shall have all the force and effect given to copyright by this Act, and shall endure until the expiration of thirty days after such deposit in the copyright office.

SEC. 22. That whenever within the period of such ad [Extension to full term.]
40 interim protection an authorized edition of such book shall be published within the United States, in accordance with the manufacturing provisions specified in section

COPYRIGHT LAW OF THE UNITED STATES.

fifteen of this Act, and whenever the provisions of this
Deposit of Act as to deposit of copies, registration, filing of affidavit,
copies, filing of
affidavit. and the printing of the copyright notice shall have been
duly complied with, the copyright shall be extended to
endure in such book for the full term elsewhere provided 5
in this Act.

Duration of Sec. 23. That the copyright secured by this Act shall
copyright: 1st
term, 28 years. endure for twenty-eight years from the date of first publication, whether the copyrighted work bears the author's
true name or is published anonymously or under an as- 10
Posthumous sumed name: *Provided,* That in the case of any posthu-
works, periodi-
cals, cyclopædic mous work or of any periodical, cyclopædic, or other com-
or composite
works. posite work upon which the copyright was originally
secured by the proprietor thereof, or of any work copyrighted by a corporate body (otherwise than as assignee 15
or licensee of the individual author) or by an employer
for whom such work is made for hire, the proprietor of
such copyright shall be entitled to a renewal and exten-
Renewal sion of the copyright in such work for the further term
term 28 years.
of twenty-eight years when application for such renewal 20
and extension shall have been made to the copyright
office and duly registered therein within one year prior
to the expiration of the original term of copyright: *And*
Other copy- *provided further,* That in the case of any other copyrighted works,
first term 28 righted work, including a contribution by an individual 25
years.
author to a periodical or to a cyclopædic or other composite work when such contribution has been separately reg-
Renewal istered, the author of such work, if still living, or the
term 28 years;
to author, wid- widow, widower, or children of the author, if the author
ow, children,
heirs or next be not living, or if such author, widow, widower, or chil- 30
of kin.
dren be not living, then the author's executors, or in the
absence of a will, his next of kin shall be entitled to a
renewal and extension of the copyright in such work for
Notice that a further term of twenty-eight years when application
renewal term
is desired. for such renewal and extension shall have been made to 35
the copyright office and duly registered therein within
one year prior to the expiration of the original term of
Copyright copyright: *And provided further,* That in default of
ends in 28
years unless the registration of such application for renewal and ex-
renewed.
tension, the copyright in any work shall determine at the 40
expiration of twenty-eight years from first publication.

685 - 914 O - 63 - 6

ACT OF MARCH 4, 1909 (IN EFFECT JULY 1, 1909).

SEC. 24. That the copyright subsisting in any work at Extension of subsisting
the time when this Act goes into effect may, at the expira- copyrights.
tion of the term provided for under existing law, be
renewed and extended by the author of such work if still
5 living, or the widow, widower, or children of the author,
if the author be not living, or if such author, widow,
widower, or children be not living, then by the author's
executors, or in the absence of a will, his next of kin,
for a further period such that the entire term shall be
10 equal to that secured by this Act, including the renewal
period: *Provided, however,* That if the work be a com- Proprietor entitled to re-
posite work upon which copyright was originally secured newal for composite work.
by the proprietor thereof, then such proprietor shall be
entitled to the privilege of renewal and extension granted
15 under this section: *Provided,* That application for such Renewal application.
renewal and extension shall be made to the copyright
office and duly registered therein within one year prior to
the expiration of the existing term.

SEC. 25. That if any person shall infringe the copyright Infringement of copyright.
20 in any work protected under the copyright laws of the
United States such person shall be liable:

(a) To an injunction restraining such infringement; Injunction.

(b) To pay to the copyright proprietor such damages Damages.
as the copyright proprietor may have suffered due to the
25 infringement, as well as all the profits which the infringer
shall have made from such infringement, and in proving
profits the plaintiff shall be required to prove sales only Proving sales.
and the defendant shall be required to prove every ele-
ment of cost which he claims, or in lieu of actual damages
30 and profits such damages as to the court shall appear to
be just, and in assessing such damages the court may, in
its discretion, allow the amounts as hereinafter stated,
but in the case of a newspaper reproduction of a copy- Newspaper reproduction of
righted photograph such damages shall not exceed the photograph; recovery, $50–
35 sum of two hundred dollars nor be less than the sum of $200.
fifty dollars, and such damages shall in no other case Maximum recovery, $5,000.
exceed the sum of five thousand dollars nor be less than Minimum recovery, $250.
the sum of two hundred and fifty dollars, and shall not be
regarded as a penalty: Painting,
40   First. In the case of a painting, statue, or sculp- statue, or sculpture, $10
ture, ten dollars for every infringing copy made or for every infringing copy.

COPYRIGHT LAW OF THE UNITED STATES.

sold by or found in the possession of the infringer or his agents or employees;

Other works. $1 for every infringing copy.

Second. In the case of any work enumerated in section five of this Act, except a painting, statue, or sculpture, one dollar for every infringing copy made 5 or sold by or found in the possession of the infringer or his agents or employees;

Lectures, $50 for every infringing delivery.

Dramatic or musical works, $100 for first and $50 for subsequent infringing performance.

Other musical compositions, $10 for every infringing performance.

Third. In the case of a lecture, sermon, or address, fifty dollars for every infringing delivery;

Fourth. In the case of dramatic or dramatico- 10 musical or a choral or orchestral composition, one hundred dollars for the first and fifty dollars for every subsequent infringing performance; in the case of other musical compositions, ten dollars for every infringing performance; 15

Delivering up infringing articles.

(c) To deliver up on oath, to be impounded during the pendency of the action, upon such terms and conditions as the court may prescribe, all articles alleged to infringe a copyright;

Destruction of infringing copies, etc.

(d) To deliver up on oath for destruction all the in- 20 fringing copies or devices, as well as all plates, molds, matrices, or other means for making such infringing copies as the court may order;

Infringement by mechanical musical instruments.

(e) Whenever the owner of a musical copyright has used or permitted the use of the copyrighted work upon 25 the parts of musical instruments serving to reproduce mechanically the musical work, then in case of infringement of such copyright by the unauthorized manufacture, use, or sale of interchangeable parts, such as disks, rolls, bands, or cylinders for use in mechanical music- 30 producing machines adapted to reproduce the copyrighted music, no criminal action shall be brought, but in a civil

Injunction may be granted.

action an injunction may be granted upon such terms as the court may impose, and the plaintiff shall be entitled

Recovery of royalty.

to recover in lieu of profits and damages a royalty as pro- 35 vided in section one, subsection (e), of this Act: *Provided also,* That whenever any person, in the absence of a license agreement, intends to use a copyrighted musical composition upon the parts of instruments serving to reproduce mechanically the musical work, relying upon the com- 40

Notice to proprietor of intention to use.

pulsory license provision of this Act, he shall serve notice of such intention, by registered mail, upon the copyright

ACT OF MARCH 4, 1909 (IN EFFECT JULY 1, 1909).

proprietor at his last address disclosed by the records of the copyright office, sending to the copyright office a duplicate of such notice; and in case of his failure so to do the court may, in its discretion, in addition to sums
5 hereinabove mentioned, award the complainant a further sum, not to exceed three times the amount provided by section one, subsection (e), by way of damages, and not as a penalty, and also a temporary injunction until the full award is paid. Damages, three times amount provided. Temporary injunction.

10 Rules and regulations for practice and procedure under this section shall be prescribed by the Supreme Court of the United States. Rules for practice and procedure.

SEC. 26. That any court given jurisdiction under section thirty-four of this Act may proceed in any action,
15 suit, or proceeding instituted for violation of any provision hereof to enter a judgment or decree enforcing the remedies herein provided. Judgment enforcing remedies.

SEC. 27. That the proceedings for an injunction, damages, and profits, and those for the seizure of infringing
20 copies, plates, molds, matrices, and so forth, aforementioned, may be united in one action. Proceedings, injunction, etc., may be united in one action.

SEC. 28. That any person who willfully and for profit shall infringe any copyright secured by this Act, or who shall knowingly and willfully aid or abet such infringe-
25 ment, shall be deemed guilty of a misdemeanor, and upon conviction thereof shall be punished by imprisonment for not exceeding one year or by a fine of not less than one hundred dollars nor more than one thousand dollars, or both, in the discretion of the court: *Provided, however,*
30 That nothing in this Act shall be so construed as to prevent the performance of religious or secular works, such as oratorios, cantatas, masses, or octavo choruses by public schools, church choirs, or vocal societies, rented, borrowed, or obtained from some public library, public
35 school, church choir, school choir, or vocal society, provided the performance is given for charitable or educational purposes and not for profit. Penalty for willful infringement. Oratorios, cantatas, etc., may be performed.

SEC. 29. That any person who, with fraudulent intent, shall insert or impress any notice of copyright required
40 by this Act, or words of the same purport, in or upon any uncopyrighted article, or with fraudulent intent shall remove or alter the copyright notice upon any article duly False notice of copyright (penalty for). Fraudulent removal of notice; fine $100-$1,000.

COPYRIGHT LAW OF THE UNITED STATES.

copyrighted shall be guilty of a misdemeanor, punishable by a fine of not less than one hundred dollars and not

Issuing, selling, or importing article bearing false notice: fine $100. more than one thousand dollars. Any person who shall knowingly issue or sell any article bearing a notice of United States copyright which has not been copyrighted 5 in this country, or who shall knowingly import any article bearing such notice or words of the same purport, which has not been copyrighted in this country, shall be liable to a fine of one hundred dollars.

Importation prohibited of articles bearing false notice and piratical copies. SEC. 30. That the importation into the United States 10 of any article bearing a false notice of copyright when there is no existing copyright thereon in the United States, or of any piratical copies of any work copyrighted in the United States, is prohibited.

Prohibition of importation of books. SEC. 31. That during the existence of the American 15 copyright in any book the importation into the United States of any piratical copies thereof or of any copies thereof (although authorized by the author or proprietor) which have not been produced in accordance with the manufacturing provisions specified in section fifteen 20 of this Act, or any plates of the same not made from type set within the limits of the United States, or any copies thereof produced by lithographic or photo-engraving process not performed within the limits of the United States, in accordance with the provisions of section fif- 25

Exceptions to prohibition of importation: teen of this Act, shall be, and is hereby, prohibited: *Provided, however,* That, except as regards piratical copies, such prohibition shall not apply:

Works for the blind. (a) To works in raised characters for the use of the blind; 30

Foreign newspapers or magazines. (b) To a foreign newspaper or magazine, although containing matter copyrighted in the United States printed or reprinted by authority of the copyright proprietor, unless such newspaper or magazine contains also copyright matter printed or reprinted without such au- 35 thorization;

Books in foreign languages of which only translations are copyrighted. (c) To the authorized edition of a book in a foreign language or languages of which only a translation into English has been copyrighted in this country;

Importation of authorized foreign books permitted. (d) To any book published abroad with the authoriza- 40 tion of the author or copyright proprietor when imported under the circumstances stated in one of the four subdivisions following, that is to say:

First. When imported, not more than one copy at one time, for individual use and not for sale; but *For individual use and not for sale.*

5 such privilege of importation shall not extend to a foreign reprint of a book by an American author copyrighted in the United States;

Second. When imported by the authority or for the use of the United States; *For the use of the United States.*

10 Third. When imported, for use and not for sale, not more than one copy of any such book in any one invoice, in good faith, by or for any society or *For the use of societies, libraries, etc.*
institution incorporated for educational, literary, philosophical, scientific, or religious purposes, or for

15 the encouragement of the fine arts, or for any college, academy, school, or seminary of learning, or for any State, school, college, university, or free public library in the United States;

Fourth. When such books form parts of libraries *Libraries purchased en bloc.*

20 or collections purchased en bloc for the use of societies, institutions, or libraries designated in the foregoing paragraph, or form parts of the libraries *Books brought personally into the United States.*
or personal baggage belonging to persons or families arriving from foreign countries and are not intended *Imported copies not to be used to violate copyright.*

25 for sale: *Provided*, That copies imported as above may not lawfully be used in any way to violate the rights of the proprietor of the American copyright or annul or limit the copyright protection secured by this Act, and such unlawful use shall be deemed

30 an infringement of copyright.

SEC. 32. That any and all articles prohibited importation by this Act which are brought into the United States *Seizure of unlawfully imported copies.*
from any foreign country (except in the mails) shall be seized and forfeited by like proceedings as those provided

35 by law for the seizure and condemnation of property imported into the United States in violation of the customs revenue laws. Such articles when forfeited shall be destroyed in such manner as the Secretary of the Treasury or the court, as the case may be, shall direct: *Provided*,

40 *however*, That all copies of authorized editions of copyright books imported in the mails or otherwise in viola- *Copies of authorized books imported may be returned.*

COPYRIGHT LAW OF THE UNITED STATES.

tion of the provisions of this Act may be exported and returned to the country of export whenever it is shown to the satisfaction of the Secretary of the Treasury, in a written application, that such importation does not involve willful negligence or fraud. 5

Secretary of Treasury and Postmaster-General to make rules to prevent unlawful importation. SEC. 33. That the Secretary of the Treasury and the Postmaster-General are hereby empowered and required to make and enforce such joint rules and regulations as shall prevent the importation into the United States in the mails of articles prohibited importation by this Act, 10 and may require notice to be given to the Treasury Department or Post-Office Department, as the case may be, by copyright proprietors or injured parties, of the actual or contemplated importation of articles prohibited importation by this Act, and which infringe the rights of 15 such copyright proprietors or injured parties.

Jurisdiction of courts in copyright cases. SEC. 34. That all actions, suits, or proceedings arising under the copyright laws of the United States shall be originally cognizable by the circuit courts of the United States, the district court of any Territory, the supreme 20 court of the District of Columbia, the district courts of Alaska, Hawaii, and Porto Rico, and the courts of first instance of the Philippine Islands.

District in which suit may be brought. SEC. 35. That civil actions, suits, or proceedings arising under this Act may be instituted in the district of which 25 the defendant or his agent is an inhabitant, or in which he may be found.

Injunctions may be granted. SEC. 36. That any such court or judge thereof shall have power, upon bill in equity filed by any party aggrieved, to grant injunctions to prevent and restrain the 30 violation of any right secured by said laws, according to the course and principles of courts of equity, on such terms as said court or judge may deem reasonable. Any injunction that may be granted restraining and enjoining the doing of anything forbidden by this Act may be 35 served on the parties against whom such injunction may be granted anywhere in the United States, and shall be operative throughout the United States and be enforceable by proceedings in contempt or otherwise by any other court or judge possessing jurisdiction of the de- 40 fendants.

ACT OF MARCH 4, 1909 (IN EFFECT JULY 1, 1909).

SEC. 37. That the clerk of the court, or judge granting *Certified copy of papers filed.*
the injunction, shall, when required so to do by the court
hearing the application to enforce said injunction, transmit without delay to said court a certified copy of all the
5 papers in said cause that are on file in his office.

SEC. 38. That the orders, judgments, or decrees of any *Judgments, etc., may be*
court mentioned in section thirty-four of this Act arising *reviewed on appeal or writ*
under the copyright laws of the United States may be *of error.*
reviewed on appeal or writ of error in the manner and to
10 the extent now provided by law for the review of cases
determined in said courts, respectively.

SEC. 39. That no criminal proceeding shall be main- *No criminal proceedings*
tained under the provisions of this Act unless the same is *shall be maintained after*
commenced within three years after the cause of action *three years.*
15 arose.

SEC. 40. That in all actions, suits, or proceedings under *Full costs shall be al-*
this Act, except when brought by or against the United *lowed.*
States or any officer thereof, full costs shall be allowed,
and the court may award to the prevailing party a reason-
20 able attorney's fee as part of the costs.

SEC. 41. That the copyright is distinct from the prop- *Copyright distinct from*
erty in the material object copyrighted, and the sale or *property in material object.*
conveyance, by gift or otherwise, of the material object
shall not of itself constitute a transfer of the copyright,
25 nor shall the assignment of the copyright constitute a
transfer of the title to the material object; but nothing in *Transfer of any copy of*
this Act shall be deemed to forbid, prevent, or restrict *copyrighted work permit-*
the transfer of any copy of a copyrighted · work the *ted.*
possession of which has been lawfully obtained.

30 SEC. 42. That copyright secured under this or previous *Copyright may be assign-*
Acts of the United States may be assigned, granted, or *ed, mortgaged, or bequeathed*
mortgaged by an instrument in writing signed by the *by will.*
proprietor of the copyright, or may be bequeathed by will.

SEC. 43. That every assignment of copyright executed *Assignment executed in*
35 in a foreign country shall be acknowledged by the as- *foreign coun-try to be ac-*
signor before a consular officer or secretary of legation of *knowledged.*
the United States authorized by law to administer oaths
or perform notarial acts. The certificate of such ac-
knowledgement under the hand and official seal of such
40 consular officer or secretary of legation shall be prima
facie evidence of the execution of the instrument.

COPYRIGHT LAW OF THE UNITED STATES.

Assignments to be recorded. SEC. 44. That every assignment of copyright shall be recorded in the copyright office within three calendar months after its execution in the United States or within six calendar months after its execution without the limits of the United States, in default of which it shall be void 5 as against any subsequent purchaser or mortgagee for a valuable consideration, without notice, whose assignment has been duly recorded.

Register of copyrights to record assignments. SEC. 45. That the register of copyrights shall, upon payment of the prescribed fee, record such assignment, 10 and shall return it to the sender with a certificate of record attached under seal of the copyright office, and upon the payment of the fee prescribed by this Act he shall furnish to any person requesting the same a certified copy thereof under the said seal. 15

Assignee's name may be substituted in copyright notice. SEC. 46. That when an assignment of the copyright in a specified book or other work has been recorded the assignee may substitute his name for that of the assignor in the statutory notice of copyright prescribed by this Act.

Copyright records. SEC. 47. That all records and other things relating to 20 copyrights required by law to be preserved shall be kept and preserved in the copyright office, Library of Congress, District of Columbia, and shall be under the control of the register of copyrights, who shall, under the direction and supervision of the Librarian of Congress, per- 25 form all the duties relating to the registration of copyrights.

Register of copyrights and assistant register of copyrights. SEC. 48. That there shall be appointed by the Librarian of Congress a register of copyrights, at a salary of four thousand dollars per annum, and one assistant register of 30 copyrights, at a salary of three thousand dollars per annum, who shall have authority during the absence of the register of copyrights to attach the copyright office seal to all papers issued from the said office and to sign such certificates and other papers as may be necessary. 35 There shall also be appointed by the Librarian such subordinate assistants to the register as may from time to time be authorized by law.

Register of copyrights to deposit and account for fees. SEC. 49. That the register of copyrights shall make daily deposits in some bank in the District of Columbia, 40 designated for this purpose by the Secretary of the Treas-

ACT OF MARCH 4, 1909 (IN EFFECT JULY 1, 1909).

ury as a national depository, of all moneys received to
be applied as copyright fees, and shall make weekly deposits with the Secretary of the Treasury, in such manner
as the latter shall direct, of all copyright fees actually
5 applied under the provisions of this Act, and annual
deposits of sums received which it has not been possible
to apply as copyright fees or to return to the remitters,
and shall also make monthly reports to the Secretary of   Shall make
the Treasury and to the Librarian of Congress of the   port of fees.
10 applied copyright fees for each calendar month, together
with a statement of all remittances received, trust funds
on hand, moneys refunded, and unapplied balances.

SEC. 50. That the register of copyrights shall give bond   Bond of reg-
to the United States in the sum of twenty thousand dol-   rights.
15 lars, in form to be approved by the Solicitor of the
Treasury and with sureties satisfactory to the Secretary
of the Treasury, for the faithful discharge of his duties.

SEC. 51. That the register of copyrights shall make an   Annual re-
annual report to the Librarian of Congress, to be printed   of copyrights.
20 in the annual report on the Library of Congress, of all
copyright business for the previous fiscal year, including
the number and kind of works which have been deposited
in the copyright office during the fiscal year, under the
provisions of this Act.

25   SEC. 52. That the seal provided under the Act of July   Seal of copy-
eighth, eighteen hundred and seventy, and at present used   right office.
in the copyright office, shall continue to be the seal
thereof, and by it all papers issued from the copyright
office requiring authentication shall be authenticated.

30   SEC. 53. That, subject to the approval of the Librarian   Rules for the
of Congress, the register of copyrights shall be authorized   registration of
copyrights.
to make rules and regulations for the registration of
claims to copyright as provided by this Act.

SEC. 54. That the register of copyrights shall provide   Record books.
35 and keep such record books in the copyright office as are
required to carry out the provisions of this Act, and when-   Entry of
ever deposit has been made in the copyright office of a   copyright.
copy of any work under the provisions of this Act he
shall make entry thereof.

40   SEC. 55. That in the case of each entry the person re-   Certificate of
corded as the claimant of the copyright shall be entitled   registration.

COPYRIGHT LAW OF THE UNITED STATES.

to a certificate of registration under seal of the copyright office, to contain his name and address, the title of the work upon which copyright is claimed, the date of the deposit of the copies of such work, and such marks as to class designation and entry number as shall fully identify the 5

Certificate for book to state receipt of affidavit. entry. In the case of a book the certificate shall also state the receipt of the affidavit as provided by section sixteen of this Act, and the date of the completion of the printing, or the date of the publication of the book, as stated in the said affidavit. The register of copyrights 10 shall prepare a printed form for the said certificate, to

Certificate may be given to any person. be filled out in each case as above provided for, which certificate, sealed with the seal of the copyright office, shall, upon payment of the prescribed fee, be given to any person making application for the same, and the said certifi- 15 cate shall be admitted in any court as prima facie evidence

Receipt for copies deposited. of the facts stated therein. In addition to such certificate the register of copyrights shall furnish, upon request, without additional fee, a receipt for the copies of the work deposited to complete the registration. 20

Index to copyright registrations. SEC. 56. That the register of copyrights shall fully index all copyright registrations and assignments and

Catalogue of copyright entries. shall print at periodic intervals a catalogue of the titles of articles deposited and registered for copyright, together with suitable indexes, and at stated intervals shall print 25 complete and indexed catalogues for each class of copyright entries, and may thereupon, if expedient, destroy

Catalogue cards. the original manuscript catalogue cards containing the titles included in such printed volumes and representing the entries made during such intervals. The current cata- 30

Catalogues and indexes prima facie evidence. logues of copyright entries and the index volumes herein provided for shall be admitted in any court as prima facie evidence of the facts stated therein as regards any copyright registration.

Distribution of catalogue of copyright entries. SEC. 57. That the said printed current catalogues as 35 they are issued shall be promptly distributed by the copyright office to the collectors of customs of the United States and to the postmasters of all exchange offices of receipt of foreign mails, in accordance with revised lists of such collectors of customs and postmasters prepared 40 by the Secretary of the Treasury and the Postmaster-

ACT OF MARCH 4, 1909 (IN EFFECT JULY 1, 1909).

General, and they shall also be furnished to all parties *Subscription price.* desiring them at a price to be determined by the register of copyrights, not exceeding five dollars per annum for the complete catalogue of copyright entries and not ex-
5 ceeding one dollar per annum for the catalogues issued during the year for any one class of subjects. The consolidated catalogues and indexes shall also be supplied to all persons ordering them at such prices as may be determined to be reasonable, and all subscriptions for the
10 catalogues shall be received by the Superintendent of *Superintendent of documents to receive subscriptions.* Public Documents, who shall forward the said publications; and the moneys thus received shall be paid into the Treasury of the United States and accounted for under such laws and Treasury regulations as shall be in force
15 at the time.

SEC. 58. That the record books of the copyright office, *Record books, etc., open to inspection.* together with the indexes to such record books, and all works deposited and retained in the copyright office, shall be open to public inspection; and copies may be taken of *Copies may be taken of entries in record books.*
20 the copyright entries actually made in such record books, subject to such safeguards and regulations as shall be prescribed by the register of copyrights and approved by the Librarian of Congress.

SEC. 59. That of the articles deposited in the copyright *Disposition of copyright deposits.*
25 office under the provisions of the copyright laws of the United States or of this Act, the Librarian of Congress shall determine what books and other articles shall be transferred to the permanent collections of the Library of Congress, including the law library, and what other
30 books or articles shall be placed in the reserve collections of the Library of Congress for sale or exchange, or be *Preservation of copyright deposits.* transferred to other governmental libraries in the District of Columbia for use therein.

SEC. 60. That of any articles undisposed of as above *Disposal of copyright deposits.*
35 provided, together with all titles and correspondence relating thereto, the Librarian of Congress and the register of copyrights jointly shall, at suitable intervals, determine what of these received during any period of years it is desirable or useful to preserve in the permanent files of
40 the copyright office, and, after due notice as hereinafter provided, may within their discretion cause the remain-

COPYRIGHT LAW OF THE UNITED STATES.

ing articles and other things to be destroyed: *Provided*, That there shall be printed in the Catalogue of Copyright Entries from February to November, inclusive, a statement of the years of receipt of such articles and a notice to permit any author, copyright proprietor, or 5 other lawful claimant to claim and remove before the expiration of the month of December of that year anything found which relates to any of his productions deposited or registered for copyright within the period of years stated, not reserved or disposed of as provided for 10

Manuscript copies to be preserved.

in this Act: *And provided further*, That no manuscript of an unpublished work shall be destroyed during its term of copyright without specific notice to the copyright proprietor of record, permitting him to claim and remove it. 15

Fees.

SEC. 61. That the register of copyrights shall receive, and the persons to whom the services designated are ren-

Fee for registration.

dered shall pay, the following fees: For the registration of any work subject to copyright, deposited under the provisons of this Act, one dollar, which sum is to include 20

Fee for certificate.

a certificate of registration under seal: *Provided*, That in the case of photographs the fee shall be fifty cents where a certificate is not demanded. For every additional cer-

Fee for recording assignment.

tificate of registration made, fifty cents. For recording and certifying any instrument of writing for the assign- 25 ment of copyright, or any such license specified in section

Fee for copy of assignment.

one, subsection (e), or for any copy of such assignment or license, duly certified, if not over three hundred words in length, one dollar; if more than three hundred and less than one thousand words in length, two dollars; if 30 more than one thousand words in length, one dollar additional for each one thousand words or fraction thereof

Fee for recording notice of user upon mechanical musical instruments.

over three hundred words. For recording the notice of user or acquiescence specified in section one, subsection (e), twenty-five cents for each notice if not over fifty 35 words, and an additional twenty-five cents for each addi-

Fee for comparing copy of assignment.

tional one hundred words. For comparing any copy of an assignment with the record of such document in the copyright office and certifying the same under seal, one

Fee for recording renewal of copyright.

dollar. For recording the extension or renewal of copy- 40 right provided for in sections twenty-three and twenty-

ACT OF MARCH 4, 1909 (IN EFFECT JULY 1, 1909).

four of this Act, fifty cents. For recording the transfer Fee for recording transfer of proprietorship. of the proprietorship of copyrighted articles, ten cents for each title of a book or other article, in addition to the fee prescribed for recording the instrument of assign-
5 ment. For any requested search of copyright office rec- Fee for search. ords, indexes, or deposits, fifty cents for each full hour of time consumed in making such search: *Provided*, That Only one registration required for work in several volumes. only one registration at one fee shall be required in the case of several volumes of the same book deposited at the
10 same time.

SEC. 62. That in the interpretation and construction of Definitions: Date of publication. this Act "the date of publication" shall in the case of a work of which copies are reproduced for sale or distribution be held to be the earliest date when copies of the first
15 authorized edition were placed on sale, sold, or publicly distributed by the proprietor of the copyright or under his authority, and the word "author" shall include an "Author." employer in the case of works made for hire.

SEC. 63. That all laws or parts of laws in conflict with Repealing clause.
20 the provisions of this Act are hereby repealed, but nothing in this Act shall affect causes of action for infringement of copyright heretofore committed now pending in courts of the United States, or which may hereafter be instituted; but such causes shall be prosecuted to a conclusion
25 in the manner heretofore provided by law.

SEC. 64. That this Act shall go into effect on the first Date of enforcement. day of July, nineteen hundred and nine.

Approved, March 4, 1909.
[60th Congress, 2d session.]

APPENDIX 3:
COPYRIGHTABLE SUBJECT MATTER

Sections 102(a) and 103 of the 1976 Act:

§ 102. Subject matter of copyright: In general

(a) Copyright protection subsists, in accordance with this title, in original works of authorship fixed in any tangible medium of expression, now known or later developed, from which they can be perceived, reproduced, or otherwise communicated, either directly or with the aid of a machine or device. Works of authorship include the following categories:

(1) literary works;

(2) musical works, including any accompanying words;

(3) dramatic works, including any accompanying music;

(4) pantomimes and choreographic works;

(5) pictorial, graphic, and sculptural works;

(6) motion pictures and other audiovisual works;

(7) sound recordings; and

(8) architectural works.

§ 103. Subject matter of copyright: Compilations and derivative works

(a) The subject matter of copyright as specified by section 102 includes compilations and derivative works, but protection for a work employing preexisting material in which copyright subsists does not extend to any part of the work in which such material has been used unlawfully.

(b) The copyright in a compilation or derivative work extends only to the material contributed by the author of such work, as distinguished from the preexisting material employed in the work, and does not imply any exclusive right in the preexisting material. The copyright in such work is independent of, and does not affect or enlarge the scope, duration, ownership, or subsistence of, any copyright protection in the preexisting material.

APPENDIX 4:
MATERIAL NOT SUBJECT TO COPYRIGHT

37 C.F.R. § 202.1: Material not subject to copyright

The following are examples of works not subject to copyright and applications for registration of such works cannot be entertained:

(a) Words and short phrases such as names, titles, and slogans; familiar symbols or designs; mere variations of typographic ornamentation, lettering or coloring; mere listing of ingredients or contents;

(b) Ideas, plans, methods, systems, or devices, as distinguished from the particular manner in which they are expressed or described in a writing;

(c) Blank forms, such as time cards, graph paper, account books, diaries, bank checks, scorecards, address books, report forms, order forms and the like, which are designed for recording information and do not in themselves convey information;

(d) Works consisting entirely of information that is common property containing no original authorship, such as, for example: Standard calendars, height and weight charts, tape measures and rulers, schedules of sporting events, and lists or tables taken from public documents or other common sources;

(e) Typeface as typeface.

APPENDIX 5:
EXCLUSIVE RIGHTS IN COPYRIGHTED WORKS AND LIMITATIONS

Section 106 of the 1976 Act:

Subject to sections 107 through 122, the owner of copyright under this title has the exclusive rights to do and to authorize any of the following:

(1) to reproduce the copyrighted work in copies or phonorecords;

(2) to prepare derivative works based upon the copyrighted work;

(3) to distribute copies or phonorecords of the copyrighted work to the public by sale or other transfer of ownership, or by rental, lease, or lending;

(4) in the case of literary, musical, dramatic, and choreographic works, pantomimes, and motion pictures and other audiovisual works, to perform the copyrighted work publicly;

(5) in the case of literary, musical, dramatic, and choreographic works, pantomimes, and pictorial, graphic, or sculptural works, including the individual images of a motion picture or other audiovisual work, to display the copyrighted work publicly; and

(6) in the case of sound recordings, to perform the copyrighted work publicly by means of a digital audio transmission.

Select excerpts from sections 108–118 of the 1976 Act:

§ 108. Limitations on exclusive rights: Reproduction by libraries and archives

(a) Except as otherwise provided in this title and notwithstanding the provisions of section 106, it is not an infringement of copyright for a library or archives, or any of its employees acting within the scope of their employment, to reproduce no more than one copy or phonorecord of a work, except as provided in subsections (b) and (c), or to distribute such copy or phonorecord, under the conditions specified by this section, if—

(1) the reproduction or distribution is made without any purpose of direct or indirect commercial advantage;

(2) the collections of the library or archives are (i) open to the public, or (ii) available not only to researchers affiliated with the library or archives or with the institution of which it is a part, but also to other persons doing research in a specialized field; and

(3) the reproduction or distribution of the work includes a notice of copyright that appears on the copy or phonorecord that is reproduced under the provisions of this section, or includes a legend stating that the work may be protected by copyright if no such notice can be found on the copy or phonorecord that is reproduced under the provisions of this section.

(b) The rights of reproduction and distribution under this section apply to three copies or phonorecords of an unpublished work duplicated solely for purposes of preservation and security or for deposit for research use in another library or archives of the type described by clause (2) of subsection (a), if—

(1) the copy or phonorecord reproduced is currently in the collections of the library or archives; and

(2) any such copy or phonorecord that is reproduced in digital format is not otherwise distributed in that format and is not made available to the public in that format outside the premises of the library or archives.

(c) The right of reproduction under this section applies to three copies or phonorecords of a published work duplicated solely for the purpose of replacement of a copy or phonorecord that is damaged, deteriorating, lost, or stolen, or if the existing format in which the work is stored has become obsolete, if—

(1) the library or archives has, after a reasonable effort, determined that an unused replacement cannot be obtained at a fair price; and

(2) any such copy or phonorecord that is reproduced in digital format is not made available to the public in that format outside the premises of the library or archives in lawful possession of such copy.

For purposes of this subsection, a format shall be considered obsolete if the machine or device necessary to render perceptible a work stored in that format is no longer manufactured or is no longer reasonably available in the commercial marketplace.

(d) The rights of reproduction and distribution under this section apply to a copy, made from the collection of a library or archives where the user makes his or her request or from that of another library or archives, of no more than one article or other contribution to a copyrighted collection or periodical issue, or to a copy or phonorecord of a small part of any other copyrighted work, if—

(1) the copy or phonorecord becomes the property of the user, and the library or archives has had no notice that the copy or phonorecord would be used for any purpose other than private study, scholarship, or research; and

(2) the library or archives displays prominently, at the place where orders are accepted, and includes on its order form, a warning of copyright in accordance with requirements that the Register of Copyrights shall prescribe by regulation.

(e) The rights of reproduction and distribution under this section apply to the entire work, or to a substantial part of it, made from the collection of a library or archives where the user makes his or her request or from that of another library or archives, if the library or archives has first determined, on the basis of a reasonable investigation, that a copy or phonorecord of the copyrighted work cannot be obtained at a fair price, if—

(1) the copy or phonorecord becomes the property of the user, and the library or archives has had no notice that the copy or phonorecord would be used for any purpose other than private study, scholarship, or research; and

(2) the library or archives displays prominently, at the place where orders are accepted, and includes on its order form, a warning of copyright in accordance with requirements that the Register of Copyrights shall prescribe by regulation.

(f) Nothing in this section—

(1) shall be construed to impose liability for copyright infringement upon a library or archives or its employees for the unsupervised use of reproducing equipment located on its premises: *Provided,* That such equipment displays a notice that the making of a copy may be subject to the copyright law;

(2) excuses a person who uses such reproducing equipment or who requests a copy or phonorecord under subsection (d) from liability for copyright infringement for any such act, or for any later use of such copy or phonorecord, if it exceeds fair use as provided by section 107;

(3) shall be construed to limit the reproduction and distribution by lending of a limited number of copies and excerpts by a library or archives of an audiovisual news program, subject to clauses (1), (2), and (3) of subsection (a); or

(4) in any way affects the right of fair use as provided by section 107, or any contractual obligations assumed at any time by the library or archives when it obtained a copy or phonorecord of a work in its collections.

§ 109. Limitations on exclusive rights: Effect of transfer of particular copy or phonorecord

(a) Notwithstanding the provisions of section 106(3), the owner of a particular copy or phonorecord lawfully made under this title, or any person authorized by such owner, is entitled, without the authority of the copyright owner, to sell or otherwise dispose of the possession of that copy or phonorecord. Notwithstanding the preceding sentence, copies or phonorecords of works subject to restored copyright under section 104A that are manufactured before the date of restoration of copyright or, with respect to reliance parties, before publication or service of notice under section 104A(e), may be sold or otherwise disposed of without the authorization of the owner of the restored copyright for purposes of direct or indirect commercial advantage only during the 12-month period beginning on—

(1) the date of the publication in the Federal Register of the notice of intent filed with the Copyright Office under section 104A(d)(2)(A), or

(2) the date of the receipt of actual notice served under section 104A(d)(2)(B), whichever occurs first.

(b)(1)(A) Notwithstanding the provisions of subsection (a), unless authorized by the owners of copyright in the sound recording or the owner of copyright in a computer program (including any tape, disk, or other medium embodying such program), and in the case of a sound recording in the musical works embodied therein, neither the owner of a particular phonorecord nor any person in possession of a particular copy of a computer program (including any tape, disk, or other medium embodying such program), may, for the purposes of direct or indirect commercial advantage, dispose of, or authorize the disposal of, the possession of that phonorecord or computer program (including any tape, disk, or other medium embodying such program) by rental, lease, or lending, or by any other act or practice in the nature of rental, lease, or lending. Nothing in the preceding sentence shall apply to the rental, lease, or lending of a phonorecord for nonprofit purposes by a nonprofit library or nonprofit educational institution. The transfer of possession of a lawfully made copy of a computer program by a nonprofit educational institution to another nonprofit educational institution or to faculty, staff, and students does not constitute rental, lease, or lending for direct or indirect commercial purposes under this subsection.

(B) This subsection does not apply to—

(i) a computer program which is embodied in a machine or product and which cannot be copied during the ordinary operation or use of the machine or product; or

(ii) a computer program embodied in or used in conjunction with a limited purpose computer that is designed for playing video games and may be designed for other purposes.

§ 110. Limitations on exclusive rights: Exemption of certain performances and displays

Notwithstanding the provisions of section 106, the following are not infringements of copyright:

(1) performance or display of a work by instructors or pupils in the course of face-to-face teaching activities of a nonprofit educational institution, in a classroom or similar place devoted to instruction, unless, in the case of a motion picture or other audiovisual work, the performance, or the display of individual images, is given by means of a copy that was not lawfully made under this title, and that the person responsible for the performance knew or had reason to believe was not lawfully made;

(2) except with respect to a work produced or marketed primarily for performance or display as part of mediated instructional activities transmitted via digital networks, or a performance or display that is given by means of a copy or phonorecord that is not lawfully made and acquired under this title, and the transmitting government body or accredited nonprofit educational institution knew or had reason to believe was not lawfully made and acquired, the performance of a nondramatic literary or musical work or reasonable and limited portions of any other work, or display of a work in an amount comparable

to that which is typically displayed in the course of a live classroom session, by or in the course of a transmission, if—

(A) the performance or display is made by, at the direction of, or under the actual supervision of an instructor as an integral part of a class session offered as a regular part of the systematic mediated instructional activities of a governmental body or an accredited nonprofit educational institution;

(B) the performance or display is directly related and of material assistance to the teaching content of the transmission;

(C) the transmission is made solely for, and, to the extent technologically feasible, the reception of such transmission is limited to—

(i) students officially enrolled in the course for which the transmission is made; or

(ii) officers or employees of governmental bodies as a part of their official duties or employment; and

(D) the transmitting body or institution—

(i) institutes policies regarding copyright, provides informational materials to faculty, students, and relevant staff members that accurately describe, and promote compliance with, the laws of the United States relating to copyright, and provides notice to students that materials used in connection with the course may be subject to copyright protection; and

(ii) in the case of digital transmissions—

(I) applies technological measures that reasonably prevent—

(aa) retention of the work in accessible form by recipients of the transmission from the transmitting body or institution for longer than the class session; and

(bb) unauthorized further dissemination of the work in accessible form by such recipients to others; and

(II) does not engage in conduct that could reasonably be expected to interfere with technological measures used by copyright owners to prevent such retention or unauthorized further dissemination;

(3) performance of a nondramatic literary or musical work or of a dramatico-musical work of a religious nature, or display of a work, in the course of services at a place of worship or other religious assembly;

(4) performance of a nondramatic literary or musical work otherwise than in a transmission to the public, without any purpose of direct or indirect commercial advantage and without payment of any fee or other compensation for the performance to any of its performers, promoters, or organizers, if—

(A) there is no direct or indirect admission charge; or

(B) the proceeds, after deducting the reasonable costs of producing the performance, are used exclusively for educational, religious, or charitable purposes and not for private financial gain, except where the copyright owner has served notice of objection to the performance under the following conditions:

(i) the notice shall be in writing and signed by the copyright owner or such owner's duly authorized agent; and

(ii) the notice shall be served on the person responsible for the performance at least seven days before the date of the performance, and shall state the reasons for the objection; and

(iii) the notice shall comply, in form, content, and manner of service, with requirements that the Register of Copyrights shall prescribe by regulation;

(5)(A) except as provided in subparagraph (B), communication of a transmission embodying a performance or display of a work by the public reception of the transmission on a single receiving apparatus of a kind commonly used in private homes, unless—

(i) a direct charge is made to see or hear the transmission; or

(ii) the transmission thus received is further transmitted to the public;

(B) communication by an establishment of a transmission or retransmission embodying a performance or display of a nondramatic musical work intended to be received by the general public, originated by a radio or television broadcast station licensed as such by the Federal Communications Commission, or, if an audiovisual transmission, by a cable system or satellite carrier, if—

(i) in the case of an establishment other than a food service or drinking establishment, either the establishment in which the communication occurs has less than 2,000 gross square feet of space (excluding space used for customer parking and for no other purpose), or the establishment in which the communication occurs has 2,000 or more gross square feet of space (excluding space used for customer parking and for no other purpose) and—

(I) if the performance is by audio means only, the performance is communicated by means of a total of not more than 6 loudspeakers, of which not more than 4 loudspeakers are located in any 1 room or adjoining outdoor space; or

(II) if the performance or display is by audiovisual means, any visual portion of the performance or display is communicated by means of a total of not more than 4 audiovisual devices, of which not more than 1 audiovisual device is located in any 1 room, and no such audiovisual device has a diagonal screen size greater than 55 inches, and any audio portion of the performance or display is communicated by means of a total of not more than 6 loudspeakers, of which not more than 4 loudspeakers are located in any 1 room or adjoining outdoor space;

(ii) in the case of a food service or drinking establishment, either the establishment in which the communication occurs has less than 3,750 gross square feet of space (excluding space used for customer parking and for no other purpose), or the establishment in which the communication occurs has 3,750 gross square feet of space or more (excluding space used for customer parking and for no other purpose) and—

(I) if the performance is by audio means only, the performance is communicated by means of a total of not more than 6 loudspeakers, of which not more than 4 loudspeakers are located in any 1 room or adjoining outdoor space; or

(II) if the performance or display is by audiovisual means, any visual portion of the performance or display is communicated by means of a total of not more than 4 audiovisual devices, of which not more than 1 audiovisual device is located in any 1 room, and no such audiovisual device has a diagonal screen size greater than 55 inches, and any audio portion of the performance or display is communicated by means of a total of not more than 6 loudspeakers, of which not more than 4 loudspeakers are located in any 1 room or adjoining outdoor space;

(iii) no direct charge is made to see or hear the transmission or retransmission;

(iv) the transmission or retransmission is not further transmitted beyond the establishment where it is received; and

(v) the transmission or retransmission is licensed by the copyright owner of the work so publicly performed or displayed;

(6) performance of a nondramatic musical work by a governmental body or a nonprofit agricultural or horticultural organization, in the course of an annual agricultural or horticultural fair or exhibition conducted by such body or organization; the exemption provided by this clause shall extend to any liability for copyright infringement that would otherwise be imposed on such body or organization, under doctrines of vicarious liability or related infringement, for a performance by a concessionnaire, business establishment, or other person at such fair or exhibition, but shall not excuse any such person from liability for the performance;

(7) performance of a nondramatic musical work by a vending establishment open to the public at large without any direct or indirect admission charge, where the sole purpose of the performance is to promote the retail sale of copies or phonorecords of the work, or of the audiovisual or other devices utilized in such performance, and the performance is not transmitted beyond the place where the establishment is located and is within the immediate area where the sale is occurring;

(8) performance of a nondramatic literary work, by or in the course of a transmission specifically designed for and primarily directed to blind or other handicapped persons who are unable to read normal printed material as a result of their handicap, or deaf or other handicapped persons who are unable to hear the aural signals accompanying a transmission of visual signals, if the performance is made without any purpose of direct or indirect commercial advantage and its transmission is made through the facilities of: (i) a governmental body; or (ii) a noncommercial educational broadcast station (as defined in section 397 of title 47); or (iii) a radio subcarrier authorization (as defined in 47 CFR 73.293–73.295 and 73.593–73.595); or (iv) a cable system (as defined in section 111 (f));

(9) performance on a single occasion of a dramatic literary work published at least ten years before the date of the performance, by or in the course of a transmission specifically designed for and primarily directed to blind or other handicapped persons who are unable to read normal printed material as a result of their handicap, if the performance is made without any purpose of direct or indirect commercial

advantage and its transmission is made through the facilities of a radio subcarrier authorization referred to in clause (8) (iii), *Provided, That* the provisions of this clause shall not be applicable to more than one performance of the same work by the same performers or under the auspices of the same organization;

(10) notwithstanding paragraph (4), the following is not an infringement of copyright: performance of a nondramatic literary or musical work in the course of a social function which is organized and promoted by a nonprofit veterans' organization or a nonprofit fraternal organization to which the general public is not invited, but not including the invitees of the organizations, if the proceeds from the performance, after deducting the reasonable costs of producing the performance, are used exclusively for charitable purposes and not for financial gain. For purposes of this section the social functions of any college or university fraternity or sorority shall not be included unless the social function is held solely to raise funds for a specific charitable purpose; and

(11) the making imperceptible, by or at the direction of a member of a private household, of limited portions of audio or video content of a motion picture, during a performance in or transmitted to that household for private home viewing, from an authorized copy of the motion picture, or the creation or provision of a computer program or other technology that enables such making imperceptible and that is designed and marketed to be used, at the direction of a member of a private household, for such making imperceptible, if no fixed copy of the altered version of the motion picture is created by such computer program or other technology.

§ 111. Limitations on exclusive rights: Secondary transmissions

(a) CERTAIN SECONDARY TRANSMISSIONS EXEMPTED.—The secondary transmission of a performance or display of a work embodied in a primary transmission is not an infringement of copyright if—

(1) the secondary transmission is not made by a cable system, and consists entirely of the relaying, by the management of a hotel, apartment house, or similar establishment, of signals transmitted by a broadcast station licensed by the Federal Communications Commission, within the local service area of such station, to the private lodgings of guests or residents of such establishment, and no direct charge is made to see or hear the secondary transmission; or

(2) the secondary transmission is made solely for the purpose and under the conditions specified by clause (2) of section 110; or

(3) the secondary transmission is made by any carrier who has no direct or indirect control over the content or selection of the primary transmission or over the particular recipients of the secondary transmission, and whose activities with respect to the secondary transmission consist solely of providing wires, cables, or other communications channels for the use of others: *Provided, That the provisions of this clause extend only to the activities of said carrier with respect to secondary transmissions and do not exempt from liability the activities of others with respect to their own primary or secondary transmissions;

(4) the secondary transmission is made by a satellite carrier pursuant to a statutory license under section 119; or

(5) the secondary transmission is not made by a cable system but is made by a governmental body, or other nonprofit organization, without any purpose of direct or indirect commercial advantage, and without charge to the recipients of the secondary transmission other than assessments necessary to defray the actual and reasonable costs of maintaining and operating the secondary transmission service.

(f) Definitions.—As used in this section, the following terms and their variant forms mean the following:

A "primary transmission" is a transmission made to the public by the transmitting facility whose signals are being received and further transmitted by the secondary transmission service, regardless of where or when the performance or display was first transmitted.

A "secondary transmission" is the further transmitting of a primary transmission simultaneously with the primary transmission, or nonsimultaneously with the primary transmission if by a "cable system" not located in whole or in part within the boundary of the forty-eight contiguous States, Hawaii, or Puerto Rico: *Provided, however,* That a nonsimultaneous further transmission by a cable system located in Hawaii of a primary transmission shall be deemed to be a secondary transmission if the carriage of the television broadcast signal comprising such further transmission is permissible under the rules, regulations, or authorizations of the Federal Communications Commission.

A "cable system" is a facility, located in any State, Territory, Trust Territory, or Possession, that in whole or in part receives signals transmitted or programs broadcast by one or more television broadcast stations licensed by the Federal Communications Commission, and makes secondary transmissions of such signals or programs by wires, cables, microwave, or other communications channels to subscribing members of the public who pay for such service. For purposes of determining the royalty fee under subsection (d)(1), two or more cable systems in contiguous communities under common ownership or control or operating from one headend shall be considered as one system.

§ 113. Scope of exclusive rights in pictorial, graphic, and sculptural works

(c) In the case of a work lawfully reproduced in useful articles that have been offered for sale or other distribution to the public, copyright does not include any right to prevent the making, distribution, or display of pictures or photographs of such articles in connection with advertisements or commentaries related to the distribution or display of such articles, or in connection with news reports.

§ 115. Scope of exclusive rights in nondramatic musical works: Compulsory license for making and distributing phonorecords

In the case of nondramatic musical works, the exclusive rights provided by clauses (1) and (3) of section 106, to make and to distribute phonorecords of such works, are subject to compulsory licensing under the conditions specified by this section.

(a) AVAILABILITY AND SCOPE OF COMPULSORY LICENSE.—

(1) When phonorecords of a nondramatic musical work have been distributed to the public in the United States under the authority of the copyright owner, any other person, including those who make phonorecords or digital phonorecord deliveries, may, by complying with the provisions of this section, obtain a compulsory license to make and distribute phonorecords of the work. A person may obtain a compulsory license only if his or her primary purpose in making phonorecords is to distribute them to the public for private use, including by means of a digital phonorecord delivery. A person may not obtain a compulsory license for use of the work in the making of phonorecords duplicating a sound recording fixed by another, unless:

(i) such sound recording was fixed lawfully; and

(ii) the making of the phonorecords was authorized by the owner of copyright in the sound recording or, if the sound recording was fixed before February 15, 1972, by any person who fixed the sound recording pursuant to an express license from the owner of the copyright in the musical work or pursuant to a valid compulsory license for use of such work in a sound recording.

(2) A compulsory license includes the privilege of making a musical arrangement of the work to the extent necessary to conform it to the style or manner of interpretation of the performance involved, but the arrangement shall not change the basic melody or fundamental character of the work, and shall not be subject to protection as a derivative work under this title, except with the express consent of the copyright owner.

§ 116. Negotiated licenses for public performances by means of coin-operated phonorecord players

(a) APPLICABILITY OF SECTION.—This section applies to any nondramatic musical work embodied in a phonorecord.

(b) NEGOTIATED LICENSES.—

(1) AUTHORITY FOR NEGOTIATIONS.—Any owners of copyright in works to which this section applies and any operators of coin-operated phonorecord players may negotiate and agree upon the terms and rates of royalty payments for the performance of such works and the proportionate division of fees paid among copyright owners, and may designate common agents to negotiate, agree to, pay, or receive such royalty payments.

(d) DEFINITIONS.—As used in this section, the following terms mean the following:

(1)A"coin-operatedphonorecordplayer"isamachineordevicethat—

(A) is employed solely for the performance of nondramatic musical works by means of phonorecords upon being activated by the insertion of coins, currency, tokens, or other monetary units or their equivalent;

(B) is located in an establishment making no direct or indirect charge for admission;

(C) is accompanied by a list which is comprised of the titles of all the musical works available for performance on it, and is affixed to the phonorecord player or posted in the establishment in a prominent position where it can be readily examined by the public; and

(D) affords a choice of works available for performance and permits the choice to be made by the patrons of the establishment in which it is located.

(2) An "operator" is any person who, alone or jointly with others—

(A) owns a coin-operated phonorecord player;

(B) has the power to make a coin-operated phonorecord player available for placement in an establishment for purposes of public performance; or

(C) has the power to exercise primary control over the selection of the musical works made available for public performance on a coin-operated phonorecord player.

§ 117. Limitations on exclusive rights: Computer programs

(a) MAKING OF ADDITIONAL COPY OR ADAPTATION BY OWNER OF COPY.— Notwithstanding the provisions of section 106, it is not an infringement for the owner of a copy of a computer program to make or authorize the making of another copy or adaptation of that computer program provided:

(1) that such a new copy or adaptation is created as an essential step in the utilization of the computer program in conjunction with a machine and that it is used in no other manner, or

(2) that such new copy or adaptation is for archival purposes only and that all archival copies are destroyed in the event that continued possession of the computer program should cease to be rightful.

(b) LEASE, SALE, OR OTHER TRANSFER OF ADDITIONAL COPY OR ADAPTATION.—Any exact copies prepared in accordance with the provisions of this section may be leased, sold, or otherwise transferred, along with the copy from which such copies were prepared, only as part of the lease, sale, or other transfer of all rights in the program. Adaptations so prepared may be transferred only with the authorization of the copyright owner.

(c) MACHINE MAINTENANCE OR REPAIR.—Notwithstanding the provisions of section 106, it is not an infringement for the owner or lessee of a machine to make or authorize the making of a copy of a computer program if such copy is made solely by virtue of the activation of a machine that lawfully contains an authorized copy of the computer program, for purposes only of maintenance or repair of that machine, if—

(1) such new copy is used in no other manner and is destroyed immediately after the maintenance or repair is completed; and

(2) with respect to any computer program or part thereof that is not necessary for that machine to be activated, such program or part thereof is not accessed or used other than to make such new copy by virtue of the activation of the machine.

(d) Definitions.—For purposes of this section—

(1) the "maintenance" of a machine is the servicing of the machine in order to make it work in accordance with its original specifications and any changes to those specifications authorized for that machine; and

(2) the "repair" of a machine is the restoring of the machine to the state of working in accordance with its original specifications and any changes to those specifications authorized for that machine.

§ 118. Scope of exclusive rights: Use of certain works in connection with noncommercial broadcasting

(a) The exclusive rights provided by section 106 shall, with respect to the works specified by subsection (b) and the activities specified by subsection (d), be subject to the conditions and limitations prescribed by this section.

(b) Notwithstanding any provision of the antitrust laws, any owners of copyright in published nondramatic musical works and published pictorial, graphic, and sculptural works and any public broadcasting entities, respectively, may negotiate and agree upon the terms and rates of royalty payments and the proportionate division of fees paid among various copyright owners, and may designate common agents to negotiate, agree to, pay, or receive payments.

(1) Any owner of copyright in a work specified in this subsection or any public broadcasting entity may submit to the Copyright Royalty Judges proposed licenses covering such activities with respect to such works.

(2) License agreements voluntarily negotiated at any time between one or more copyright owners and one or more public broadcasting entities shall be given effect in lieu of any determination by the Librarian of Congress or the Copyright Royalty Judges, if copies of such agreements are filed with the Copyright Royalty Judges within 30 days of execution in accordance with regulations that the Copyright Royalty Judges shall issue.

Section 602 of the 1976 Act:

§ 602. Infringing importation of copies or phonorecords

(a) Importation into the United States, without the authority of the owner of copyright under this title, of copies or phonorecords of a work that have been acquired outside the United States is an infringement of the exclusive right to distribute copies or phonorecords under section 106, actionable under section 501. This subsection does not apply to—

(1) importation of copies or phonorecords under the authority or for the use of the Government of the United States or of any State or political subdivision of a State, but not including copies or phonorecords for use in schools, or copies of any audiovisual work imported for purposes other than archival use;

(2) importation, for the private use of the importer and not for distribution, by any person with respect to no more than one copy or phonorecord of any one work at any one time, or by any person arriving from outside the United States with respect to copies or phonorecords forming part of such person's personal baggage; or

(3) importation by or for an organization operated for scholarly, educational, or religious purposes and not for private gain, with respect to no more than one copy of an audiovisual work solely for its archival purposes, and no more than five copies or phonorecords of any other work for its library lending or archival purposes, unless the importation of such copies or phonorecords is part of an activity consisting of systematic reproduction or distribution, engaged in by such organization in violation of the provisions of section 108(g)(2).

(b) In a case where the making of the copies or phonorecords would have constituted an infringement of copyright if this title had been applicable, their importation is prohibited. In a case where the copies or phonorecords were lawfully made, the United States Customs Service has no authority to prevent their importation unless the provisions of section 601 are applicable. In either case, the Secretary of the Treasury is authorized to prescribe, by regulation, a procedure under which any person claiming an interest in the copyright in a particular work may, upon payment of a specified fee, be entitled to notification by the Customs Service of the importation of articles that appear to be copies or phonorecords of the work.

APPENDIX 6:
COPYRIGHT NOTICE REQUIREMENTS

Sections 401 and 402 of the 1976 Act:

§ 401. Notice of copyright: Visually perceptible copies

(a) GENERAL PROVISIONS.—Whenever a work protected under this title is published in the United States or elsewhere by authority of the copyright owner, a notice of copyright as provided by this section may be placed on publicly distributed copies from which the work can be visually perceived, either directly or with the aid of a machine or device.

(b) FORM OF NOTICE.—If a notice appears on the copies, it shall consist of the following three elements:

(1) the symbol © (the letter C in a circle), or the word "Copyright," or the abbreviation "Copr."; and

(2) the year of first publication of the work; in the case of compilations or derivative works incorporating previously published material, the year date of first publication of the compilation or derivative work is sufficient. The year date may be omitted where a pictorial, graphic, or sculptural work, with accompanying text matter, if any, is reproduced in or on greeting cards, postcards, stationery, jewelry, dolls, toys, or any useful articles; and

(3) the name of the owner of copyright in the work, or an abbreviation by which the name can be recognized, or a generally known alternative designation of the owner.

(c) POSITION OF NOTICE.—The notice shall be affixed to the copies in such manner and location as to give reasonable notice of the claim of copyright. The Register of Copyrights shall prescribe by regulation, as examples, specific methods of affixation and positions of the notice on various types of works that will satisfy this requirement, but these specifications shall not be considered exhaustive.

(d) EVIDENTIARY WEIGHT OF NOTICE.—If a notice of copyright in the form and position specified by this section appears on the published copy or copies to which a defendant in a copyright infringement suit had access, then no weight shall be given to such a defendant's interposition of a defense based on innocent infringement in mitigation of actual or statutory damages, except as provided in the last sentence of section 504(c)(2).

§ 402. Notice of copyright: Phonorecords of sound recordings

(a) GENERAL PROVISIONS.—Whenever a sound recording protected under this title is published in the United States or elsewhere by authority of the copyright owner, a notice of copyright as provided by this section may be placed on publicly distributed phonorecords of the sound recording.

(b) FORM OF NOTICE.—If a notice appears on the phonorecords, it shall consist of the following three elements:

(1) the symbol ℗ (the letter P in a circle); and

(2) the year of first publication of the sound recording; and

(3) the name of the owner of copyright in the sound recording, or an abbreviation by which the name can be recognized, or a generally known alternative designation of the owner; if the producer of the sound recording is named on the phonorecord labels or containers, and if no other name appears in conjunction with the notice, the producer's name shall be considered a part of the notice.

(c) POSITION OF NOTICE.—The notice shall be placed on the surface of the phonorecord, or on the phonorecord label or container, in such manner and location as to give reasonable notice of the claim of copyright.

(d) EVIDENTIARY WEIGHT OF NOTICE.—If a notice of copyright in the form and position specified by this section appears on the published phonorecord or phonorecords to which a defendant in a copyright infringement suit had access, then no weight shall be given to such a defendant's interposition of a defense based on innocent infringement in mitigation of actual or statutory damages, except as provided in the last sentence of section 504(c)(2).

APPENDIX 7:
DURATION OF COPYRIGHT

Excerpt from section 301 of the 1976 Act:

§ 301. Preemption with respect to other laws

(a) On and after January 1, 1978, all legal or equitable rights that are equivalent to any of the exclusive rights within the general scope of copyright as specified by section 106 in works of authorship that are fixed in a tangible medium of expression and come within the subject matter of copyright as specified by sections 102 and 103, whether created before or after that date and whether published or unpublished, are governed exclusively by this title. Thereafter, no person is entitled to any such right or equivalent right in any such work under the common law or statutes of any State.

(b) Nothing in this title annuls or limits any rights or remedies under the common law or statutes of any State with respect to—

(1) subject matter that does not come within the subject matter of copyright as specified by sections 102 and 103, including works of authorship not fixed in any tangible medium of expression; or

(2) any cause of action arising from undertakings commenced before January 1, 1978;

(3) activities violating legal or equitable rights that are not equivalent to any of the exclusive rights within the general scope of copyright as specified by section 106; or

(4) State and local landmarks, historic preservation, zoning, or building codes, relating to architectural works protected under section 102(a)(8).

(c) With respect to sound recordings fixed before February 15, 1972, any rights or remedies under the common law or statutes of any

State shall not be annulled or limited by this title until February 15, 2067. The preemptive provisions of subsection (a) shall apply to any such rights and remedies pertaining to any cause of action arising from undertakings commenced on and after February 15, 2067. Notwithstanding the provisions of section 303, no sound recording fixed before February 15, 1972, shall be subject to copyright under this title before, on, or after February 15, 2067.

(d) Nothing in this title annuls or limits any rights or remedies under any other Federal statute.

(e) The scope of Federal preemption under this section is not affected by the adherence of the United States to the Berne Convention or the satisfaction of obligations of the United States thereunder.

Excerpt from section 302 of the 1976 Act:

§ 302. Duration of copyright: Works created on or after January 1, 1978

(a) IN GENERAL.—Copyright in a work created on or after January 1, 1978, subsists from its creation and, except as provided by the following subsections, endures for a term consisting of the life of the author and 70 years after the author's death.

(b) JOINT WORKS.—In the case of a joint work prepared by two or more authors who did not work for hire, the copyright endures for a term consisting of the life of the last surviving author and 70 years after such last surviving author's death.

(c) ANONYMOUS WORKS, PSEUDONYMOUS WORKS, AND WORKS MADE FOR HIRE.—In the case of an anonymous work, a pseudonymous work, or a work made for hire, the copyright endures for a term of 95 years from the year of its first publication, or a term of 120 years from the year of its creation, whichever expires first. If, before the end of such term, the identity of one or more of the authors of an anonymous or pseudonymous work is revealed in the records of a registration made for that work under subsections (a) or (d) of section 408, or in the records provided by this subsection, the copyright in the work endures for the term specified by subsection (a) or (b), based on the life of the author or authors whose identity has been revealed. Any person having an interest in the copyright in an anonymous or pseudonymous work may at any time record, in records to be maintained by the Copyright Office for that purpose, a statement identifying one or more authors of the work; the statement shall also identify the person filing it, the nature of that person's interest, the source of the information recorded, and the particular work affected, and shall comply in form and content with requirements that the Register of Copyrights shall prescribe by regulation.

Excerpt from section 303 of the 1976 Act:

§ 303. Duration of copyright: Works created but not published or copyrighted before January 1, 1978

(a) Copyright in a work created before January 1, 1978, but not theretofore in the public domain or copyrighted, subsists from January 1, 1978, and endures for the term provided by section 302. In no case, however, shall the term of copyright in such a work expire before December 31, 2002; and, if the work is published on or before December 31, 2002, the term of copyright shall not expire before December 31, 2047.

(b) The distribution before January 1, 1978, of a phonorecord shall not for any purpose constitute a publication of the musical work embodied therein.

. . .

(b) Copyrights in Their Renewal Term at the Time of the Effective Date of the Sonny Bono Copyright Term Extension Act—Any copyright still in its renewal term at the time that the Sonny Bono Copyright Term Extension Act becomes effective shall have a copyright term of 95 years from the date copyright was originally secured.

§ 305. Duration of copyright: Terminal date

All terms of copyright provided by sections 302 through 304 run to the end of the calendar year in which they would otherwise expire.

APPENDIX 8:
SEARCH REQUEST FORM

 **Search Request Form**

Library of Congress
Copyright Office
101 Independence Avenue SE
Washington, DC 20559-6000

Reference & Bibliography Section
8:30 AM to 5:00 PM eastern
Monday through Friday.
Phone: (202) 707-6850
Fax: (202) 252-3485

TYPE OF WORK

☐ Book   ☐ Music   ☐ Motion picture   ☐ Drama   ☐ Sound recording   ☐ Computer program
☐ Photograph/artwork   ☐ Map   ☐ Periodical   ☐ Contribution   ☐ Architectural work   ☐ Mask work

SEARCH INFORMATION YOU REQUIRE

☐ Registration   ☐ Renewal   ☐ Assignment   ☐ Address

SPECIFICS OF WORK TO BE SEARCHED

Title _____

Author _____

Copyright claimant _____
(Name in © notice)

Approximate year date of publication/creation _____

Registration number (if known) _____

If you need more space please attach additional pages.

The fee for a search report is based on a set statutory fee* for the hour(s) or fraction of an hour consumed. The more information you furnish as a basis for the search, the better service we can provide. The time between the date of receipt of your fee for the search and your receiving a report will vary, depending on the method of payment (personal check, money order, or credit card) and on the workload. If you desire an estimate for the cost of the search and report, indicate your preference by checking the box below. There is a separate fee for an estimate.

Names, titles, and short phrases are not copyrightable.

SEARCH REQUEST FORM

Please read Circular 22 for more information on copyright searches.

Your name _____   Date _____

Address _____
_____

Daytime telephone _____   Email _____

Convey results of estimate/search by telephone?   ☐ Yes   ☐ No

Fee enclosed?   ☐ Yes: AMOUNT: $ _____   ☐ No

*NOTE: Copyright Office fees are subject to change. For current fees for estimates or searches, check the Copyright Office website at *www.copyright.gov*, write the Copyright Office, or call the Reference & Bibliography Section at (202) 707-6850.

APPENDIX 9:
FORM TX FOR THE REGISTRATION OF
A LITERARY WORK

 Instructions for Short Form TX

For nondramatic literary works, including fiction and nonfiction, books, short stories, poems, collections of poetry, essays, articles in serials, and computer programs

USE THIS FORM IF—
1. You are the *only* author and copyright owner of this work, *and*
2. The work was *not* made for hire, *and*
3. The work is completely new (does not contain a substantial amount of material that has been previously published or registered or is in the public domain).

If any of the above does not apply, you must use standard Form TX.
Note: *Short Form TX is not appropriate for an anonymous author who does not wish to reveal his or her identity.*

HOW TO COMPLETE SHORT FORM TX
• Type or print in black ink.
• Be clear and legible. (Your certificate of registration will be copied from your form.)
• Give only the information requested.

Note: You may use a continuation sheet (Form __/CON) to list individual titles in a collection. Complete Space A and list the individual titles under Space C on the back page. Space B is not applicable to short forms.

 Title of This Work

You must give a title. If there is no title, state "UNTITLED." If you are registering an unpublished collection, give the collection title you want to appear in our records (for example: "Joan's Poems, Volume 1"). Alternative title: If the work is known by two titles, you also may give the second title. If the work has been published as part of a larger work (including a periodical), give the title of that larger work in addition to the title of the contribution.

 Name and Address of Author and Owner of the Copyright

Give your name and mailing address. You may include your pseudonym followed by "pseud." Also, give the nation of which you are a citizen or where you have your domicile (i.e., permanent residence).
Give daytime phone and fax numbers and email address, if available.

 Year of Creation

Give the latest year in which you completed the work you are registering at this time. A work is "created" when it is written down, stored in a computer, or otherwise "fixed" in a tangible form.

 Publication

If the work has been published (i.e., if copies have been distributed to the public), give the complete date of publication (month, day, and year) and the nation where the publication first took place.

 Type of Authorship in This Work

Check the box or boxes that describe your authorship in the copy you are sending with the application. For example, if you are

registering a story and are planning to add illustrations later, check only the box for "text."
A "compilation" of terms or of data is a selection, coordination, or arrangement of such information into a chart, directory, or other form. A compilation of previously published or public domain material must be registered using a standard Form TX.

 Signature of Author

Sign the application in black ink and check the appropriate box. The person signing the application should be the author or his/her authorized agent.

 Person to Contact for Rights and Permissions

This space is optional. You may give the name and address of the person or organization to contact for permission to use the work. You may also provide phone, fax, or email information.

 Certificate Will Be Mailed

This space must be completed. Your certificate of registration will be mailed in a window envelope to this address. Also, if the Copyright Office needs to contact you, we will write to this address.

 Deposit Account

Complete this space only if you currently maintain a deposit account in the Copyright Office.

FORM TX FOR THE REGISTRATION OF A LITERARY WORK

- The filing fee in the form of a check or money order (*no cash*) payable to *Register of Copyrights*, and
- One or two copies of the work. If the work is unpublished, send one copy. If published, send two copies of the best published edition. (If first published outside the U.S., send one copy either as first published or of the best edition.) **Note:** Inquire about special requirements for works first published before 1978. Copies submitted become the property of the U.S. Government.

Mail everything (application form, copy or copies, and fee) *in one package* to:

Library of Congress
Copyright Office-TX
101 Independence Avenue SE
Washington, DC 20559-6222

QUESTIONS? Call (202) 707-3000 between 8:30 AM and 5:00 PM eastern time, Monday through Friday except federal holidays. For forms and informational circulars, call (202) 707-9100 24 hours a day, 7 days a week. For further information, go to *www.copyright.gov*.

PRIVACY ACT ADVISORY STATEMENT Required by the Privacy Act of 1974 (P.L. 93-579)
The authority for requesting this information is title 17 USC, secs. 409 and 410. Furnishing the requested information is voluntary. But if the information is not furnished, it may be necessary to delay or refuse registration and you may not be entitled to certain relief, remedies, and benefits provided in chapters 4 and 5 of title 17 USC.
The principal uses of the requested information are the establishment and maintenance of a public record and the examination of the application for compliance with the registration requirements of the copyright law.
Other routine uses include public inspection and copying, preparation of public indexes, preparation of public catalogs of copyright registrations, and preparation of search reports upon request.
NOTE: No other advisory statement will be given in connection with this application. Please keep this statement and refer to it if we communicate with you regarding this application.

Understanding Copyright Law: A Beginner's Guide

Copyright Office fees are subject to change. For current fees, check the Copyright Office website at *www.copyright.gov*, write the Copyright Office, or call (202) 707-3000.

Privacy Act Notice: Sections 408-410 of title 17 of the *United States Code* authorize the Copyright Office to collect the personally identifying information requested on this form in order to process the application for copyright registration. By providing this information you are agreeing to routine uses of the information that include publication to give legal notice of your copyright claim as required by 17 *U.S.C.* § 705. It will appear in the Office's online catalog. If you do not provide the information requested, registration may be refused or delayed, and you may not be entitled to certain relief, remedies, and benefits under the copyright law.

Short Form TX
For a Nondramatic Literary Work
UNITED STATES COPYRIGHT OFFICE
REGISTRATION NUMBER

TX   TXU
Effective Date of Registration

Application Received

Examined By

Deposit Received
One   Two
Correspondence ☐   Fee Received

TYPE OR PRINT IN BLACK INK. DO NOT WRITE ABOVE THIS LINE.

1 — **Title of This Work:** Alternative title or title of larger work in which this work was published:

2 — **Name and Address of Author and Owner of the Copyright:** Nationality or domicile: Phone, fax, and email:
Phone ( )   Fax ( )
Email

3 — **Year of Creation:**

4 — *If work has been published,* **Date and Nation of Publication:**
a. Date _____ Month _____ Day _____ Year   *(Month, day, and year all required)*
b. Nation

5 — **Type of Authorship in This Work:** Check all that this author created.
☐ Text (includes fiction, nonfiction, poetry, computer programs, etc.)
☐ Illustrations
☐ Photographs
☐ Compilation of terms or data

6 — **Signature:** Registration cannot be completed without a signature.
I certify that the statements made by me in this application are correct to the best of my knowledge. Check one:
☐ Author   ☐ Authorized agent
X _____

7 — **Name and Address of Person to Contact for Rights and Permissions:** Phone, fax, and email:
☐ Check here if same as #2 above.
Phone ( )   Fax ( )
Email

OPTIONAL

8
Certificate will be mailed in window envelope to this address:
Name ▼
Number/Street/Apt ▼
City/State/Zip ▼

9
Deposit account # _____
Name _____
Complete this space only if you currently hold a Deposit Account in the Copyright Office.

DO NOT WRITE HERE   Page 1 of ____ pages

*17 USC § 506(e): Any person who knowingly makes a false representation of a material fact in the application for copyright registration provided for by section 409, or in any written statement filed in connection with the application, shall be fined not more than $2,500.

Form TX-Short   Rev: 11/2005   Print: 11/2005— xx,000   Printed on recycled paper

U.S. Government Printing Office: 2005-xxx-xxx/xx,xxx

Form TX

Detach and read these instructions before completing this form.
Make sure all applicable spaces have been filled in before you return this form.

BASIC INFORMATION

When to Use This Form: Use Form TX for registration of published or unpublished nondramatic literary works, excluding periodicals or serial issues. This class includes a wide variety of works: fiction, nonfiction, poetry, textbooks, reference works, directories, catalogs, advertising copy, compilations of information, and computer programs. For periodicals and serials, use Form SE.

Deposit to Accompany Application: An application for copyright registration must be accompanied by a deposit consisting of copies or phonorecords representing the entire work for which registration is to be made. The following are the general deposit requirements as set forth in the statute:

Unpublished Work: Deposit one complete copy (or phonorecord)
Published Work: Deposit two complete copies (or one phonorecord) of the best edition.
Work First Published Outside the United States: Deposit one complete copy (or phonorecord) of the first foreign edition.
Contribution to a Collective Work: Deposit one complete copy (or phonorecord) of the best edition of the collective work.
The Copyright Notice: Before March 1, 1989, the use of copyright notice was mandatory on all published works, and any work first published before that date should have carried a notice. For works first

published on and after March 1, 1989, use of the copyright notice is optional. For more information about copyright notice, see Circular 3, "Copyright Notices."

For Further Information: To speak to an information specialist, call (202) 707-3000 (TTY: (202) 707-6737). Recorded information is available 24 hours a day. Order forms and other publications from the address in space 9 or call the Forms and Publications Hotline at (202) 707-9100. Most circulars (but not forms) are available via fax. Call (202) 707-2600 from a touchtone phone. Access and download circulars, forms, and other information from the Copyright Office Website at *www.copyright.gov.*

> **PRIVACY ACT ADVISORY STATEMENT Required by the Privacy Act of 1974 (P.L. 93-579)**
> The authority for requesting this information is title 17, U.S.C., secs. 409 and 410. Furnishing the requested information is voluntary. But if the information is not furnished, it may be necessary to delay or refuse registration and you may not be entitled to certain relief, remedies, and benefits provided in chapters 4 and 5 of title 17, U.S.C.
> The principal uses of the requested information are the establishment and maintenance of a public record and the examination of the application for compliance with the registration requirements of the copyright code.
> Other routine uses include public inspection and copying, preparation of public indexes, preparation of public catalogs of copyright registrations, and preparation of search reports upon request.
> NOTE: No other advisory statement will be given in connection with this application. Please keep this statement and refer to it if we communicate with you regarding this application.

LINE-BY-LINE INSTRUCTIONS

Please type or print using black ink. The form is used to produce the certificate.

 SPACE 1: Title

Title of This Work: Every work submitted for copyright registration must be given a title to identify that particular work. If the copies or phonorecords of the work bear a title or an identifying phrase that could serve as a title, transcribe that wording *completely* and *exactly* on the application. Indexing of the registration and future identification of the work will depend on the information you give here.

Previous or Alternative Titles: Complete this space if there are any additional titles for the work under which someone searching for the registration might be likely to look or under which a document pertaining to the work might be recorded.

Publication as a Contribution: If the work being registered is a contribution to a periodical, serial, or collection, give the title of the contribution in the "Title of This Work" space. Then, in the line headed "Publication as a Contribution," give information about the collective work in which the contribution appeared.

 SPACE 2: Author(s)

General Instructions: After reading these instructions, decide who are the "authors" of this work for copyright purposes. Then, unless the work is a "collective work," give the requested information about every "author" who contributed any appreciable amount of copyrightable matter to this version of the work. If you need further space, request Continuation Sheets. In the case of a collective work, such as an anthology, collection of essays, or encyclopedia, give information about the author of the collective work as a whole.

Name of Author: The fullest form of the author's name should be given. Unless the work was "made for hire," the individual who actually created the work is its "author." In the case of a work made

for hire, the statute provides that "the employer or other person for whom the work was prepared is considered the author."

What is a "Work Made for Hire"? A "work made for hire" is defined as (1) "a work prepared by an employee within the scope of his or her employment"; or (2) "a work specially ordered or commissioned for use as a contribution to a collective work, as a part of a motion picture or other audiovisual work, as a translation, as a supplementary work, as a compilation, as an instructional text, as a test, as answer material for a test, or as an atlas, if the parties expressly agree in a written instrument signed by them that the works shall be considered a work made for hire." If you have checked "Yes" to indicate that the work was "made for hire," you must give the full legal name of the employer (or other person for whom the work was prepared). You may also include the name of the employee along with the name of the employer (for example: "Elster Publishing Co., employer for hire of John Ferguson").

"Anonymous" or "Pseudonymous" Work: An author's contribution to a work is "anonymous" if that author is not identified on the copies or phonorecords of the work. An author's contribution to a work is "pseudonymous" if that author is identified on the copies or phonorecords under a fictitious name. If the work is "anonymous" you may: (1) leave the line blank; or (2) state "anonymous" on the line; or (3) reveal the author's identity. If the work is "pseudonymous" you may: (1) leave the line blank; or (2) give the pseudonym and identify it as such (for example: "Huntley Haverstock, pseudonym"); or (3) reveal the author's name, making clear which is the real name and which is the pseudonym (for example, "Judith Barton, whose pseudonym is Madeline Elster"). However, the citizenship or domicile of the author **must** be given in all cases.

Dates of Birth and Death: If the author is dead, the statute requires that the year of death be included in the application unless the work is anonymous or pseudonymous. The author's birth date is optional but is useful as a form of identification. Leave this space blank if the author's contribution was a "work made for hire."

Understanding Copyright Law: A Beginner's Guide

Author's Nationality or Domicile: Give the country of which the author is a citizen or the country in which the author is domiciled. Nationality or domicile **must** be given in all cases.

Nature of Authorship: After the words "Nature of Authorship," give a brief general statement of the nature of this particular author's contribution to the work. Examples: "Entire text"; "Coauthor of entire text"; "Computer program"; "Editorial revisions"; "Compilation and English translation"; "New text."

SPACE 3: Creation and Publication

General Instructions: Do not confuse "creation" with "publication." Every application for copyright registration must state "the year in which creation of the work was completed." Give the date and nation of first publication only if the work has been published.

Creation: Under the statute, a work is "created" when it is fixed in a copy or phonorecord for the first time. Where a work has been prepared over a period of time, the part of the work existing in fixed form on a particular date constitutes the created work on that date. The date you give here should be the year in which the author completed the particular version for which registration is now being sought, even if other versions exist or if further changes or additions are planned.

Publication: The statute defines "publication" as "the distribution of copies or phonorecords of a work to the public by sale or other transfer of ownership, or by rental, lease, or lending." A work is also "published" if there has been an "offering to distribute copies or phonorecords to a group of persons for purposes of further distribution, public performance, or public display." Give the full date (month, day, year) when, and the country where, publication first occurred. If first publication took place simultaneously in the United States and other countries, it is sufficient to state "U.S.A."

SPACE 4: Claimant(s)

Name(s) and Address(es) of Copyright Claimant(s): Give the name(s) and address(es) of the copyright claimant(s) in this work even if the claimant is the same as the author. Copyright in a work belongs initially to the author of the work (including, in the case of a work made for hire, the employer or other person for whom the work was prepared). The copyright claimant is either the author of the work or a person or organization to whom the copyright initially belonging to the author has been transferred.

Transfer: The statute provides that, if the copyright claimant is not the author, the application for registration must contain "a brief statement of how the claimant obtained ownership of the copyright." If any copyright claimant named in space 4 is not an author named in space 2, give a brief statement explaining how the claimant(s) obtained ownership of the copyright. Examples: "By written contract"; "Transfer of all rights by author"; "Assignment"; "By will." Do not attach transfer documents or other attachments or riders.

SPACE 5: Previous Registration

General Instructions: The questions in space 5 are intended to show whether an earlier registration has been made for this work and, if so, whether there is any basis for a new registration. As a general rule, only one basic copyright registration can be made for the same version of a particular work.

Same Version: If this version is substantially the same as the work covered by a previous registration, a second registration is not generally possible unless: (1) the work has been registered in unpublished form and a second registration is now being sought to cover this first published edition; or (2) someone other than the

author is identified as copyright claimant in the earlier registration, and the author is now seeking registration in his or her own name. If either of these two exceptions applies, check the appropriate box and give the earlier registration number and date. Otherwise, do not submit Form TX. Instead, write the Copyright Office for information about supplementary registration or recordation of transfers of copyright ownership.

Changed Version: If the work has been changed and you are now seeking registration to cover the additions or revisions, check the last box in space 5, give the earlier registration number and date, and complete both parts of space 6 in accordance with the instructions below.

Previous Registration Number and Date: If more than one previous registration has been made for the work, give the number and date of the latest registration.

SPACE 6: Derivative Work or Compilation

General Instructions: Complete space 6 if this work is a "changed version," "compilation," or "derivative work" and if it incorporates one or more earlier works that have already been published or registered for copyright or that have fallen into the public domain. A "compilation" is defined as "a work formed by the collection and assembling of preexisting materials or of data that are selected, coordinated, or arranged in such a way that the resulting work as a whole constitutes an original work of authorship." A "derivative work" is "a work based on one or more preexisting works." Examples of derivative works include translations, fictionalizations, abridgments, condensations, or "any other form in which a work may be recast, transformed, or adapted." Derivative works also include works "consisting of editorial revisions, annotations, or other modifications" if these changes, as a whole, represent an original work of authorship.

Preexisting Material (space 6a): For derivative works, complete this space **and** space 6b. In space 6a identify the preexisting work that has been recast, transformed, or adapted. The preexisting work may be material that has been previously published, previously registered, or that is in the public domain. An example of preexisting material might be: "Russian version of Goncharov's 'Oblomov.'"

Material Added to This Work (space 6b): Give a brief, general statement of the new material covered by the copyright claim for which registration is sought. **Derivative work** examples include: "Foreword, editing, critical annotations"; "Translation"; "Chapters 11-17." If the work is a **compilation**, describe both the compilation itself and the material that has been compiled. Example: "Compilation of certain 1917 Speeches by Woodrow Wilson." A work may be both a derivative work and compilation, in which case a sample statement might be: "Compilation and additional new material."

 ## SPACE 7,8,9: Fee, Correspondence, Certification, Return Address

Deposit Account: If you maintain a Deposit Account in the Copyright Office, identify it in space 7a. Otherwise leave the space blank and send the fee of $30 with your application and deposit.

Correspondence (space 7b): This space should contain the name, address, area code, telephone number, fax number, and email address (if available) of the person to be consulted if correspondence about this application becomes necessary.

Certification (space 8): The application cannot be accepted unless it bears the date and the **handwritten signature** of the author or other copyright claimant, or of the owner of exclusive right(s), or of the duly authorized agent of author, claimant, or owner of exclusive right(s).

Address for Return of Certificate (space 9): The address box must be completed legibly since the certificate will be returned in a window envelope.

FORM TX FOR THE REGISTRATION OF A LITERARY WORK

Copyright Office fees are subject to change. For current fees, check the Copyright Office website at *www.copyright.gov*, write the Copyright Office, or call (202) 707-3000.

Privacy Act Notice: Sections 408-410 of title 17 of the *United States Code* authorize the Copyright Office to collect the personally identifying information requested on this form in order to process the application for copyright registration. By providing this information you are agreeing to routine uses of the information that include publication to give legal notice of your copyright claim as required by 17 *U.S.C.* § 705. It will appear in the Office's online catalog. If you do not provide the information requested, registration may be refused or delayed, and you may not be entitled to certain relief, remedies, and benefits under the copyright law.

C Form TX
For a Nondramatic Literary Work
UNITED STATES COPYRIGHT OFFICE

REGISTRATION NUMBER

TX   TXU

EFFECTIVE DATE OF REGISTRATION

Month   Day   Year

DO NOT WRITE ABOVE THIS LINE. IF YOU NEED MORE SPACE, USE A SEPARATE CONTINUATION SHEET.

1

TITLE OF THIS WORK ▼

PREVIOUS OR ALTERNATIVE TITLES ▼

PUBLICATION AS A CONTRIBUTION If this work was published as a contribution to a periodical, serial, or collection, give information about the collective work in which the contribution appeared.   Title of Collective Work ▼

If published in a periodical or serial give: Volume ▼   Number ▼   Issue Date ▼   On Pages ▼

2 **a**

NAME OF AUTHOR ▼

DATES OF BIRTH AND DEATH
Year Born ▼   Year Died ▼

Was this contribution to the work a "work made for hire"?
☐ Yes
☐ No

AUTHOR'S NATIONALITY OR DOMICILE
Name of Country
OR { Citizen of _____
     Domiciled in _____

WAS THIS AUTHOR'S CONTRIBUTION TO THE WORK
Anonymous?   ☐ Yes ☐ No
Pseudonymous? ☐ Yes ☐ No
If the answer to either of these questions is "Yes," see detailed instructions

NATURE OF AUTHORSHIP Briefly describe nature of material created by this author in which copyright is claimed. ▼

NOTE
Under the law, the "author" of a "work made for hire" is generally the employer, not the employee (see instructions). For any part of this work that was "made for hire" check "Yes" in the space provided, give the employer (or other person for whom the work was prepared) as "Author" of that part, and leave the space for dates of birth and death blank.

b

NAME OF AUTHOR ▼

DATES OF BIRTH AND DEATH
Year Born ▼   Year Died ▼

Was this contribution to the work a "work made for hire"?
☐ Yes
☐ No

AUTHOR'S NATIONALITY OR DOMICILE
Name of Country
OR { Citizen of _____
     Domiciled in _____

WAS THIS AUTHOR'S CONTRIBUTION TO THE WORK
Anonymous?   ☐ Yes ☐ No
Pseudonymous? ☐ Yes ☐ No
If the answer to either of these questions is "Yes," see detailed instructions

NATURE OF AUTHORSHIP Briefly describe nature of material created by this author in which copyright is claimed. ▼

c

NAME OF AUTHOR ▼

DATES OF BIRTH AND DEATH
Year Born ▼   Year Died ▼

Was this contribution to the work a "work made for hire"?
☐ Yes
☐ No

AUTHOR'S NATIONALITY OR DOMICILE
Name of Country
OR { Citizen of _____
     Domiciled in _____

WAS THIS AUTHOR'S CONTRIBUTION TO THE WORK
Anonymous?   ☐ Yes ☐ No
Pseudonymous? ☐ Yes ☐ No
If the answer to either of these questions is "Yes," see detailed instructions

NATURE OF AUTHORSHIP Briefly describe nature of material created by this author in which copyright is claimed. ▼

3 **a**

YEAR IN WHICH CREATION OF THIS WORK WAS COMPLETED This information must be given Year in all cases.

b DATE AND NATION OF FIRST PUBLICATION OF THIS PARTICULAR WORK
Complete this information ONLY if this work has been published.   Month _____ Day _____ Year _____   Nation

4

COPYRIGHT CLAIMANT(S) Name and address must be given even if the claimant is the same as the author given in space 2. ▼

See instructions before completing this space.

TRANSFER If the claimant(s) named here in space 4 is (are) different from the author(s) named in space 2, give a brief statement of how the claimant(s) obtained ownership of the copyright. ▼

APPLICATION RECEIVED

ONE DEPOSIT RECEIVED

TWO DEPOSITS RECEIVED

FUNDS RECEIVED

DO NOT WRITE HERE OFFICE USE ONLY

MORE ON BACK ▶ · Complete all applicable spaces (numbers 5-9) on the reverse side of this page.
· See detailed instructions   · Sign the form at line 8.

DO NOT WRITE HERE
Page 1 of _____ pages

EXAMINED BY	FORM TX
CHECKED BY	
☐ CORRESPONDENCE Yes	FOR COPYRIGHT OFFICE USE ONLY

DO NOT WRITE ABOVE THIS LINE. IF YOU NEED MORE SPACE, USE A SEPARATE CONTINUATION SHEET.

PREVIOUS REGISTRATION Has registration for this work, or for an earlier version of this work, already been made in the Copyright Office?
☐ Yes ☐ No If your answer is "Yes," why is another registration being sought? (Check appropriate box.) ▼
a. ☐ This is the first published edition of a work previously registered in unpublished form.
b. ☐ This is the first application submitted by this author as copyright claimant.
c. ☐ This is a changed version of the work, as shown by space 6 on this application.
If your answer is "Yes," give: Previous Registration Number ▶   Year of Registration ▶

5

DERIVATIVE WORK OR COMPILATION
Preexisting Material Identify any preexisting work or works that this work is based on or incorporates. ▼

a

6

See instructions before completing this space.

Material Added to This Work Give a brief, general statement of the material that has been added to this work and in which copyright is claimed. ▼

b

DEPOSIT ACCOUNT If the registration fee is to be charged to a Deposit Account established in the Copyright Office, give name and number of Account.
Name ▼   Account Number ▼

a

7

CORRESPONDENCE Give name and address to which correspondence about this application should be sent. Name/Address/Apt/City/State/Zip ▼

b

Area code and daytime telephone number ▶   (   )   Fax number ▶   (   )

Email ▶

CERTIFICATION* I, the undersigned, hereby certify that I am the
Check only one ▶
☐ author
☐ other copyright claimant
☐ owner of exclusive right(s)
☐ authorized agent of
of the work identified in this application and that the statements made by me in this application are correct to the best of my knowledge.
Name of author or other copyright claimant, or owner of exclusive right(s) ▲

8

Typed or printed name and date ▼ If this application gives a date of publication in space 3, do not sign and submit it before that date.
     Date ▶

Handwritten signature ▼

Certificate will be mailed in window envelope to this address:

Name ▼	
Number/Street/Apt ▼	
City/State/Zip ▼	

YOU MUST:
· Complete all necessary spaces
· Sign your application in space 8
SEND ALL 3 ELEMENTS IN THE SAME PACKAGE:
1. Application form
2. Nonrefundable filing fee in check or money order payable to Register of Copyrights
3. Deposit material
MAIL TO:
Library of Congress
Copyright Office-TX
101 Independence Avenue SE
Washington, DC 20559-6222

9

Form TX–Full Rev: 11/2008 Print: 11/2008 — xx,000 Printed on recycled paper   U.S. Government Printing Office: 2008-xx-xxx/xx,xxx

APPENDIX 10:
FORM VA FOR THE REGISTRATION OF VISUAL ARTS

ⓒ Instructions for Short Form VA
For pictorial, graphic, and sculptural works

USE THIS FORM IF—
1. You are the *only* author and copyright owner of this work, *and*
2. The work was *not* made for hire, *and*
3. The work is completely new (does not contain a substantial amount of material that has been previously published or registered or is in the public domain).

If any of the above does not apply, you must use standard Form VA.

NOTE: *Short Form VA is not appropriate for an anonymous author who does not wish to reveal his or her identity.*

HOW TO COMPLETE SHORT FORM VA
- Type or print in black ink.
- Be clear and legible. (Your certificate of registration will be copied from your form.)
- Give only the information requested.

Note: You may use a continuation sheet (Form ___/CON) to list individual titles in a collection. Complete Space A and list the individual titles under Space C on the back page. Space B is not applicable to short forms.

Title of This Work
You must give a title. If there is no title, state "UNTITLED." If you are registering an unpublished collection, give the collection title you want to appear in our records (for example: "Jewelry by Josephine, 1995 Volume"). Alternative title: If the work is known by two titles, you also may give the second title. If the work has been published as part of a larger work (including a periodical), give the title of that larger work instead of an alternative title, in addition to the title of the contribution.

Name and Address of Author and Owner of the Copyright
Give your name and mailing address. You may include your pseudonym followed by "pseud." Also, give the nation of which you are a citizen or where you have your domicile (i.e., permanent residence). Give daytime phone and fax numbers and email address, if available.

Year of Creation
Give the latest year in which you completed the work you are registering at this time. A work is "created" when it is "fixed" in a tangible form. Examples: drawn on paper, molded in clay, stored in a computer.

Publication
If the work has been published (i.e., if copies have been distributed to the public), give the complete date of publication (month, day, and year) and the nation where the publication first took place.

Type of Authorship in This Work
Check the box or boxes that describe your authorship in the material you are sending. For example, if you are registering illustrations but have not written the story yet, check only the box for "2-dimensional artwork."

Signature of Author
Sign the application in black ink and check the appropriate box. The person signing the application should be the author or his/her authorized agent.

Person to Contact for Rights/Permissions
This space is optional. You may give the name and address of the person or organization to contact for permission to use the work. You may also provide phone, fax, or email information.

Certificate Will Be Mailed
This space must be completed. Your certificate of registration will be mailed in a window envelope to this address. Also, if the Copyright Office needs to contact you, we will write to this address.

Deposit Account
Complete this space only if you currently maintain a deposit account in the Copyright Office.

FORM VA FOR THE REGISTRATION OF VISUAL ARTS

- The filing fee in the form of a check or money order (*no cash*) payable to *Register of Copyrights*. (Copyright Office fees are subject to change. For current fees, check the Copyright Office website at *www.copyright.gov*, write the Copyright Office, or call (202) 707-3000.) — *and*
- One or two copies of the work or identifying material consisting of photographs or drawings showing the work. See table (right) for requirements for most works. **Note:** Request Circular 40a for information about the requirements for other works. Copies submitted become the property of the U.S. Government.

Mail everything (application form, copy or copies, and fee) *in one package* to:

Library of Congress
Copyright Office
101 Independence Avenue SE
Washington, DC 20559-6000

Questions? Call (202) 707-3000 [TTY: (202) 707-6737] between 8:30 a.m. and 5:00 p.m. eastern time, Monday through Friday except federal holidays. For forms and informational circulars, call (202) 707-9100 24 hours a day, 7 days a week, or download them from the Copyright Office website at *www.copyright.gov*.

If you are registering:	And the work is *unpublished/published* send:
• 2-dimensional artwork in a book, map, poster, or print	a. And the work is *unpublished*, send one complete copy or identifying material
	b. And the work is *published*, send two copies of the best published edition
• 3-dimensional sculpture, • 2-dimensional artwork applied to a T-shirt	a. And the work is *unpublished*, send identifying material
	b. And the work is *published*, send identifying material
• a greeting card, pattern, commercial print or label, fabric, wallpaper	a. And the work is *unpublished*, send one complete copy or identifying material
	b. And the work is *published*, send one copy of the best published edition

PRIVACY ACT ADVISORY STATEMENT Required by the Privacy Act of 1974 (P.L. 93-579) The authority for requesting this information is title 17 *USC*, secs. 409 and 410. Furnishing the requested information is voluntary. But if the information is not furnished, it may be necessary to delay or refuse registration and you may not be entitled to certain relief, remedies, and benefits provided in chapters 4 and 5 of title 17 *USC*.
The principal uses of the requested information are the establishment and maintenance of a public record and the examination of the application for compliance with the registration requirements of the copyright law.
Other routine uses include public inspection and copying, preparation of public indexes, preparation of public catalogs of copyright registrations, and preparation of search reports upon request.
NOTE: No other advisory statement will be given in connection with this application. Please keep this statement and refer to it if we communicate with you regarding this application.

Understanding Copyright Law: A Beginner's Guide

Copyright Office fees are subject to change. For current fees, check the Copyright Office website at www.copyright.gov, write the Copyright Office, or call (202) 707-3000.

Short Form VA
For a Work of the Visual Arts
UNITED STATES COPYRIGHT OFFICE

REGISTRATION NUMBER

VA   VAU

Effective Date of Registration

Examined By

Application Received

Deposit Received
One   Two

Correspondence ☐

Fee Received

TYPE OR PRINT IN BLACK INK. DO NOT WRITE ABOVE THIS LINE.

1 **Title of This Work:**

Alternative title or title of larger work in which this work was published:

2 **Name and Address of Author and Owner of the Copyright:**

Nationality or domicile:
Phone, fax, and email:

Phone (   )   Fax (   )
Email

3 **Year of Creation:**

4 **If work has been published, Date and Nation of Publication:**

a. Date _____ Month _____ Day _____ Year _____ (Month, day, and year all required)

b. Nation

5 **Type of Authorship in This Work:**
Check all that this author created.

☐ 3-Dimensional sculpture   ☐ Photograph   ☐ Map
☐ 2-Dimensional artwork   ☐ Jewelry design ☐ Text
☐ Technical drawing

6 **Signature:**

Registration cannot be completed without a signature.

I certify that the statements made by me in this application are correct to the best of my knowledge.* Check one:
☐ Author   ☐ Authorized agent

X _

7 **Name and Address of Person to Contact for Rights and Permissions:**
Phone, fax, and email:

☐ Check here if same as #2 above.

Phone (   )   Fax (   )
Email

OPTIONAL

8

Certificate will be mailed in window envelope to this address:

Name ▼
Number/Street/Apt ▼
City/State/Zip ▼

Complete this space only if you currently hold a Deposit Account in the Copyright Office.

9 Deposit Account # _____
Name _____

DO NOT WRITE HERE   Page 1 of ____ pages

*17 USC §506(e): Any person who knowingly makes a false representation of a material fact in the application for copyright registration provided for by section 409, or in any written statement filed in connection with the application, shall be fined not more than $2,500.

Form VA-Short   Rev: 07/2006   Print: 07/2006—30,000   Printed on recycled paper

U.S. Government Printing Office: 2005-320-958/60,127

Form VA

Detach and read these instructions before completing this form.
Make sure all applicable spaces have been filled in before you return this form.

BASIC INFORMATION

When to Use This Form: Use Form VA for copyright registration of published or unpublished works of the visual arts. This category consists of "pictorial, graphic, or sculptural works," including two-dimensional and three-dimensional works of fine, graphic, and applied art, photographs, prints and art reproductions, maps, globes, charts, technical drawings, diagrams, and models.

What Does Copyright Protect? Copyright in a work of the visual arts protects those pictorial, graphic, or sculptural elements that, either alone or in combination, represent an "original work of authorship." The statute declares: "In no case does copyright protection for an original work of authorship extend to any idea, procedure, process, system, method of operation, concept, principle, or discovery, regardless of the form in which it is described, explained, illustrated, or embodied in such work."

Works of Artistic Craftsmanship and Designs: "Works of artistic craftsmanship" are registrable on Form VA, but the statute makes clear that protection extends to "their form" and not to "their mechanical or utilitarian aspects." The "design of a useful article" is considered copyrightable "only if, and only to the extent that, such design incorporates pictorial, graphic, or sculptural features that can be identified separately from, and are capable of existing independently of, the utilitarian aspects of the article."

Labels and Advertisements: Works prepared for use in connection with the sale or advertisement of goods and services are registrable if they contain "original work of authorship." Use Form VA if the copyrightable material in the work you are registering is mainly pictorial or graphic; use Form TX if it consists mainly of text. **Note:** Words and short phrases such as names, titles, and slogans cannot be protected by copyright, and the same is true of standard symbols, emblems, and other commonly used graphic designs that are in the public domain. When used commercially, material of that sort can sometimes be protected under state laws of unfair competition or under the federal trademark laws. For information about trademark registration, write to the U.S. Patent and Trademark Office, PO Box 1450, Alexandria, VA 22313-1450.

Architectural Works: Copyright protection extends to the design of buildings created for the use of human beings. Architectural works created on or after December 1, 1990, or that on December 1, 1990, were unconstructed and embodied only in unpublished plans or drawings are eligible. Request Circular 41, *Copyright Claims in Architectural Works*, for more information. Architectural works and technical drawings cannot be registered on the same application.

Deposit to Accompany Application: An application for copyright registration must be accompanied by a deposit consisting of copies representing the entire work for which registration is to be made.

Unpublished Work: Deposit one complete copy.

Published Work: Deposit two complete copies of the best edition.

Work First Published Outside the United States: Deposit one complete copy of the first foreign edition.

Contribution to a Collective Work: Deposit one complete copy of the best edition of the collective work.

The Copyright Notice: Before March 1, 1989, the use of copyright notice was mandatory on all published works, and any work first published before that date should have carried a notice. For works first published on and after March 1, 1989, use of the copyright notice is optional. For more information about copyright notice, see Circular 3, *Copyright Notice*.

For Further Information: To speak to a Copyright Office staff member, call (202) 707-3000 (TTY: (202) 707-6737). Recorded information is available 24 hours a day. Order forms and other publications from the address in space 9 or call the Forms and Publications Hotline at (202) 707-9100. Access and download circulars, forms, and other information from the Copyright Office website at *www.copyright.gov.*

LINE-BY-LINE INSTRUCTIONS

Please type or print using black ink. The form is used to produce the certificate.

SPACE 1: Title

Title of This Work: Every work submitted for copyright registration must be given a title to identify that particular work. If the copies of the work bear a title (or an identifying phrase that could serve as a title), transcribe that wording *completely* and *exactly* on the application. Indexing of the registration and future identification of the work will depend on the information you give here. For an architectural work that has been constructed, add the date of construction after the title; if unconstructed at this time, add "not yet constructed."

Publication as a Contribution: If the work being registered is a contribution to a periodical, serial, or collection, give the title of the contribution in the "Title of This Work" space. Then, in the line headed "Publication as a Contribution," give information about the collective work in which the contribution appeared.

Nature of This Work: Briefly describe the general nature or character of the pictorial, graphic, or sculptural work being registered for copyright.Examples: "Oil Painting"; "Charcoal Drawing"; "Etching"; "Sculpture"; "Map"; "Photograph"; "Scale Model"; "Lithographic Print"; "Jewelry Design"; "Fabric Design."

Previous or Alternative Titles: Complete this space if there are any additional titles for the work under which someone searching for the registration might be likely to look, or under which a document pertaining to the work might be recorded.

SPACE 2: Author(s)

General Instruction: After reading these instructions, decide who are the "authors" of this work for copyright purposes. Then, unless the work is a "collective work," give the requested information about every "author" who contributed any appreciable amount of copyrightable matter to this version of the work. If you need further space, request Continuation Sheets. In the case of a collective work, such as a catalog of paintings or collection of cartoons by various authors, give information about the author of the collective work as a whole.

Name of Author: The fullest form of the author's name should be given. Unless the work was "made for hire," the individual who actually created the work is "author." In the case of a work made for hire, the statute provides that "the employer or other person for whom the work was prepared is considered the author."

What Is a "Work Made for Hire"? A "work made for hire" is defined as: (1) "a work prepared by an employee within the scope of his or her employment"; or (2) "a work specially ordered or commissioned for use as a contribution to a collective work, as a part of a motion picture or other audiovisual work, as a translation, as a supplementary work, as a compilation, as an instructional text, as a test, as answer material for a test, or as an atlas, if the parties expressly agree in a written instrument signed by them that the work shall be considered a work made for hire." If you have checked "Yes" to indicate that the work was "made for hire," you must give the full legal name of the employer (or other person for whom the work was prepared). You may also include the name of the employee along with the name of the employer (for example: "Elster Publishing Co., employer for hire of John Ferguson").

"Anonymous" or "Pseudonymous" Work: An author's contribution to a work is "anonymous" if that author is not identified on the copies or phonorecords of the work. An author's contribution to a work is "pseudonymous" if that author is identified on the copies or phonorecords under a fictitious name. If the work is "anonymous" you may: (1) leave the line blank; or (2) state "anonymous" on the line; or (3) reveal the author's identity.If the work is "pseudonymous" you may: (1) leave the line blank; or (2) give the pseudonym and identify it as such (for example: "Huntley Haverstock, pseudonym"); or (3) reveal the author's name, making clear which is the real name and which is the pseudonym (for example: "Henry Leek, whose pseudonym is Priam Farrel"). However, the citizenship or domicile of the author *must* be given in all cases.

Dates of Birth and Death: If the author is dead, the statute requires that the year of death be included in the application unless the work is anonymous or pseudonymous. The author's birth date is optional but is useful as a form of identification. Leave this space blank if the author's contribution was a "work made for hire."

Author's Nationality or Domicile: Give the country of which the author is a citizen or the country in which the author is domiciled. Nationality or domicile *must* be given in all cases.

Nature of Authorship: Catagories of pictorial, graphic, and sculptural authorship are listed below. Check the box(es) that best describe(s) each author's contribution to the work.

3-Dimensional sculptures: fine art sculptures, toys, dolls, scale models, and sculptural designs applied to useful articles.

2-Dimensional artwork: watercolor and oil paintings; pen and ink drawings; logo illustrations; greeting cards; collages; stencils; patterns; computer graphics; graphics appearing in screen displays; artwork appearing on posters, calendars, games, commercial prints and labels, and packaging, as well as 2-dimensional artwork applied to useful articles, and designs reproduced on textiles, lace, and other fabrics; on wallpaper, carpeting, floor tile, wrapping paper, and clothing.

Reproductions of works of art: reproductions of preexisting artwork made by, for example, lithography, photoengraving, or etching.

Maps: cartographic representations of an area, such as state and county maps, atlases, marine charts, relief maps, and globes.

Photographs: pictorial photographic prints and slides and holograms.

Jewelry designs: 3-dimensional designs applied to rings, pendants, earrings, necklaces, and the like.

Technical drawings: diagrams illustrating scientific or technical information in linear form, such as architectural blueprints or mechanical drawings.

Text: textual material that accompanies pictorial, graphic, or sculptural works, such as comic strips, greeting cards, games rules, commercial prints or labels, and maps.

Architectural works: designs of buildings, including the overall form as well as the arrangement and composition of spaces and elements of the design.

NOTE: Any registration for the underlying architectural plans must be applied for on a separate Form VA, checking the box "Technical drawing."

SPACE 3: Creation and Publication

General Instructions: Do not confuse "creation" with "publication." Every application for copyright registration must state "the year in which creation of the work was completed." Give the date and nation of first publication only if the work has been published.

Creation: Under the statute, a work is "created" when it is fixed in a copy or phonorecord for the first time. Where a work has been prepared over a period of time, the part of the work existing in fixed on a particular date constitutes the created work on that date. The date you give here should be the year in which the author completed the particular version for which registration is now being sought, even if other versions exist or if further changes or additions are planned.

Publication: The statute defines "publication" as "the distribution of copies or phonorecords of a work to the public by sale or other transfer of ownership, or by rental, lease, or lending"; a work is also "published" if there has been an "offering to distribute copies or phonorecords to a group of persons for purposes of further distribution, public performance, or public display." Give the full date (month, day, year) when, and the country where, publication first occurred. If first publication took place simultaneously in the United States and other countries, it is sufficient to state "U.S.A."

SPACE 4: Claimant(s)

Name(s) and Address(es) of Copyright Claimant(s): Give the name(s) and address(es) of the copyright claimant(s) in this work even if the claimant is the same as the author. Copyright in a work belongs initially to the author of the work (including, in the case of a work made for hire, the employer or other person for whom the work was prepared). The copyright claimant is either the author of the work or a person or organization to whom the copyright initially belonging to the author has been transferred.

Transfer: The statute provides that, if the copyright claimant is not the author, the application for registration must contain "a brief statement of how the claimant obtained ownership of the copyright." If any copyright claimant named in space 4 is not an author named in space 2, give a brief statement explaining how the claimant(s) obtained ownership of the copyright. Examples: "By written contract"; "Transfer of all rights by author"; "Assignment"; "By will." Do not attach transfer documents or other attachments or riders.

SPACE 5: Previous Registration

General Instructions: The questions in space 5 are intended to find out whether an earlier registration has been made for this work and, if so, whether there is any basis for a new registration. As a rule, only one basic

copyright registration can be made for the same version of a particular work.

Same Version: If this version is substantially the same as the work covered by a previous registration, a second registration is not generally possible unless: (1) the work has been registered in unpublished form and a second registration is now being sought to cover this first published edition; or (2) someone other than the author is identified as a copyright claimant in the earlier registration, and the author is now seeking registration in his or her own name. If either of these two exceptions applies, check the appropriate box and give the earlier registration number and date. Otherwise, do not submit Form VA; instead, write the Copyright Office for information about supplementary registration or recordation of transfers of copyright ownership.

Changed Version: If the work has been changed and you are now seeking registration to cover the additions or revisions, check the last box in space 5, give the earlier registration number and date, and complete both parts of space 6 in accordance with the instruction below.

Previous Registration Number and Date: If more than one previous registration has been made for the work, give the number and date of the latest registration.

SPACE 6: Derivative Work or Compilation

General Instructions: Complete space 6 if this work is a "changed version," "compilation," or "derivative work," and if it incorporates one or more earlier works that have already been published or registered for copyright, or that have fallen into the public domain. A "compilation" is defined as "a work formed by the collection and assembling of preexisting materials or of data that are selected, coordinated, or arranged in such a way that the resulting work as a whole constitutes an original work of authorship." A "derivative work" is "a work based on one or more preexisting works." Examples of derivative works include reproductions of works of art, sculptures based on drawings, lithographs based on paintings, maps based on previously published sources, or "any other form in which a work may be recast, transformed, or adapted." Derivative works also include works "consisting of editorial revisions, annotations, or other modifications" if these changes, as a whole, represent an original work of authorship.

Preexisting Material (space 6a): Complete this space *and* space 6b for derivative works. In this space identify the preexisting work that has been recast, transformed, or adapted. Examples of preexisting material might be "Grunewald Altarpiece" or "19th century quilt design." Do not complete this space for compilations.

Material Added to This Work (space 6b): Give a brief, general statement of the *additional* new material covered by the copyright claim for which registration is sought. In the case of a derivative work, identify this new material. Examples: "Adaptation of design and additional artistic work"; "Reproduction of painting by photolithography"; "Additional cartographic material"; "Compilation of photographs." If the work is a compilation, give a brief, general statement describing both the material that has been compiled *and* the compilation itself. Example: "Compilation of 19th century political cartoons."

SPACE 7, 8, 9: Fee, Correspondence, Certification, Return Address

Deposit Account: If you maintain a Deposit Account in the Copyright Office, identify it in space 7a. Otherwise, leave the space blank and send the fee with your application and deposit.

Correspondence (space 7b): Give the name, address, area code, telephone number, email address, and fax number (if available) of the person to be consulted if correspondence about this application becomes necessary.

Certification (space 8): The application cannot be accepted unless it bears the date and the *handwritten signature* of the author or other copyright claimant, or of the owner of exclusive right(s), or of the duly authorized agent of the author, claimant, or owner of exclusive right(s).

Address for Return of Certificate (space 9): The address box must be completed legibly since the certificate will be returned in a window envelope.

Copyright Office fees are subject to change. For current fees, check the Copyright Office website at www.copyright.gov, write the Copyright Office, or call (202) 707-3000.

Form VA
For a Work of the Visual Arts
UNITED STATES COPYRIGHT OFFICE

REGISTRATION NUMBER

VA   VAU
EFFECTIVE DATE OF REGISTRATION

Month   Day   Year

DO NOT WRITE ABOVE THIS LINE. IF YOU NEED MORE SPACE, USE A SEPARATE CONTINUATION SHEET.

1

Title of This Work ▼   NATURE OF THIS WORK ▼ See Instructions

Previous or Alternative Titles ▼

Publication as a Contribution If this work was published as a contribution to a periodical, serial, or collection, give information about the collective work in which the contribution appeared. Title of Collective Work ▼

If published in a periodical or serial give: Volume ▼   Number ▼   Issue Date ▼   On Pages ▼

2 a

NAME OF AUTHOR ▼   DATES OF BIRTH AND DEATH
                                        Year Born ▼   Year Died ▼

NOTE

Under the law, the "author" of a "work made for hire" is generally the employer, not the employee (see instructions). For any part of this work that was "made for hire" check "Yes" in the space provided, give the employer (or other person for whom the work was prepared) as "Author" of that part, and leave the space for dates of birth and death blank.

Was this contribution to the work a "work made for hire"?
☐ Yes
☐ No

Author's Nationality or Domicile
Name of Country
OR ☐ Citizen of _____
    ☐ Domiciled in _____

Was This Author's Contribution to the Work
Anonymous?   ☐ Yes ☐ No
Pseudonymous? ☐ Yes ☐ No
If the answer to either of these questions is "Yes," see detailed instructions.

Nature of Authorship Check appropriate box(es). **See instructions**
☐ 3-Dimensional sculpture   ☐ Map   ☐ Technical drawing
☐ 2-Dimensional artwork   ☐ Photograph   ☐ Text
☐ Reproduction of work of art ☐ Jewelry design ☐ Architectural work

b

Name of Author ▼   Dates of Birth and Death
                                        Year Born ▼   Year Died ▼

Was this contribution to the work a "work made for hire"?
☐ Yes
☐ No

Author's Nationality or Domicile
Name of Country
OR ☐ Citizen of _____
    ☐ Domiciled in _____

Was This Author's Contribution to the Work
Anonymous?   ☐ Yes ☐ No
Pseudonymous? ☐ Yes ☐ No
If the answer to either of these questions is "Yes," see detailed instructions.

Nature of Authorship Check appropriate box(es). **See instructions**
☐ 3-Dimensional sculpture   ☐ Map   ☐ Technical drawing
☐ 2-Dimensional artwork   ☐ Photograph   ☐ Text
☐ Reproduction of work of art ☐ Jewelry design ☐ Architectural work

3 a

Year in Which Creation of This Work Was Completed
This information must be given
Year in all cases.

b Date and Nation of First Publication of This Particular Work
Complete this information
ONLY if this work
has been published.
Month _____ Day _____ Year _____
                                    Nation

4

See instructions before completing this space.

COPYRIGHT CLAIMANT(S) Name and address must be given even if the claimant is the same as the author given in space 2. ▼

Transfer If the claimant(s) named here in space 4 is (are) different from the author(s) named in space 2, give a brief statement of how the claimant(s) obtained ownership of the copyright. ▼

APPLICATION RECEIVED

ONE DEPOSIT RECEIVED

TWO DEPOSITS RECEIVED

FUNDS RECEIVED

DO NOT WRITE HERE
OFFICE USE ONLY

MORE ON BACK ▶ • Complete all applicable spaces (numbers 5-9) on the reverse side of this page.
                    • See detailed instructions.   • Sign the form at line 8.

DO NOT WRITE HERE
Page 1 of _____ pages

EXAMINED BY	FORM VA
CHECKED BY	
CORRESPONDENCE ☐ Yes	FOR COPYRIGHT OFFICE USE ONLY

DO NOT WRITE ABOVE THIS LINE. IF YOU NEED MORE SPACE, USE A SEPARATE CONTINUATION SHEET.

PREVIOUS REGISTRATION Has registration for this work, or for an earlier version of this work, already been made in the Copyright Office?
☐ Yes ☐ No If your answer is "Yes," why is another registration being sought? (Check appropriate box.) ▼
a. ☐ This is the first published edition of a work previously registered in unpublished form.
b. ☐ This is the first application submitted by this author as copyright claimant.
c. ☐ This is a changed version of the work, as shown by space 6 on this application.
If your answer is "Yes," give: **Previous Registration Number** ▼   **Year of Registration** ▼

5

DERIVATIVE WORK OR COMPILATION Complete both space 6a and 6b for a derivative work; complete only 6b for a compilation.
a. **Preexisting Material** Identify any preexisting work or works that this work is based on or incorporates. ▼

b. **Material Added to This Work** Give a brief, general statement of the material that has been added to this work and in which copyright is claimed. ▼

6
a
b
See instructions before completing this space.

DEPOSIT ACCOUNT If the registration fee is to be charged to a Deposit Account established in the Copyright Office, give name and number of Account.
Name ▼   **Account Number** ▼

CORRESPONDENCE Give name and address to which correspondence about this application should be sent. Name/Address/Apt/City/State/Zip ▼

7
a
b

Area code and daytime telephone number   (   )   Fax number   (   )
Email

CERTIFICATION* I, the undersigned, hereby certify that I am the
check only one ▶
☐ author
☐ other copyright claimant
☐ owner of exclusive right(s)
☐ authorized agent of _____
Name of author or other copyright claimant, or owner of exclusive right(s) ▲
of the work identified in this application and that the statements made by me in this application are correct to the best of my knowledge.

8

Typed or printed name and date ▼ If this application gives a date of publication in space 3, do not sign and submit it before that date.
Date _____

Handwritten signature (X) ▼
X _____

Certificate will be mailed in window envelope to this address:	Name ▼	YOU MUST: • Complete all necessary spaces • Sign your application in space 8
	Number/Street/Apt ▼	SEND ALL 3 ELEMENTS IN THE SAME PACKAGE: 1. Application form 2. Nonrefundable filing fee in check or money order payable to Register of Copyrights 3. Deposit material
	City/State/Zip ▼	MAIL TO: Library of Congress Copyright Office 101 Independence Avenue SE Washington, DC 20559-6000

9

*17 USC §506(e): Any person who knowingly makes a false representation of a material fact in the application for copyright registration provided for by section 409, or in any written statement filed in connection with the application, shall be fined not more than $2,500.

Form VA – Full Rev: 07/2006 Print: 07/2006—30,000 Printed on recycled paper   U.S. Government Printing Office: 2006-320-958 /60,125

APPENDIX 11:
FORM PA FOR THE REGISTRATION OF
PERFORMING ARTS

 ## Instructions for Short Form PA
For works in the performing arts (except audiovisual works)

USE THIS FORM IF—

1. You are the only author and copyright owner of this work, and
2. The work was not made for hire, and
3. The work is completely new (does not contain a substantial amount of material that has been previously published or registered or is in the public domain) and is not an audiovisual work.

If any of the above does not apply, you must use standard Form PA.

NOTE: *Short Form PA is not appropriate for an anonymous author who does not wish to reveal his or her identity and may not be used for audiovisual works, including motion pictures.*

HOW TO COMPLETE SHORT FORM PA

- Type or print in black ink.
- Be clear and legible. (Your certificate of registration will be copied from your form.)
- Give only the information requested.

NOTE: You may use a continuation sheet (Form ___/CON) to list individual titles in a collection. Complete Space A and list the individual titles under Space C on the back page. Space B is not applicable to short forms.

 ### Title of This Work

You must give a title. If there is no title, state "UNTITLED." Alternative title: If the work is known by two titles, you also may give the second title. Or if the work has been published as part of a larger work, give the title of that larger work, in addition to the title of the contribution.

If you are registering an unpublished collection, give the collection title you want to appear in our records (for example: "Songs by Alice, Volume 1"). Be sure to keep a personal record of the songs you have included in the collection. If you want the certificate of registration to list the individual titles as well as the collection title, use a continuation sheet (Form___/CON).

Name and Address of Author and Owner of the Copyright

Give your name and mailing address. You may include your pseudonym followed by "pseud." Also, give the nation of which you are a citizen or where you have your domicile (i.e., permanent residence). Give daytime phone and fax numbers and email address, if available.

Year of Creation

Give the latest year in which you completed the work you are registering at this time. A work is "created" when it is written down, recorded, or otherwise "fixed" in a tangible form.

Publication

If the work has been published (i.e., if copies have been distributed to the public), give the complete date of publication (month, day, and year) and the nation where the publication first took place.

 ### Type of Authorship in This Work

Check the box or boxes that describe the kind of material you are registering. Check *only* the authorship included in the copy, tape, or CD you are sending with the application. For example, if you are registering lyrics and plan to add music later, check only the box for "lyrics."

 ### Signature of Author

Sign the application in black ink and check the appropriate box. The person signing the application should be the author or his/her authorized agent.

 ### Person to Contact for Rights and Permissions

This space is optional. You may give the name and address of the person or organization to contact for permission to use the work. You may also provide phone, fax, or email information.

 ### Certificate Will Be Mailed

This space must be completed. Your certificate of registration will be mailed in a window envelope to this address. Also, if the Copyright Office needs to contact you, we will write to this address.

 ### Deposit Account

Complete this space only if you currently maintain a deposit account in the Copyright Office.

MAIL WITH THE FORM—
- The filing fee, in the form of a check or money order (*no cash*) payable to *Register of Copyrights*, and
- One or two copies of the work. If the work is unpublished, send one copy, tape, or CD. If published, send two copies of the best published edition if the work is in printed form, such as sheet music, or one copy of the best published edition if the work is recorded on a tape or disk.

Note: Inquire about special requirements for works first published outside the United States or before 1978. Copies submitted become the property of the U.S. Government.

Mail everything (application form, copy or copies, and fee) *in one package* to: *Library of Congress, Copyright Office-PA, 101 Independence Avenue SE, Washington, DC 20559-6233*

QUESTIONS? Call (202) 707-3000 between 8:30 AM and 5:00 PM, eastern time, Monday through Friday, except federal holidays. For forms and informational circulars, call (202) 707-9100 24 hours a day, 7 days a week. Download circulars and certain forms at *www.copyright.gov*.

Copyright Office fees are subject to change.
For current fees, check the Copyright Office
website at *www.copyright.gov*, write the
Copyright Office, or call (202) 707-3000.

Privacy Act Notice: Sections 408-410 of title 17 of the *United States Code* authorize the Copyright Office to collect the personally identifying information requested on this form in order to process the application for copyright registration. By providing this information you are agreeing to routine uses of the information that include publication to give legal notice of your copyright claim as required by 17 *U.S.C.* § 705. It will appear in the Office's online catalog. If you do not provide the information requested, registration may be refused or delayed, and you may not be entitled to certain relief, remedies, and benefits under the copyright law.

Short Form PA
For a Work of Performing Arts
UNITED STATES COPYRIGHT OFFICE

REGISTRATION NUMBER

PA	PAU

Effective Date of Registration

Application Received

Examined By

Deposit Received	
One	Two

Correspondence ☐

Fee Received

TYPE OR PRINT IN BLACK INK. DO NOT WRITE ABOVE THIS LINE.

1 **Title of This Work:**

Alternative title or title of larger work in which this work was published:

2 **Name and Address of Author and Owner of the Copyright:**

Nationality or domicile:
Phone, fax, and email:

Phone (   )   Fax (   )
Email:

3 **Year of Creation:**

4 *If work has been published,* **Date and Nation of Publication:**

a. Date _____ Month _____ Day _____ Year _____ (*Month, day, and year all required*)

b. Nation

5 **Type of Authorship in This Work:**
Check all that this author created.

☐ Music   ☐ Other text (includes dramas, screenplays, etc.)
☐ Lyrics   (*If your work is a motion picture or other audiovisual work, use the Standard Form PA.*)

6 **Signature:**
(Registration cannot be completed without a signature.)

I certify that the statements made by me in this application are correct to the best of my knowledge. Check one:
☐ Author
☐ Authorized agent   X _ _ _ _ _ _ _ _ _ _ _ _ _ _ _ _ _ _

7 **OPTIONAL** **Name and Address of Person to Contact for Rights and Permissions:**

☐ Check here if same as #2 above.

Phone, fax, and email:

Phone (   )   Fax (   )
Email:

8 **Certificate will be mailed in window envelope to this address:**

Name ▼
Number/Street/Apt ▼
City/State/Zip ▼

Complete this space only if you currently hold a Deposit Account in the Copyright Office.

9 Deposit Account #_____
Name _____

DO NOT WRITE HERE   Page 1 of ____ pages

*17 U.S.C. §506(e): Any person who knowingly makes a false representation of a material fact in the application for copyright registration provided for by section 409, or in any written statement filed in connection with the application, shall be fined not more than $2,500.

Form PA-Short   Rev: 09/2008   Print: 09/2008 — 20,000   Printed on recycled paper

U.S. Government Printing Office: 2008-339-733/80,006

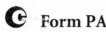

Form PA

Detach and read these instructions before completing this form.
Make sure all applicable spaces have been filled in before you return this form.

BASIC INFORMATION

When to Use This Form: Use Form PA for registration of published or unpublished works of the performing arts. This class includes works prepared for the purpose of being "performed" directly before an audience or indirectly "by means of any device or process." Works of the performing arts include: (1) musical works, including any accompanying words; (2) dramatic works, including any accompanying music; (3) pantomimes and choreographic works; and (4) motion pictures and other audiovisual works.

Deposit to Accompany Application: An application for copyright registration must be accompanied by a deposit consisting of copies or phonorecords representing the entire work for which registration is made. The following are the general deposit requirements as set forth in the statute:

Unpublished Work: Deposit one complete copy (or phonorecord).

Published Work: Deposit two complete copies (or one phonorecord) of the best edition.

Work First Published Outside the United States: Deposit one complete copy (or phonorecord) of the first foreign edition.

Contribution to a Collective Work: Deposit one complete copy (or phonorecord) of the best edition of the collective work.

Motion Pictures: Deposit *both* of the following: (1) a separate written description of the contents of the motion picture; and (2) for a published work, one complete copy of the best edition of the motion picture; or, for an unpublished work, one complete copy of the motion picture or identifying material. Identifying material may be either an audiorecording of the

entire soundtrack or one frame enlargement or similar visual print from each 10-minute segment.

The Copyright Notice: Before March 1, 1989, the use of copyright notice was mandatory on all published works, and any work first published before that date should have carried a notice. For works first published on and after March 1, 1989, use of the copyright notice is optional. For more information about copyright notice, see Circular 3, *Copyright Notice.*

For Further Information: To speak to a Copyright Office staff member, call (202) 707-3000. Recorded information is available 24 hours a day. Order forms and other publications from the Forms and Publications Hotline at (202) 707-9100. Access and download circulars, certain forms, and other information from the Copyright Office website at *www.copyright.gov.*

LINE-BY-LINE INSTRUCTIONS

Please type or print using black ink. The form is used to produce the certificate.

SPACE 1: Title

Title of This Work: Every work submitted for copyright registration must be given a title to identify that particular work. If the copies or phonorecords of the work bear a title (or an identifying phrase that could serve as a title), transcribe that wording *completely* and *exactly* on the application. Indexing of the registration and future identification of the work will depend on the information you give here. If the work you are registering is an entire "collective work" (such as a collection of plays or songs), give the overall title of the collection. If you are registering one or more individual contributions to a collective work, give the title of each contribution, followed by the title of the collection. For an unpublished collection, you may give the titles of the individual works after the collection title.

Previous or Alternative Titles: Complete this space if there are any additional titles for the work under which someone searching for the registration might be likely to look, or under which a document pertaining to the work might be recorded.

Nature of This Work: Briefly describe the general nature or character of the work being registered for copyright. Examples: "Music"; "Song Lyrics"; "Words and Music"; "Drama"; "Musical Play"; "Choreography"; "Pantomime"; "Motion Picture"; "Audiovisual Work."

SPACE 2: Author(s)

General Instructions: After reading these instructions, decide who are the "authors" of this work for copyright purposes. Then, unless the work is a "collective work," give the requested information about every "author" who contributed any appreciable amount of copyrightable matter to this version of the work. If you need further detail, request additional Continuation Sheets. In the case of a collective work such as a songbook or a collection of plays, give information about the author of the collective work as a whole.

Name of Author: The fullest form of the author's name should be given. Unless the work was "made for hire," the individual who actually created the work is its "author." In the case of a work made for hire, the statute provides that "the employer or other person for whom the work was prepared is considered the author."

What Is a "Work Made for Hire"? A "work made for hire" is defined as: (1) "a work prepared by an employee within the scope of his or her employment"; or (2) "a work specially ordered or commissioned for use as a contribution to a collective work, as a part of a motion picture or other audiovisual work, as a translation, as a supplementary work, as a compilation, as an instructional text, as a test, as answer material for a test, or as an atlas, if the parties expressly agree in a written instrument signed by them that the work shall be considered a work made for hire." If you have checked "Yes" to indicate that the work was "made for hire," you must give the full legal name of the employer (or other person for whom the work was prepared). You may also include the name of the employee along with the name of the employer (for example: "Elster Music Co., employer for hire of John Ferguson").

"Anonymous" or "Pseudonymous" Work: An author's contribution to a work is "anonymous" if that author is not identified on the copies or phonorecords of the work. An author's contribution to a work is "pseudonymous" if that author is identified on the copies or phonorecords under a fictitious name. If the work is "anonymous" you may: (1) leave the line blank; or (2) state "anonymous" on the line; or (3) reveal the author's identity. If the work is "pseudonymous" you may: (1) leave the line blank; or (2) give the pseudonym and identify it as such (example: "Huntley Haverstock, pseudonym"); or (3) reveal the author's name, making clear which is the real name and which is the pseudonym (for example: "Judith Barton, whose pseudonym is Madeline Elster"). However, the citizenship or domicile of the author *must* be given in all cases.

Dates of Birth and Death: If the author is dead, the statute requires that the year of death be included in the application unless the work is anonymous or pseudonymous. The author's birth date is optional, but is useful as a form of identification. Leave this space blank if the author's contribution was a "work made for hire."

Author's Nationality or Domicile: Give the country of which the author is a citizen, or the country in which the author is domiciled. Nationality or domicile *must* be given in all cases.

Nature of Authorship: Give a brief general statement of the nature of this particular author's contribution to the work. Examples: "Words"; "Coauthor of Music"; "Words and Music"; "Arrangement"; "Coauthor of Book and Lyrics"; "Dramatization"; "Screen Play"; "Compilation and English Translation"; "Editorial Revisions."

Understanding Copyright Law: A Beginner's Guide

SPACE 3: Creation and Publication

General Instructions: Do not confuse "creation" with "publication." Every application for copyright registration must state "the year in which creation of the work was completed." Give the date and nation of first publication only if the work has been published.

Creation: Under the statute, a work is "created" when it is fixed in a copy or phonorecord for the first time. Where a work has been prepared over a period of time, the part of the work existing in fixed form on a particular date constitutes the created work on that date. The date you give here should be the year in which the author completed the particular version for which registration is now being sought, even if other versions exist or if further changes or additions are planned.

Publication: The statute defines "publication" as "the distribution of copies or phonorecords of a work to the public by sale or other transfer of ownership, or by rental, lease, or lending"; a work is also "published" if there has been an "offering to distribute copies or phonorecords to a group of persons for purposes of further distribution, public performance, or public display." Give the full date (month, day, year) when, and the country where, publication first occurred. If first publication took place simultaneously in the United States and other countries, it is sufficient to state "U.S.A."

SPACE 4: Claimant(s)

Name(s) and Address(es) of Copyright Claimant(s): Give the name(s) and address(es) of the copyright claimant(s) in this work even if the claimant is the same as the author. Copyright in a work belongs initially to the author of the work (including, in the case of a work made for hire, the employer or other person for whom the work was prepared). The copyright claimant is either the author of the work or a person or organization to whom the copyright initially belonging to the author has been transferred.

Transfer: The statute provides that, if the copyright claimant is not the author, the application for registration must contain "a brief statement of how the claimant obtained ownership of the copyright." If any copyright claimant named in space 4 is not an author named in space 2, give a brief statement explaining how the claimant(s) obtained ownership of the copyright. Examples: "By written contract"; "Transfer of all rights by author"; "Assignment"; "By will." Do not attach transfer documents or other attachments or riders.

SPACE 5: Previous Registration

General Instructions: The questions in space 5 are intended to show whether an earlier registration has been made for this work and, if so, whether there is any basis for a new registration. As a general rule, only one basic copyright registration can be made for the same version of a particular work.

Same Version: If this version is substantially the same as the work covered by a previous registration, a second registration is not generally possible unless: (1) the work has been registered in unpublished form and a second registration is now being sought to cover this first published edition; or (2) someone other than the author is identified as copyright claimant in the earlier registration, and the author is now seeking registration in his or her own name. If either of these two exceptions applies, check the appropriate box and give the earlier registration number and date. Otherwise, do not submit Form PA; instead, write the Copyright Office.

for information about supplementary registration or recordation of transfers of copyright ownership.

Changed Version: If the work has been changed and you are now seeking registration to cover the additions or revisions, check the last box in space 5, give the earlier registration number and date, and complete both parts of space 6 in accordance with the instructions below.

Previous Registration Number and Date: If more than one previous registration has been made for the work, give the number and date of the latest registration.

SPACE 6: Derivative Work or Compilation

General Instructions: Complete space 6 if this work is a "changed version," "compilation," or "derivative work," and if it incorporates one or more earlier works that have already been published or registered for copyright or that have fallen into the public domain. A "compilation" is defined as "a work formed by the collection and assembling of preexisting materials or of data that are selected, coordinated, or arranged in such a way that the resulting work as a whole constitutes an original work of authorship." A "derivative work" is "a work based on one or more preexisting works." Examples of derivative works include musical arrangements, dramatizations, translations, abridgments, condensations, motion picture versions, or "any other form in which a work may be recast, transformed, or adapted." Derivative works also include works "consisting of editorial revisions, annotations, or other modifications" if these changes, as a whole, represent an original work of authorship.

Preexisting Material (space 6a): Complete this space and space 6b for derivative works. In this space identify the preexisting work that has been recast, transformed, or adapted. For example, the preexisting material might be: "French version of Hugo's 'Le Roi s'amuse.'" Do not complete this space for compilations.

Material Added to This Work (space 6b): Give a brief general statement of the additional new material covered by the copyright claim for which registration is sought. In the case of a derivative work, identify this new material. Examples: "Arrangement for piano and orchestra"; "Dramatization for television"; "New film version"; "Revisions throughout; Act III completely new." If the work is a compilation, give a brief general statement describing both the material that has been compiled and the compilation itself. Example: "Compilation of 19th Century Military Songs."

SPACE 7, 8, 9: Fee, Correspondence, Certification, Return Address

Deposit Account: If you maintain a Deposit Account in the Copyright Office, identify it in space 7a. Otherwise, leave the space blank and send the fee with your application and deposit.

Correspondence (space 7b): Give the name, address, area code, telephone number, fax number, and email address (if available) of the person to be consulted if correspondence about this application becomes necessary.

Certification (space 8): The application cannot be accepted unless it bears the date and the **handwritten signature** of the author or other copyright claimant, or of the owner of exclusive right(s), or of the duly authorized agent of the author, claimant, or owner of exclusive right(s).

Address for Return of Certificate (space 9): The address box must be completed legibly since the certificate will be returned in a window envelope.

MORE INFORMATION

How to Register a Recorded Work: If the musical or dramatic work that you are registering has been recorded (as a tape, disk, or cassette), you may choose either copyright application Form PA (Performing Arts) or Form SR (Sound Recordings), depending on the purpose of the registration.

Use Form PA to register the underlying musical composition or dramatic work. Form SR has been developed specifically to register a "sound recording" as defined by the Copyright Act — a work resulting from the "fixation of a series of sounds," separate and distinct from the underlying musical or dramatic work. Form SR should be used when the copyright claim is limited to the sound recording itself. (In one instance, Form SR may also be used to file for a copyright registration for both kinds of works — see (4) below.) Therefore:

(1) File Form PA if you are seeking to register the musical or dramatic work, not the "sound recording," even though what you deposit for copyright purposes may be in the form of a phonorecord.

(2) File Form PA if you are seeking to register the audio portion of an audiovisual work, such as a motion picture soundtrack; these are considered integral parts of the audiovisual work.

(3) File Form SR if you are seeking to register the "sound recording" itself, that is, the work that results from the fixation of a series of musical, spoken, or other sounds, but not the underlying musical or dramatic work.

(4) File Form SR if you are the copyright claimant for both the underlying musical or dramatic work and the sound recording, and you prefer to register both on the same form.

(5) File both forms PA and SR if the copyright claimant for the underlying work and sound recording differ, or you prefer to have separate registration for them.

"Copies" and "Phonorecords": To register for copyright, you are required to deposit "copies" or "phonorecords." These are defined as follows:

Musical compositions may be embodied (fixed) in "copies," objects from which a work can be read or visually perceived, directly or with the aid of a machine or device, such as manuscripts, books, sheet music, film, and videotape. They may also be fixed in "phonorecords," objects embodying fixations of sounds, such as tapes and phonograph disks, commonly known as phonograph records. For example, a song (the work to be registered) can be reproduced in sheet music ("copies") or phonograph records ("phonorecords"), or both.

Copyright Office fees are subject to change. For current fees, check the Copyright Office website at www.copyright.gov, write the Copyright Office, or call (202) 707-3000.

Privacy Act Notice: Sections 408-410 of title 17 of the *United States Code* authorize the Copyright Office to collect the personally identifying information requested on this form in order to process the application for copyright registration. By providing this information you are agreeing to routine uses of the information that include publication to give legal notice of your copyright claim as required by 17 U.S.C. § 705. It will appear in the Office's online catalog. If you do not provide the information requested, registration may be refused or delayed, and you may not be entitled to certain relief, remedies, and benefits under the copyright law.

Form PA
For a Work of Performing Arts
UNITED STATES COPYRIGHT OFFICE

REGISTRATION NUMBER

PA   PAU

EFFECTIVE DATE OF REGISTRATION

Month   Day   Year

DO NOT WRITE ABOVE THIS LINE. IF YOU NEED MORE SPACE, USE A SEPARATE CONTINUATION SHEET.

1

TITLE OF THIS WORK ▼

PREVIOUS OR ALTERNATIVE TITLES ▼

NATURE OF THIS WORK ▼ See instructions

2 a

NAME OF AUTHOR ▼

DATES OF BIRTH AND DEATH
Year Born ▼   Year Died ▼

Was this contribution to the work a "work made for hire"?
☐ Yes
☐ No

AUTHOR'S NATIONALITY OR DOMICILE
Name of Country
OR { Citizen of _____
Domiciled in _____

WAS THIS AUTHOR'S CONTRIBUTION TO THE WORK
Anonymous?   ☐ Yes ☐ No
Pseudonymous? ☐ Yes ☐ No
If the answer to either of these questions is "Yes," see detailed instructions.

NATURE OF AUTHORSHIP Briefly describe nature of material created by this author in which copyright is claimed. ▼

NOTE

Under the law, the "author" of a "work made for hire" is generally the employer, not the employee (see instructions). For any part of this work that was "made for hire" check "Yes" in the space provided, give the employer (or other person for whom the work was prepared) as "Author" of that part, and leave the space for dates of birth and death blank.

b

NAME OF AUTHOR ▼

DATES OF BIRTH AND DEATH
Year Born ▼   Year Died ▼

Was this contribution to the work a "work made for hire"?
☐ Yes
☐ No

AUTHOR'S NATIONALITY OR DOMICILE
Name of Country
OR { Citizen of _____
Domiciled in _____

WAS THIS AUTHOR'S CONTRIBUTION TO THE WORK
Anonymous?   ☐ Yes ☐ No
Pseudonymous? ☐ Yes ☐ No
If the answer to either of these questions is "Yes," see detailed instructions.

NATURE OF AUTHORSHIP Briefly describe nature of material created by this author in which copyright is claimed. ▼

c

NAME OF AUTHOR ▼

DATES OF BIRTH AND DEATH
Year Born ▼   Year Died ▼

Was this contribution to the work a "work made for hire"?
☐ Yes
☐ No

AUTHOR'S NATIONALITY OR DOMICILE
Name of Country
OR { Citizen of _____
Domiciled in _____

WAS THIS AUTHOR'S CONTRIBUTION TO THE WORK
Anonymous?   ☐ Yes ☐ No
Pseudonymous? ☐ Yes ☐ No
If the answer to either of these questions is "Yes," see detailed instructions.

NATURE OF AUTHORSHIP Briefly describe nature of material created by this author in which copyright is claimed. ▼

3 a

YEAR IN WHICH CREATION OF THIS WORK WAS COMPLETED This information must be given in all cases.
_____ Year

b DATE AND NATION OF FIRST PUBLICATION OF THIS PARTICULAR WORK
Complete this information ONLY if this work has been published.
Month _____ Day _____ Year _____
_____ Nation

4

See instructions before completing this space.

COPYRIGHT CLAIMANT(S) Name and address must be given even if the claimant is the same as the author given in space 2. ▼

APPLICATION RECEIVED

ONE DEPOSIT RECEIVED

TWO DEPOSITS RECEIVED

FUNDS RECEIVED

DO NOT WRITE HERE OFFICE USE ONLY

TRANSFER If the claimant(s) named here in space 4 is (are) different from the author(s) named in space 2, give a brief statement of how the claimant(s) obtained ownership of the copyright. ▼

MORE ON BACK ▶ • Complete all applicable spaces (numbers 5-9) on the reverse side of this page.
• See detailed instructions. • Sign the form at line 8.

DO NOT WRITE HERE

EXAMINED BY		FORM PA
CHECKED BY		
☐ CORRESPONDENCE Yes		FOR COPYRIGHT OFFICE USE ONLY

DO NOT WRITE ABOVE THIS LINE. IF YOU NEED MORE SPACE, USE A SEPARATE CONTINUATION SHEET.

5

PREVIOUS REGISTRATION Has registration for this work, or for an earlier version of this work, already been made in the Copyright Office?

☐ Yes ☐ No If your answer is "Yes," why is another registration being sought? (Check appropriate box.) ▼ If your answer is No, do not check box A, B, or C.

a. ☐ This is the first published edition of a work previously registered in unpublished form.

b. ☐ This is the first application submitted by this author as copyright claimant.

c. ☐ This is a changed version of the work, as shown by space 6 on this application.

If your answer is "Yes," give: **Previous Registration Number** ▼   **Year of Registration** ▼

6 a

DERIVATIVE WORK OR COMPILATION Complete both space 6a and 6b for a derivative work; complete only 6b for a compilation.

Preexisting Material Identify any preexisting work or works that this work is based on or incorporates. ▼

See instructions
before completing
this space.

6 b

Material Added to This Work Give a brief, general statement of the material that has been added to this work and in which copyright is claimed. ▼

7 a

DEPOSIT ACCOUNT If the registration fee is to be charged to a Deposit Account established in the Copyright Office, give name and number of Account.

Name ▼   **Account Number** ▼

7 b

CORRESPONDENCE Give name and address to which correspondence about this application should be sent. Name/Address/Apt/City/State/Zip▼

Area code and daytime telephone number   (   )   Fax number   (   )

Email

8

CERTIFICATION* I, the undersigned, hereby certify that I am the

Check only one ▶
☐ author
☐ other copyright claimant
☐ owner of exclusive right(s)
☐ authorized agent of _____
Name of author or other copyright claimant, or owner of exclusive right(s) ▲

of the work identified in this application and that the statements made by me in this application are correct to the best of my knowledge.

Typed or printed name and date ▼ If this application gives a date of publication in space 3, do not sign and submit it before that date.

_____ Date _____

Handwritten signature (X) ▼

X _____

9

Certificate will be mailed in window envelope to this address:	Name ▼
	Number/Street/Apt ▼
	City/State/Zip ▼

YOU MUST:
· Complete all necessary spaces
· Sign your application in space 8

**SEND ALL 3 ELEMENTS
IN THE SAME PACKAGE:**
1. Application form
2. Nonrefundable filing fee in check or money order payable to Register of Copyrights
3. Deposit material

MAIL TO:
Library of Congress
Copyright Office-PAD
101 Independence Avenue SE
Washington, DC 20559-6230

*17 USC §506(e): Any person who knowingly makes a false representation of a material fact in the application for copyright registration provided for by section 409, or in any written statement filed in connection with the application, shall be fined not more than $2,500.

U.S. Government Printing Office: 2008-XXX-XXX/XX.XXX

APPENDIX 12:
FORM SR FOR THE REGISTRATION OF
A SOUND RECORDING

 ## Form SR

Detach and read these instructions before completing this form.
Make sure all applicable spaces have been filled in before you return this form.

BASIC INFORMATION

When to Use This Form: Use Form SR for registration of published or unpublished sound recordings. It should be used when the copyright claim is limited to the sound recording itself, and it may also be used where the same copyright claimant is seeking simultaneous registration of the underlying musical, dramatic, or literary work embodied in the phonorecord.

With one exception, "sound recordings" are works that result from the fixation of a series of musical, spoken, or other sounds. The exception is for the audio portions of audiovisual works, such as a motion picture soundtrack or an audio cassette accompanying a filmstrip. These are considered a part of the audiovisual work as a whole.

Deposit to Accompany Application: An application for copyright registration must be accompanied by a deposit consisting of phonorecords representing the entire work for which registration is to be made.

Unpublished Work: Deposit one complete phonorecord.

Published Work: Deposit two complete phonorecords of the best edition, together with "any printed or other visually perceptible material" published with the phonorecords.

Work First Published Outside the United States: Deposit one complete phonorecord of the first foreign edition.

Contribution to a Collective Work: Deposit one complete phonorecord of the best edition of the collective work.

The Copyright Notice: Before March 1, 1989, the use of copyright notice was mandatory on all published works, and any work first published before that date should have carried a notice. For works first published on and after March 1, 1989, use of the copyright notice is optional. For more information about copyright notice, see Circular 3, *Copyright Notices.*

For Further Information: To speak to a Copyright Office staff member, call (202) 707-3000 (TTY: (202) 707-6737). Recorded information is available 24 hours a day. Order forms and other publications from Library of Congress, Copyright Office, 101 Independence Avenue SE, Washington, DC 20559-6000 or call the Forms and Publications Hotline at (202) 707-9100. Access and download circulars, forms, and other information from the Copyright Office website at *www.copyright.gov.*

FORM SR FOR THE REGISTRATION OF A SOUND RECORDING

Please type or print neatly using black ink. The form is used to produce the certificate.

SPACE 1: Title

Title of This Work: Every work submitted for copyright registration must be given a title to identify that particular work. If the phonorecords or any accompanying printed material bears a title (or an identifying phrase that could serve as a title), transcribe that wording completely and exactly on the application. Indexing of the registration and future identification of the work may depend on the information you give here.

Previous, Alternative, or Contents Titles: Complete this space if there are any previous or alternative titles for the work under which someone searching for the registration might be likely to look, or under which a document pertaining to the work might be recorded. You may also give the individual contents titles, if any, in this space or you may use a Continuation Sheet. Circle the term that describes the titles given.

SPACE 2: Author(s)

General Instructions: After reading these instructions, decide who are the "authors" of this work for copyright purposes. Then, unless the work is a "collective work," give the requested information about every "author" who contributed any appreciable amount of copyrightable matter to this version of the work. If you need further space, request additional Continuation Sheets. In the case of a collective work such as a collection of previously published or registered sound recordings, give information about the author of the collective work as a whole. If you are submitting this Form SR to cover the recorded musical, dramatic, or literary work as well as the sound recording itself, it is important for space 2 to include full information about the various authors of all of the material covered by the copyright claim, making clear the nature of each author's contribution.

Name of Author: The fullest form of the author's name should be given. Unless the work was "made for hire," the individual who actually created the work is its "author." In the case of a work made for hire, the statute provides that "the employer or other person for whom the work was prepared is considered the author."

What Is a "Work Made for Hire"? A "work made for hire" is defined as: (1) "a work prepared by an employee within the scope of his or her employment"; or (2) "a work specially ordered or commissioned for use as a contribution to a collective

work, as a part of a motion picture or other audiovisual work, as a translation, as a supplementary work, as a compilation, as an instructional text, as a test, as answer material for a test, or as an atlas, if the parties expressly agree in a written instrument signed by them that the work shall be considered a work made for hire." If you have checked "Yes" to indicate that the work was "made for hire," you must give the full legal name of the employer (or other person for whom the work was prepared). You may also include the name of the employee along with the name of the employer (for example: "Elster Record Co., employer for hire of John Ferguson").

"Anonymous" or "Pseudonymous" Work: An author's contribution to a work is "anonymous" if that author is not identified on the copies or phonorecords of the work. An author's contribution to a work is "pseudonymous" if that author is identified on the copies or phonorecords under a fictitious name. If the work is "anonymous" you may: (1) leave the line blank; or (2) state "anonymous" on the line; or (3) reveal the author's identity. If the work is "pseudonymous" you may: (1) leave the line blank; or (2) give the pseudonym and identify it as such (for example: "Huntley Haverstock, pseudonym"); or (3) reveal the author's name, making clear which is the real name and which is the pseudonym (for example: "Judith Barton, whose pseudonym is Madeline Elster"). However, the citizenship or domicile of the author *must* be given in all cases.

Dates of Birth and Death: If the author is dead, the statute requires that the year of death be included in the application unless the work is anonymous or pseudonymous. The author's birth date is optional, but is useful as a form of identification. Leave this space blank if the author's contribution was a "work made for hire."

Author's Nationality or Domicile: Give the country in which the author is a citizen, or the country in which the author is domiciled. Nationality or domicile *must* be given in all cases.

Nature of Authorship: Sound recording authorship is the performance, sound production, or both, that is fixed in the recording deposited for registration. Describe this authorship in space 2 as "sound recording." If the claim also covers the underlying work(s), include the appropriate authorship terms for each author, for example, "words," "music," "arrangement of music," or "text."

Generally, for the claim to cover both the sound recording and the underlying work(s), every author should have contributed to both the sound recording *and* the underlying work(s). If the claim includes artwork or photographs, include the appropriate term in the statement of authorship.

SPACE 3: Creation and Publication

General Instructions: Do not confuse "creation" with "publication." Every application for copyright registration must state "the year in which creation of the work was completed." Give the date and nation of first publication only if the work has been published.

Creation: Under the statute, a work is "created" when it is fixed in a copy or phonorecord for the first time. Where a work has been prepared over a period of time, the part of the work existing in fixed form on a particular date constitutes the created work on that date. The date you give here should be the year in which the author completed the particular version for which registration is now being sought, even if other versions exist or if further changes or additions are planned.

Publication: The statute defines "publication" as "the distribution of copies or phonorecords of a work to the public by sale or other transfer of ownership, or by rental, lease, or lending"; a work is also "published" if there has been an "offering to distribute copies or phonorecords to a group of persons for purposes of further distribution, public performance, or public display." Give the full date (month, date, year) when, and the country where, publication first occurred. If first publication took place simultaneously in the United States and other countries, it is sufficient to state "U.S.A."

SPACE 4: Claimant(s)

Name(s) and Address(es) of Copyright Claimant(s): Give the name(s) and address(es) of the copyright claimant(s) in the work even if the claimant is the same as the author. Copyright in a work belongs initially to the author of the work (including, in the case of a work made for hire, the employer or other person for whom the work was prepared). The copyright claimant is either the author of the work or a person or organization to whom the copyright initially belonging to the author has been transferred.

Transfer: The statute provides that, if the copyright claimant is not the author, the application for registration must contain "a brief statement of how the claimant obtained ownership of the copyright." If any copyright claimant named in space 4a is not an author named in space 2, give a brief statement explaining how the claimant(s) obtained ownership of the copyright. Examples: "By written contract"; "Transfer of all rights by author"; "Assignment"; "By will." Do not attach transfer documents or other attachments or riders.

SPACE 5: Previous Registration

General Instructions: The questions in space 5 are intended to show whether an earlier registration has been made for this work and, if so, whether there is any basis for a new registration. As a rule, only one basic copyright registration can be made for the same version of a particular work.

Same Version: If this version is substantially the same as the work covered by a previous registration, a second registration is not generally possible unless: (1) the work has been registered in unpublished form and a second registration is now being sought to cover this first published edition; or (2) someone other than the author is identified as copyright claimant in the earlier registration and the author is now seeking registration in his or her own name. If either of these two exceptions applies, check the appropriate box and give the earlier registration number and date. Otherwise, do not submit Form SR. Instead, write the Copyright Office for information about supplementary registration or recordation of transfers of copyright ownership.

Changed Version: If the work has been changed and you are now seeking registration to cover the additions or revisions, check the last box in space 5, give the earlier registration number and date, and complete both parts of space 6 in accordance with the instructions below.

Previous Registration Number and Date: If more than one previous registration has been made for the work, give the number and date of the latest registration.

SPACE 6: Derivative Work or Compilation

General Instructions: Complete space 6 if this work is a "changed version," "compilation," or "derivative work," and if it incorporates one or more earlier works that have already been published or registered for copyright, or that have fallen into the public domain, or sound recordings that were fixed before February 15, 1972. A "compilation" is defined as "a work formed by the collection and assembling of preexisting materials or of data that are selected, coordinated, or arranged in such a way that the resulting work as a whole constitutes an original work of authorship." A "derivative work" is "a work based on one or more preexisting works." Examples of derivative works include recordings reissued with substantial editorial revisions or abridgments of the recorded sounds, and recordings republished with new recorded material, or "any other form in which a work may be recast, transformed, or adapted." Derivative works also include works "consisting of editorial revisions, annotations, or other modifications" if these changes, as a whole, represent an original work of authorship.

Preexisting Material (space 6a): Complete this space *and* space 6b for derivative works. In this space identify the preexisting work that has been recast, transformed, or adapted. The preexisting work may be material that has been previously published, previously registered, or that is in the public domain. For example, the preexisting material might be: "1970 recording by Sperryville Symphony of Bach Double Concerto."

Material Added to This Work (space 6b): Give a brief, general statement of the additional new material covered by the copyright claim for which registration is sought. In the case of a derivative work, identify this new material. Examples: "Recorded performances on bands 1 and 3"; "Remixed sounds from original multitrack sound sources"; "New words, arrangement, and additional sounds." If the work is a compilation, give a brief, general statement describing both the material that has been compiled *and* the compilation itself. Example: "Compilation of 1938 Recordings by various swing bands."

SPACE 7, 8, 9: Fee, Correspondence, Certification, Return Address

Deposit Account: If you maintain a Deposit Account in the Copyright Office, identify it in space 7a. Otherwise, leave the space blank and send the filing fee with your application and deposit. (See space 8 on form.) (**Note:** Copyright Office fees are subject to change. For current fees, check the Copyright Office website at *www.copyright.gov*, write the Copyright Office, or call (202) 707-3000.)

Correspondence (space 7b): Give the name, address, area code, telephone number, fax number, and email address (if available) of the person to be consulted if correspondence about this application becomes necessary.

Certification (space 8): This application cannot be accepted unless it bears the date and the *handwritten signature* of the author or other copyright claimant, or of the owner of exclusive right(s), or of the duly authorized agent of the author, claimant, or owner of exclusive right(s).

Address for Return of Certificate (space 9): The address box must be completed legibly since the certificate will be returned in a window envelope.

MORE INFORMATION

"Works": "Works" are the basic subject matter of copyright; they are what authors create and copyright protects. The statute draws a sharp distinction between the "work" and "any material object in which the work is embodied."

"Copies" and "Phonorecords": These are the two types of material objects in which "works" are embodied. In general, "copies" are objects from which a work can be read or visually perceived, directly or with the aid of a machine or device, such as manuscripts, books, sheet music, film, and videotape. "Phonorecords" are objects embodying fixations of sounds, such as audio tapes and phonograph disks ("phonorecords"). For example, a song (the "work") can be reproduced in sheet music ("copies") or phonograph disks ("phonorecords"), or both.

"Sound Recordings": These are "works," not "copies" or "phonorecords." "Sound recordings" are "works that result from the fixation of a series of musical, spoken, or other sounds, but not including the sounds accompanying a motion picture or other audiovisual work." Example: When a record company issues a new release, the release will typically involve two distinct "works": the "musical work" that has been recorded, and the "sound recording" as a separate work in itself. The material objects that the record company sends out are "phonorecords": physical reproductions of both the "musical work" and the "sound recording."

Should You File More Than One Application? If your work consists of a recorded musical, dramatic, or literary work and if both that "work" and the sound recording as a separate "work" are eligible for registration, the application form you should file depends on the following:

File Only Form SR if: The copyright claimant is the same for both the musical, dramatic, or literary work and for the sound recording, and you are seeking a single registration to cover both of these "works."

File Only Form PA (or Form TX) if: You are seeking to register only the musical, dramatic, or literary work, not the sound recording. Form PA is appropriate for works of the performing arts; Form TX is for nondramatic literary works.

Separate Applications Should Be Filed on Form PA (or Form TX) and on Form SR if: (1) The copyright claimant for the musical, dramatic, or literary work is different from the copyright claimant for the sound recording; or (2) You prefer to have separate registrations for the musical, dramatic, or literary work and for the sound recording.

Understanding Copyright Law: A Beginner's Guide   **145**

FORM SR FOR THE REGISTRATION OF A SOUND RECORDING

Copyright Office fees are subject to change.
For current fees, check the Copyright Office
website at www.copyright.gov, write the Copyright Office, or call (202) 707-3000.

Form SR
For a Sound Recording
UNITED STATES COPYRIGHT OFFICE

REGISTRATION NUMBER

SR   SRU

EFFECTIVE DATE OF REGISTRATION

Month   Day   Year

DO NOT WRITE ABOVE THIS LINE. IF YOU NEED MORE SPACE, USE A SEPARATE CONTINUATION SHEET.

1

TITLE OF THIS WORK ▼

PREVIOUS, ALTERNATIVE, OR CONTENTS TITLES (CIRCLE ONE) ▼

2 a

NAME OF AUTHOR ▼

DATES OF BIRTH AND DEATH
Year Born ▼   Year Died ▼

Was this contribution to the work a "work made for hire"?
☐ Yes
☐ No

AUTHOR'S NATIONALITY OR DOMICILE
Name of Country
OR { Citizen of ▶_____
Domiciled in ▶_____

WAS THIS AUTHOR'S CONTRIBUTION TO THE WORK
Anonymous?   ☐ Yes ☐ No
Pseudonymous?   ☐ Yes ☐ No

If the answer to either of these questions is "Yes," see detailed instructions.

NATURE OF AUTHORSHIP   Briefly describe nature of material created by this author in which copyright is claimed. ▼

NOTE

Under the law, the "author" of a "work made for hire" is generally the employer, not the employee (see instructions). For any part of this work that was "made for hire," check "Yes" in the space provided, give the employer (or other person for whom the work was prepared) as "Author" of that part, and leave the space for dates of birth and death blank.

b

NAME OF AUTHOR ▼

DATES OF BIRTH AND DEATH
Year Born ▼   Year Died ▼

Was this contribution to the work a "work made for hire"?
☐ Yes
☐ No

AUTHOR'S NATIONALITY OR DOMICILE
Name of Country
OR { Citizen of ▶_____
Domiciled in ▶_____

WAS THIS AUTHOR'S CONTRIBUTION TO THE WORK
Anonymous?   ☐ Yes ☐ No
Pseudonymous?   ☐ Yes ☐ No

If the answer to either of these questions is "Yes," see detailed instructions.

NATURE OF AUTHORSHIP   Briefly describe nature of material created by this author in which copyright is claimed. ▼

c

NAME OF AUTHOR ▼

DATES OF BIRTH AND DEATH
Year Born ▼   Year Died ▼

Was this contribution to the work a "work made for hire"?
☐ Yes
☐ No

AUTHOR'S NATIONALITY OR DOMICILE
Name of Country
OR { Citizen of ▶_____
Domiciled in ▶_____

WAS THIS AUTHOR'S CONTRIBUTION TO THE WORK
Anonymous?   ☐ Yes ☐ No
Pseudonymous?   ☐ Yes ☐ No

If the answer to either of these questions is "Yes," see detailed instructions.

NATURE OF AUTHORSHIP   Briefly describe nature of material created by this author in which copyright is claimed. ▼

3 a

YEAR IN WHICH CREATION OF THIS WORK WAS COMPLETED

This information must be given
_____ Year in all cases.

b Complete this information ONLY if this work has been published.

DATE AND NATION OF FIRST PUBLICATION OF THIS PARTICULAR WORK
Month ▶_____ Day ▶_____ Year ▶_____ ◀ Nation

4 a

COPYRIGHT CLAIMANT(S) Name and address must be given even if the claimant is the same as the author given in space 2. ▼

See instructions before completing this space.

b TRANSFER If the claimant(s) named here in space 4 is (are) different from the author(s) named in space 2, give a brief statement of how the claimant(s) obtained ownership of the copyright. ▼

APPLICATION RECEIVED

ONE DEPOSIT RECEIVED

TWO DEPOSITS RECEIVED

FUNDS RECEIVED

DO NOT WRITE HERE OFFICE USE ONLY

MORE ON BACK ▶
• Complete all applicable spaces (numbers 5-9) on the reverse side of this page.
• See detailed instructions.
• Sign the form at line 8.

DO NOT WRITE HERE
Page 1 of _____ pages

EXAMINED BY	FORM SR
CHECKED BY	
CORRESPONDENCE ☐ Yes	FOR COPYRIGHT OFFICE USE ONLY

DO NOT WRITE ABOVE THIS LINE. IF YOU NEED MORE SPACE, USE A SEPARATE CONTINUATION SHEET.

PREVIOUS REGISTRATION Has registration for this work, or for an earlier version of this work, already been made in the Copyright Office?
☐ Yes ☐ No If your answer is "Yes," why is another registration being sought? (Check appropriate box) ▼
a. ☐ This work was previously registered in unpublished form and now has been published for the first time.
b. ☐ This is the first application submitted by this author as copyright claimant.
c. ☐ This is a changed version of the work, as shown by space 6 on this application.
If your answer is "Yes," give: **Previous Registration Number** ▼   **Year of Registration** ▼

5

DERIVATIVE WORK OR COMPILATION
Preexisting Material Identify any preexisting work or works that this work is based on or incorporates. ▼

a

6

See instructions before completing this space.

Material Added to This Work Give a brief, general statement of the material that has been added to this work and in which copyright is claimed. ▼

b

DEPOSIT ACCOUNT If the registration fee is to be charged to a deposit account established in the Copyright Office, give name and number of Account.
Name ▼   Account Number ▼

a

7

CORRESPONDENCE Give name and address to which correspondence about this application should be sent. Name / Address / Apt / City / State / Zip ▼

b

Area code and daytime telephone number   Fax number
Email

CERTIFICATION* I, the undersigned, hereby certify that I am the
Check only one ▼
☐ author
☐ other copyright claimant
☐ owner of exclusive right(s)
☐ authorized agent of _____
                    Name of author or other copyright claimant, or owner of exclusive right(s) ▲

8

of the work identified in this application and that the statements made by me in this application are correct to the best of my knowledge.

Typed or printed name and date ▼ If this application gives a date of publication in space 3, do not sign and submit it before that date.

_____ Date _____

Handwritten signature ▼
_____

Certificate will be mailed in window envelope to this address	Name ▼	**YOU MUST:** • Complete all necessary spaces • Sign your application in space 8
	Number/Street/Apt ▼	**SEND ALL 3 ELEMENTS IN THE SAME PACKAGE:** 1. Application form 2. Nonrefundable filing fee in check or money order payable to Register of Copyrights 3. Deposit material
	City/State/Zip ▼	**MAIL TO:** Library of Congress Copyright Office 101 Independence Avenue SE Washington, DC 20559-6000

9

*17 USC §506(e): Any person who knowingly makes a false representation of a material fact in the application for copyright registration provided for by section 409, or in any written statement filed in connection with the application, shall be fined not more than $2,500.

Form SR-Full Rev: 11/2006 Print: 11/2006—60,000 Printed on recycled paper   U.S. Government Printing Office: 2007-330-945/80,138

APPENDIX 13:
CONTINUATION SHEET FOR
APPLICATION FORMS

Continuation Sheet
for Application Forms

Form ____ /CON
UNITED STATES COPYRIGHT OFFICE

REGISTRATION NUMBER

- This Continuation Sheet is used in conjunction with Forms CA, PA, SE, SR, TX, and VA only. Indicate which basic form you are continuing in the space in the upper right-hand corner.
- Try to fit the information called for into the spaces provided on the basic form.
- If you do not have enough space on the basic form, use this Continuation Sheet, and submit it with the basic form.
- If you submit this Continuation Sheet, clip (do not tape or staple) it to the basic form and fold the two together before submitting them.
- Space A of this sheet is intended to identify the basic application.
  Space B is a continuation of space 2 on the basic application.
  Space B is not applicable to Short Forms.
  Space C (on the reverse side of this sheet) is for the continuation of Spaces 1, 4, or 6 on the basic application or for the continuation of Space 1 on any of the three Short Forms PA, TX, or VA.

Privacy Act Notice: Sections 408–410 of title 17 of the *United States Code* authorize the Copyright Office to collect the personally identifying information requested on this form in order to process the application for copyright registration. By providing this information you are agreeing to routine uses of the information that include publication to give legal notice of your copyright claim as required by 17 U.S.C. § 705. It will appear in the Office's online catalog. If you do not provide the information requested, registration may be refused or delayed, and you may not be entitled to certain relief, remedies, and benefits under the copyright law.

| PA | PAU | SE | SEG | SEU | SR | SRU | TX | TXU | VA | VAU |

EFFECTIVE DATE OF REGISTRATION

_____
(Month)   (Day)   (Year)

CONTINUATION SHEET RECEIVED

Page _____ of _____ pages

DO NOT WRITE ABOVE THIS LINE. FOR COPYRIGHT OFFICE USE ONLY

A

Identification
of
Application

IDENTIFICATION OF CONTINUATION SHEET: This sheet is a continuation of the application for copyright registration on the basic form submitted for the following work:

- TITLE: Give the title as given under the heading "Title of this Work" in space 1 of the basic form.

. . . .

- NAME(S) AND ADDRESS(ES) OF COPYRIGHT CLAIMANT(S) : Give the name and address of at least one copyright claimant as given in space 4 of the basic form or space 2 of any of the Short Forms PA, TX, or VA.

B

Continuation
of Space 2

d

NAME OF AUTHOR ▼

DATES OF BIRTH AND DEATH
Year Born▼   Year Died▼

Was this contribution to the work a "work made for hire"?
☐ Yes
☐ No

AUTHOR'S NATIONALITY OR DOMICILE
Name of Country
OR { Citizen of ▶ _____
Domiciled in ▶ _____

WAS THIS AUTHOR'S CONTRIBUTION TO THE WORK
Anonymous?   ☐ Yes ☐ No
Pseudonymous? ☐ Yes ☐ No

If the answer to either of these questions is "Yes," see detailed instructions.

NATURE OF AUTHORSHIP Briefly describe nature of the material created by the author in which copyright is claimed. ▼

NAME OF AUTHOR ▼

DATES OF BIRTH AND DEATH
Year Born ▼   Year Died ▼

---

e

Was this contribution to the work a "work made for hire"?	AUTHOR'S NATIONALITY OR DOMICILE Name of Country	WAS THIS AUTHOR'S CONTRIBUTION TO THE WORK	
☐ Yes	OR ⎰ Citizen of ▶ _____	Anonymous? ☐ Yes ☐ No	If the answer to either of these questions is
☐ No	⎱ Domiciled in ▶ _____	Pseudonymous? ☐ Yes ☐ No	"Yes," see detailed instructions.

NATURE OF AUTHORSHIP Briefly describe nature of the material created by the author in which copyright is claimed. ▼

NAME OF AUTHOR ▼	DATES OF BIRTH AND DEATH
	Year Born ▼ Year Died ▼

f

Was this contribution to the work a "work made for hire"?	AUTHOR'S NATIONALITY OR DOMICILE Name of Country	WAS THIS AUTHOR'S CONTRIBUTION TO THE WORK	
☐ Yes	OR ⎰ Citizen of ▶ _____	Anonymous? ☐ Yes ☐ No	If the answer to either of these questions is
☐ No	⎱ Domiciled in ▶ _____	Pseudonymous? ☐ Yes ☐ No	"Yes," see detailed instructions.

NATURE OF AUTHORSHIP Briefly describe nature of the material created by the author in which copyright is claimed. ▼

Use the reverse side of this sheet if you need more space for continuation of spaces 1, 4, or 6 of the basic form or for the continuation of Space 1 on any of the Short Forms PA, TX, or VA.

CONTINUATION OF (Check which):　　❏ Space 1　　❏ Space 4　　❏ Space 6

C

**Continuation
of other
Spaces**

**Certificate
will be
mailed in
window
envelope
to this
address:**

Name ▼

Number/Street/Apt ▼

City/State/Zip ▼

YOU MUST:
• Complete all necessary spaces
• Sign your application

**SEND ALL 3 ELEMENTS
IN THE SAME PACKAGE:**
1. Application form
2. Nonrefundable fee in check or
   money order payable to Register
   of Copyrights
3. Deposit Material

MAIL TO:
Library of Congress, Copyright Office
101 Independence Avenue SE
Washington, DC 20559-6000

D

Form CON　Rev: 02/2008　Print: 09/2008 — 20,000　Printed on recycled paper

U.S. Government Printing Office: 2008-339-733/80.005

APPENDIX 14:
FORM CO

UNITED STATES COPYRIGHT OFFICE

Form CO · Instructions

Use this form to register a

- *Literary work*
- *Visual arts work*
- *Performing arts work*
- *Motion picture or other audiovisual work*
- *Sound recording*
- *Single serial issue*

Before you register your work

Review the appropriate circulars on the Copyright Office website, www.copyright. gov, for detailed information about how to register particular types of works and the requirements for what copy or copies of your work to send. Also, consider using the electronic Copyright Office (eCO) for faster service and a lower filing fee.

What may be included

The following may be included in one registration on Form CO:

- *Unpublished works: works by the same author(s) and owned by the same copyright claimant(s), organized in a collection under a collection title.*

- *Published works: works published in a single unit of publication and owned by the same copyright claimant.*

What to send

1 Completed and signed application

2 $45 filing fee payable to *Register of Copyrights*

3 Deposit—the required copy or copies of your work

- *Unpublished works:* one complete copy.

- *Published works:* generally, two complete copies of the "best edition." There are exceptions for certain types of works. See Circular 1, *Copyright Basics,* for details.

To avoid damage to your deposit from Library security measures, please package the following items in boxes rather than envelopes for mailing to the Copyright Office:
· electronic media such as audiocassettes, videocassettes, CDs, and DVDs
· microform
· photographs
· slick advertisements, color photocopies, and other print items that are rubber- and vegetable-based
Also please note that CDs packaged in standard full-sized jewel boxes are more likely to survive the mail irradiation process than those packaged in slim-line cases.

Send all three elements in the same envelope or package to:

Library of Congress
Copyright Office
101 Independence Avenue, SE
Washington, DC 20559-****

Use the appropriate four-digit zip code extension to expedite the processing of your claim. In place of ****, use the following:

Literary work: -6222
Visual arts work: -6211
Performing arts work: -6233
Motion picture/AV work: -6238
Sound recording: -6237
Serial issue: -6226

How to use this 2D barcode form

- Complete this form online and then print it out. Do not attempt to print out a blank form. (Form CO is available only online.)

- Print out a second copy for your records. Do not save the form online.

- *Never alter the form by hand after you print it out.* The information you enter is stored in the barcodes on the form.

- If you want to make more than one registration with similar information, keep the form open after you print it; then make the necessary changes and print that version. Repeat as needed. Once you close the form, all the information entered will be lost.

- Both single- and double-sided printing is acceptable.

- *Important printer information:* To achieve best results, use a laser printer. Inkjet printer copies require enlarging if you use the shrink-to-fit-page option. Dot-matrix printer copies are not acceptable.

FORM CO

Line-by-line Instructions   * Indicates required fields.   ** Indicates required alternate fields (one of two required).

Section 1 - Work Being Registered

1A* *Type of work being registered* · Check the appropriate box. If your work contains more than one type of authorship, choose the type for the predominant authorship in the work.

1B* *Title of work* · Give only one title in this space. To enter an additional title(s), such as titles of individual works in an unpublished collection or works owned by the same claimant in a single unit of publication, click the "additional title" button. Repeat as needed, up to a maximum of 50 titles. (For a registration with more than 50 titles, file electronically or request the appropriate paper application with continuation sheets by mail. See also 1D and 1I below. Give the complete title exactly as it appears on the copy. If there is no title on the copy, give an identifying phrase to serve as the title or state "untitled." Use standard title capitalization without quotation marks; for example, The Old Man and the Sea.

1C *Serial issue* · For serials only, give the required information. **NOTE:** For copyright registration purposes, a serial is a work issued or intended to be issued in successive parts bearing numerical or chronological designations and intended to be continued indefinitely. The classification "serial" includes periodicals, newspapers, magazines, bulletins, newsletters, annuals, journals, proceedings of societies, and other similar works. Enter the ISSN (International Standard Serial Number) without dashes. The Copyright Office does not assign these numbers. For information on obtaining an ISSN, go to *www.loc.gov/issn/*.

1D *Previous or alternative title* · If the work is known by another title, give that title here.

1E* *Year of completion* · Give the year in which creation of *the work you are submitting* was completed. Do not give a year for earlier or later versions. If the work has been published, the year of completion cannot be later than the year of first publication.

1F–1H *Date of publication* · Give the complete date, in mm/dd/yyyy format, on which the work was first published. Do not give a date that is in the future. **NOTE:** Leave this line blank if the work is unpublished. "Publication" is the distribution of copies or phonorecords of a work to the public by sale or other transfer of ownership or by rental, lease, or lending. The offering to distribute copies or phonorecords to a group of persons for purposes of further distribution, public performance, or public display constitutes publication. A public performance or display of a work does not of itself constitute publication. 17 U.S.C. § 101.

1G *ISBN* · Give the International Standard Book Number (ISBN), if one has been assigned to this work, without dashes. The Copyright Office does not assign these numbers. For information on obtaining an ISBN, contact R.R. Bowker at *www.bowker.com*.

1H *Nation of publication* · Give the nation where the work was first published. Check "United States" in any of the following circumstances: (1) if the work was first published in the United States; (2) if the work was published simultaneously in the United States and another country; or (3) if the work was first published

in another country that is not a "treaty party," and published in the United States within 30 days of first publication. A treaty party is a country other than the United States that is a party to an international copyright agreement. Almost all countries of the world are currently treaty parties. See Circular 38a, *International Copyright Relations of the United States*, for more information. **NOTE:** Leave this line blank if the work is unpublished.

1I *Published as a contribution in a larger work entitled* · If this work has been published as part of a larger work, enter the title of that larger work in this space. Examples of a work published as part of a larger work include a song on a CD, an article in a magazine, and a poem in an anthology. If the larger work includes a volume, number, and/or issue date, add that information on the lines provided.

Section 2 - Author Information

2A** *Personal name* · Complete line 2A *or* line 2B but not both. The individual who actually created the work is the author except in the case of a "work made for hire," as explained below at 2G. Complete line 2A if the author is an individual. Give the fullest form of the name and skip line 2B.

2B** *Organization name* · Complete line 2A *or* line 2B but not both. Complete line 2B only if the work is made for hire and a corporation or organization is the author. "Work made for hire" is explained below at 2G. Give the fullest form of the corporate or organizational name.

2C *Doing business as* · You may give the name under which an author does business (doing business as; trading as; sole owner of; also known as).

2D *Year of birth* · Give the year the author was born. The year of birth is optional but is very useful as a form of author identification. Many authors have the same name. **NOTE:** If the year of birth is provided, it will be made part of the online public records produced by the Copyright Office and accessible on the Internet. This information cannot be removed later from those public records.

2E *Year of death* · This information is required if the author is deceased.

2F *Citizenship/domicile* · Check to indicate U.S. citizenship. If the author is a citizen of another country, enter the name of this nation. Alternatively, identify the nation where the author is domiciled (resides permanently).

2G *Author's contribution is* · If this line is applicable, check only one box.

• *Made for hire* · Check this box only if the work was made for hire. This means that:

   1 the work, or an author's contribution to the work, is prepared by an employee as a regular part of his or her employment, or

Understanding Copyright Law: A Beginner's Guide

2 a work is specially ordered or commissioned in certain instances: for use as a contribution to a collective work, as a part of a motion picture or other audiovisual work, as a translation, as a supplementary work, as a compilation, as an instructional text, as a test, as answer material for a test, or as an atlas, providing the parties agree in writing that the contribution shall be considered a work made for hire. **NOTE:** In this case, name the employer as the author in line 2A or 2B. The employee should not be given. See Circular 9, *Works Made for Hire Under the 1976 Copyright Act*, for more information.

• *Anonymous* · Check this box if no natural person is named as author on copies of the work and the work is not made for hire. In this case, at line 2A, you should either (1) give the author's legal name or (2) state "anonymous" in the "first name" field. Do not leave line 2A blank. If the name is given in line 2A, it will be made part of the online public records produced by the Copyright Office and accessible on the Internet. This information cannot be removed later from those public records.

• *Pseudonymous* · Check this box if the author is identified on copies of the work only under a fictitious name and the work is not made for hire. In this case, check the box and give the pseudonym on the associated line. At line 2A, you should either (1) give the author's legal name or (2) state "anonymous" in the "first name" field. Do not leave line 2A blank. If the name is given in line 2A, it will be made part of the online public records produced by the Copyright Office and accessible on the Internet. This information cannot be removed later from those public records.

2H✱ *This author created* · Check the appropriate box(es) that describe this author's contribution to this work. Give a brief statement on the line after "other" only if it is necessary to give a more specific description of the authorship or if none of the check boxes applies. Examples of other authorship statements are choreography, musical arrangement, translation, dramatization, or fictionalization. **NOTE:** Do not give any of the following terms: idea, process, procedure, system, method of operation, concept, principle, discovery, title, or name. These terms refer to elements not subject to copyright. For information on compilations, see the instructions for line 4C.

For a single serial issue, the preferred description of the authorship is typically "collective work." Give this statement at the "other" line. This indicates that the claim is in the collective work as a whole and may include text, editing, compilation, and contribution(s) in which copyright has been transferred to the claimant.

For sound recordings and musical works: Sound recordings and musical works are separate works. To register a claim in both, the copyright claimant(s)/owner(s) must be the same. This requirement generally means the author(s) must be the same. The author of a sound recording is the performer or producer, and the authorship is "sound recording/performance." The author of a musical work—a song, for example—is the composer or song writer and the authorship is "music" or "music and lyrics." See Circular 56A, *Copyright Registration of Musical Compositions and Sound Recordings*, for more information.

Additional authors · To add another author, click the "additional author" button. Repeat as needed.

Section 3 - Copyright Claimant Information

3A✱✱ *Personal name* · Complete line 3A or line 3B but not both. Complete line 3A if the claimant is an individual. The copyright claimant (owner) is either the author of the work or the person or organization to whom the copyright has been transferred by an author or other authorized copyright owner. Give the fullest form of the name and skip line 3B.

3B✱✱ *Organization name* · Complete line 3A or line 3B but not both. Complete line 3B if the claimant is a corporation or organization. The copyright claimant (owner) is either the author of the work or the person or organization to whom the copyright has been transferred by an author or other authorized copyright owner. Give the fullest form of the corporate or organizational name.

3C *Doing business as* · You may give the name under which a claimant does business (doing business as; trading as; sole owner of; also known as).

3C *Address, email, and phone* · Give this information in the lines provided. **NOTE:** The claimant postal address will be made part of the online public records produced by the Copyright Office and accessible on the Internet. This information cannot be removed later from those public records. The email address and phone number will not appear in the public record unless also included in section 5, Rights and Permissions Contact. Be sure to review section 5 accordingly.

3E *Copyright ownership acquired by* · If the claimant is the author of the work, skip this line. Transfer information is required if this claimant is not an author but has obtained ownership of the copyright from the author or another owner. In this case, check the appropriate box to indicate how ownership was acquired. **NOTE:** "Written agreement" includes a transfer by assignment or by contract. "Will or inheritance" applies only if the person from whom copyright was transferred is deceased. If necessary, check "other" and give a brief statement indicating how copyright was transferred.

Additional claimants · To add another claimant, click the "additional claimant" button. Repeat as needed.

Section 4 - Limitation of Copyright Claim

NOTE: Skip this section unless this work contains or is based on previously registered or previously published material, material in the public domain, or material not owned by this claimant. The purpose of section 4 is to exclude such material from the claim and identify the new material upon which the present claim is based.

4A *Material excluded from this claim* · Check the appropriate box or boxes to exclude any previously registered or previously published material, material in the public domain, or material not owned by this claimant. "Text" may include fiction or nonfiction text, computer program code, lyrics, poetry, or scripts. "Artwork" may include two- or three-dimensional artwork, technical drawings, or photographs. "Audiovisual work" may include video clips, motion picture footage, or a series of images on a CD-ROM. (See the shaded box at the bottom of page 4 for specific examples.) Give a brief statement on the line after "other" only if it is necessary to give a more specific description of the material excluded from this claim or if none of the check boxes applies. **NOTE:** To use someone else's material in your work lawfully, you must have permission from the copyright owner of that material.

4B *Previous registration* · If the work for which you are now seeking registration, or an earlier version of it, has been registered, give the registration number and the year of registration. If there have been multiple registrations, you may give information regarding the last two.

Special situation · If you are registering the first published edition of a work that is identical to a previously registered unpublished version (contains no new material not already registered), check the "other" box in line 4A and state "First publication of work registered as unpublished." In this case, skip line 4C.

4C *New material included in this claim* · Check the appropriate box or boxes to identify the new material you are claiming in this registration. (See the shaded box at the bottom of this paage for specific examples.) Give a brief statement on the line after "other" only if it is necessary to give a more specific description of the new material included in this claim or if none of the check boxes applies. **NOTE:** "Compilation" is a work formed by the collection and assembling of preexisting materials or of data that are selected, coordinated, or arranged in such a way that the resulting work as a whole constitutes an original work of authorship. A claim in "compilation" does not include the material that has been compiled. If that material should also be included in the claim, check the appropriate additional boxes.

Section 5 - Rights and Permissions

This is the person to contact to obtain permission to use this work. If this is the same as the first copyright claimant, simply check the

box. **NOTE:** All the information given in section 5, including name, postal address, email address, and phone number, will be made part of the online public records produced by the Copyright Office and accessible on the Internet. This information cannot be removed later from those public records.

Section 6 - Correspondence Contact *

This is the person the Copyright Office should contact with any questions about this application. If this is the same as the first copyright claimant or the rights and permissions contact, simply check the appropriate box. (Information given only in this space will not appear in the online public record.)

Section 7 - Mail Certificate To *

This is the person to whom the registration certificate should be mailed. If this is the same as the first copyright claimant, the rights and permissions contact, or the correspondence contact, simply check the appropriate box. (Information given only in this space will not appear in the online public record.)

Section 8 - Certification

8A* *Handwritten signature* · After you print out the completed application, be sure to sign it at this space.

8B* *Printed name* · Enter the name of the person who will sign the form.

8C* *Date signed* · Choose "today's date" or "write date by hand." In the latter case, be sure to date the application by hand when you sign it. **NOTE:** If this application gives a date of publication, do not certify using a date prior to the publication date.

8D *Deposit account* · Leave this line blank unless you have a Copyright Office deposit account and are charging the filing fee to that account.

8E *Applicant's internal tracking number* · Enter your own internal tracking number, if any.

Section 4 — Examples

Your work	How to complete line 4a (excluded material)	How to complete line 4c (new, additional, or revised material)
New arrangement of a public domain song	Check the "text" and "music" boxes.	State "new arrangement" at the "other" line.
Revised version of a previously published book	Check the "text" box.	Check the "text" box.
English translation of a Spanish novel	Check the "text" box.	State "English translation" at the "other" line.
Movie based on a previously registered screenplay	Check the "text" box.	State "All other cinematographic material" at the "other" line.

Understanding Copyright Law: A Beginner's Guide

UNITED STATES COPYRIGHT OFFICE
Form CO · Application for Copyright Registration

APPLICATION FOR COPYRIGHT REGISTRATION

* Designates Required Fields

1 WORK BEING REGISTERED

1a. * Type of work being registered (*Fill in one only*)

☐ Literary work   ☐ Performing arts work

☐ Visual arts work   ☐ Motion picture/audiovisual work

☐ Sound recording   ☐ Single serial issue

ApplicationForCopyrightRegistration

1b. * Title of this work (*one title per space*)

WorkTitles

1c. For a serial issue: Volume [   ] Number [   ] Issue [   ] ISSN [   ]

Frequency of publication: [   ] Other [   ]

1d. Previous or alternative title

1e. * Year of completion [   ][   ][   ][   ]

Publication (*If this work has not been published, skip to section 2*)

1f. Date of publication [   ] (*mm/dd/yyyy*) **1g.** ISBN [   ]

1h. Nation of publication ☐ United States ☐ Other   Other [   ]

1i. Published as a contribution in a larger work entitled

1j. If line 1i above names a serial issue Volume [   ] Number [   ] Issue [   ]

1k. If work was preregistered Number PRE-[   ]

For Office Use Only

WorkBeingRegistered

Page of

UNITED STATES COPYRIGHT OFFICE

Form CO · Application for Copyright Registration

2 AUTHOR INFORMATION - Entry Number

2a. Personal name   *complete either 2a or 2b*

First Name   Middle   Last

2b. Organization name

2c. Doing business as

2d. Year of birth   **2e.** Year of death

2f. ☐ Citizenship   ☐ United States   ☐ Other   Other

☐ Domicile   ☐ United States   ☐ Other   Other

2g. Author's contribution: ☐ Made for hire   ☐ Anonymous

☐ Pseudonymous   (Pseudonym is:

Continuation of Author Information

2h. * This author created (*Fill in only the authorship that applies to this author*)

☐ Text   ☐ Compilation   ☐ Map/technical drawing   ☐ Music

☐ Poetry   ☐ Sculpture   ☐ Architectural work   ☐ Lyrics

☐ Computer program   ☐ Jewelry design   ☐ Photography   ☐ Motion picture/audiovisual

☐ Editing   ☐ 2-dimensional artwork   ☐ Script/play/screenplay   ☐ Sound recording/performance

Other:

For Office Use Only

AuthorInformation

Page   of

UNITED STATES COPYRIGHT OFFICE
Form CO · Application for Copyright Registration

3 COPYRIGHT CLAIMANT INFORMATION   - Entry Number

Claimant   *complete either 3a or 3b* – If you do not know the address for a claimant, enter "not known" in the Street address and City fields. You must give the address for at least one claimant.

3a. Personal name
First Name _____ Middle _____ Last _____

3b. Organization name
_____

3c. Doing business as
_____

3d. Street address * _____

Street address (line 2) _____

City * _____ State _____ ZIP / Postal code _____ Country _____

Email _____ Phone number _____

3e. If claimant is **not** an author, copyright ownership acquired by: ☐ Written agreement ☐ Will or inheritance ☐ Other

Other |

For Office Use Only

CopyrightClaimantInformation

Page of

UNITED STATES COPYRIGHT OFFICE

Form CO · Application for Copyright Registration

4 LIMITATION OF COPYRIGHT CLAIM

Skip section 4 if this work is all new.

4a. Material excluded from this claim *(Material previously registered, previously published, or not owned by this claimant)*

☐ Text   ☐ Artwork   ☐ Music   ☐ Sound recording/performance   ☐ Motion picture/audiovisual

Other: |

4b. Previous registration(s)   Number | Year ☐☐☐☐

Number | Year ☐☐☐☐

4c. New material included in this claim *(This work contains new, additional, or revised material)*

☐ Text	☐ Compilation	☐ Map/technical drawing	☐ Music
☐ Poetry	☐ Sculpture	☐ Architectural work	☐ Lyrics
☐ Computer program	☐ Jewelry design	☐ Photography	☐ Motion picture/audiovisual
☐ Editing	☐ 2-dimensional artwork	☐ Script/play/screenplay	☐ Sound recording/performance

Other: |

For Office Use Only

LimitationOfCopyrightClaim

Privacy Act Notice
Sections 408-410 of title 17 of the United States Code authorize the Copyright Office to collect the personally identifying information requested on this form in order to process the application for copyright registration. By providing this information you are agreeing to routine uses of the information that include publication to give legal notice of your copyright claim as required by 17 U.S.C. § 705. It will appear in the Office's online catalog. If you do not provide the information requested, registration may be refused or delayed, and you may not be entitled to certain relief, remedies, and benefits under the copyright law.

Page of

UNITED STATES COPYRIGHT OFFICE
Form CO · Application for Copyright Registration

5 RIGHTS AND PERMISSIONS CONTACT

☐ Check if information below should be copied from the **first** copyright claimant

First Name _____ Middle _____ Last _____

Name of organization _____

Street address _____

Street address (line 2) _____

City _____ State _____ ZIP / Postal code _____ Country _____

Email _____ Phone number _____

For Office Use Only

RightsAndPermissionsContact

Page of

UNITED STATES COPYRIGHT OFFICE

Form CO · Application for Copyright Registration

6 CORRESPONDENCE CONTACT

☐ Copy from **first** copyright claimant   ☐ Copy from rights and permissions contact

First name *   Middle   Last *

Name of organization

Street address *

Street address (line 2)

City *   State   ZIP / Postal code   Country

Email *   Daytime phone number

For Office Use Only

CorrespondenceContact

Page   of

UNITED STATES COPYRIGHT OFFICE
Form CO · Application for Copyright Registration

7 MAIL CERTIFICATE TO:

* Complete either 7a, 7b, or both

☐ Copy from **first** copyright claimant   ☐ Copy from rights and permissions contact   ☐ Copy from correspondence contact

7a. First Name   Middle   Last

7b. Name of organization

7c. Street address *

Street address (line 2)

City *   State   ZIP / Postal code   Country

For Office Use Only

MailCertificateTo

Page   of

UNITED STATES COPYRIGHT OFFICE

Form CO · Application for Copyright Registration

8 CERTIFICATION

17 U.S.C. § 506(e): Any person who knowingly makes a false representation of a material fact in the application for copyright registration provided for by section 409, or in any written statement filed in connection with the application, shall be fined not more than $2,500.

I certify that I am the author, copyright claimant, or owner of exclusive rights, or the authorized agent of the author, copyright claimant, or owner of exclusive rights, of this work, and that the information given in this application is correct to the best of my knowledge.

Sign Here →

8a. Handwritten signature

8b. Printed name   **8c.** Date signed

8d. Deposit account number   Account holder

8e. Applicant's internal tracking number (optional)

For Office Use Only

Certification

What are these barcodes for?

The Adobe® LiveCycle® Barcoded Forms bar-codes provide a facility to automate the extraction of data from paper forms and deliver it to core systems for processing. This dramatically reduces costs, **errors**, and time compared to manual data entry and solutions based on optical character recognition (OCR).

Page of

APPENDIX 15:
DEFINITIONS RELATED TO AUTHORSHIP

Excerpts from section 101 of the 1976 Act:

An "anonymous work" is a work on the copies or phonorecords of which no natural person is identified as author.

A "joint work" is a work prepared by two or more authors with the intention that their contributions be merged into inseparable or interdependent parts of a unitary whole.

A "pseudonymous work" is a work on the copies or phonorecords of which the author is identified under a fictitious name.

A "work made for hire" is—

(1) a work prepared by an employee within the scope of his or her employment; or

(2) a work specially ordered or commissioned for use as a contribution to a collective work, as a part of a motion picture or other audiovisual work, as a translation, as a supplementary work, as a compilation, as an instructional text, as a test, as answer material for a test, or as an atlas, if the parties expressly agree in a written instrument signed by them that the work shall be considered a work made for hire. For the purpose of the foregoing sentence, a "supplementary work" is a work prepared for publication as a secondary adjunct to a work by another author for the purpose of introducing, concluding, illustrating, explaining, revising, commenting upon, or assisting in the use of the other work, such as forewords, afterwords, pictorial illustrations, maps, charts, tables, editorial notes, musical arrangements, answer material for tests, bibliographies, appendixes, and indexes, and an "instructional text" is a literary, pictorial, or graphic work prepared for publication and with the purpose of use in systematic instructional activities.

APPENDIX 16:
COPYRIGHT DEPOSIT REQUIREMENTS

Excerpt from section 408 of the 1976 Copyright Act:

§ 408. Copyright registration in general

(b) DEPOSIT FOR COPYRIGHT REGISTRATION.—Except as provided by subsection (c), the material deposited for registration shall include—

(1) in the case of an unpublished work, one complete copy or phonorecord;

(2) in the case of a published work, two complete copies or phonorecords of the best edition;

(3) in the case of a work first published outside the United States, one complete copy or phonorecord as so published;

(4) in the case of a contribution to a collective work, one complete copy or phonorecord of the best edition of the collective work.

Copies or phonorecords deposited for the Library of Congress under section 407 may be used to satisfy the deposit provisions of this section, if they are accompanied by the prescribed application and fee, and by any additional identifying material that the Register may, by regulation, require. The Register shall also prescribe regulations establishing requirements under which copies or phonorecords acquired for the Library of Congress under subsection (e) of section 407, otherwise than by deposit, may be used to satisfy the deposit provisions of this section.

(c) ADMINISTRATIVE CLASSIFICATION AND OPTIONAL DEPOSIT.—

(1) The Register of Copyrights is authorized to specify by regulation the administrative classes into which works are to be placed for purposes of deposit and registration, and the nature of the copies or phonorecords to be deposited in the various classes specified. The regulations may require or permit, for particular

classes, the deposit of identifying material instead of copies or phonorecords, the deposit of only one copy or phonorecord where two would normally be required, or a single registration for a group of related works. This administrative classification of works has no significance with respect to the subject matter of copyright or the exclusive rights provided by this title.

Section 202.20 of title 37 of the CFR:

§ 202.20 Deposit of copies and phonorecords for copyright registration.

(a) *General.* This section prescribes rules pertaining to the deposit of copies and phonorecords of published and unpublished works for the purpose of copyright registration under section 408 of title 17 of the United States Code, as amended by Pub. L. 94–553. The provisions of this section are not applicable to the deposit of copies and phonorecords for the Library of Congress under section 407 of title 17, except as expressly adopted in §202.19 of these regulations.

(b) *Definitions.* For the purposes of this section:

(1) *The best edition* of a work has the meaning set forth in §202.19 (b)(1). For purposes of this section, if a work is first published in both hard copy, *i.e.*, in a physically tangible format, and also in an electronic format, the current Library of Congress Best Edition Statement requirements pertaining to the hard copy format apply.

(2) A *complete* copy or phonorecord means the following:

(i) *Unpublished works.* Subject to the requirements of paragraph (b)(2)(vii) of this section, a "complete" copy or phonorecord of an unpublished work is a copy or phonorecord representing the entire copyrightable content of the work for which registration is sought;

(ii) *Published works.* Subject to the requirements of paragraphs (b)(2) (iv) through (vii) of this section, a "complete" copy or phonorecord of a published work includes all elements comprising the applicable unit of publication of the work, including elements that, if considered separately, would not be copyrightable subject matter. However, even where certain physically separable elements included in the applicable unit of publication are missing from the deposit, a copy or phonorecord will be considered "complete" for purposes of registration where:

(A) The copy or phonorecord deposited contains all parts of the work for which copyright registration is sought; and

(B) The removal of the missing elements did not physically damage the copy or phonorecord or garble its contents; and

(C) The work is exempt from the mandatory deposit requirements under section 407 of title 17 of the United States Code and §202.19(c) of these regulations, or the copy deposited consists entirely of a container, wrapper, or holder, such as an envelope, sleeve, jacket, slipcase, box, bag, folder, binder, or other receptacle acceptable for deposit under paragraph (c)(2) of this section;

(iii) *Works submitted for registration in digital formats.* A 'complete' electronically filed work is one which is embodied in a digital file which contains:

(A) if the work is unpublished, all authorship elements for which registration is sought; and

(B) if the work is published solely in an electronic format, all elements constituting the work in its published form, *i.e.*, the complete work as published, including metadata and authorship for which registration is not sought. Publication in an electronic only format requires submission of the digital file[s] in exact first–publication form and content.

(C) For works submitted electronically, any of the following file formats are acceptable for registration: PDF; TXT; WPD; DOC; TIF; SVG; JPG; XML; HTML; WAV; and MPEG family of formats, including MP3. This list of file formats is non-exhaustive and it may change, or be added to periodically. Changes will be noted in the list of acceptable formats on the Copyright Office website.

(D) Contact with the registration applicant may be necessary if the Copyright Office cannot access, view, or examine the content of any particular digital file that has been submitted for the registration of a work. For purposes of section 410(d) of 17 U.S.C., a deposit has not been received in the Copyright Office until a copy that can be reviewed by the Office is received.

(iv) *Contributions to collective works.* In the case of a published contribution to a collective work, a "complete" copy is one complete copy of the best edition of the entire collective work, the complete section containing the contribution if published in a newspaper, the contribution cut from the paper in which it appeared, or a photocopy of the contribution itself as it was published in the collective work.

(v) *Sound recordings.* In the case of published sound recordings, a "complete" phonorecord has the meaning set forth in §202.19(b)(2) of these regulations;

(vi) *Musical scores.* In the case of a musical composition published in copies only, or in both copies and phonorecords:

(A) If the only publication of copies took place by the rental, lease, or lending of a full score and parts, a full score is a "complete" copy; and

(B) If the only publication of copies took place by the rental, lease, or lending of a conductor's score and parts, a conductor's score is a "complete" copy;

(vii) *Motion pictures.* In the case of a published or unpublished motion picture, a copy is "complete" if the reproduction of all of the visual and aural elements comprising the copyrightable subject matter in the work is clean, undamaged, undeteriorated, and free of splices, and if the copy itself and its physical housing are free of any defects that would interfere with the performance of the work or that would cause mechanical, visual, or audible defects or distortions.

(3) The terms *architectural works, copy, collective work, device, fixed, literary work, machine, motion picture, phonorecord, publication, sound recording, transmission program,* and *useful article,* and their variant forms, have the meanings given to them in 17 U.S.C. 101.

(4) A *secure test* is a nonmarketed test administered under supervision at specified centers on specific dates, all copies of which are accounted for and either destroyed or returned to restricted locked storage following each administration. For these purposes a test is not marketed if copies are not sold but it is distributed and used in such a manner that ownership and control of copies remain with the test sponsor or publisher.

(5) *Title 17* means title 17 of the United States Code, as amended by Pub. L. 94–553.

(6) For the purposes of determining the applicable deposit requirements under this §202.20 only, the following shall be considered as unpublished motion pictures: motion pictures that consist of television transmission programs and that have been published,

if at all, only by reason of a license or other grant to a nonprofit institution of the right to make a fixation of such programs directly from a transmission to the public, with or without the right to make further uses of such fixations.

(c) *Nature of required deposit.*

(1) Subject to the provisions of paragraph (c)(2) of this section, the deposit required to accompany an application for registration of claim to copyright under section 408 of title 17 shall consist of:

(i) In the case of unpublished works, one complete copy or phonorecord.

(ii) In the case of works first published in the United States before January 1, 1978, two complete copies or phonorecords of the work as first published.

(iii) In the case of works first published in the United States on or after January 1, 1978, two complete copies or phonorecords of the best edition.

(iv) In the case of works first published outside of the United States, one complete copy or phonorecord of the work either as first published or of the best edition. For purposes of this section, any works simultaneously first published within and outside of the United States shall be considered to be first published in the United States.

(2) In the case of certain works, the special provisions set forth in this clause shall apply. In any case where this clause specifies that one copy or phonorecord may be submitted, that copy or phonorecord shall represent the best edition, or the work as first published, as set forth in paragraph (c)(1) of this section.

(i) *General.* In the following cases the deposit of one complete copy or phonorecord will suffice in lieu of two copies or phonorecords:

(A) Published three-dimensional cartographic representations of area, such as globes and relief models;

(B) Published diagrams illustrating scientific or technical works or formulating scientific or technical information in linear or other two-dimensional form, such as an architectural or engineering blueprint, or a mechanical drawing;

(C) Published greeting cards, picture postcards, and stationery;

(D) Lectures, sermons, speeches, and addresses published individually and not as a collection of the works of one or more authors;

(E) Musical compositions published in copies only, or in both copies and phonorecords, if the only publication of copies took place by rental, lease, or lending;

(F) Published multimedia kits or any part thereof;

(G) Works exempted from the requirement of depositing identifying material under paragraph (c)(2)(xi)(B)(5) of this section;

(H) Literary, dramatic, and musical works published only as embodied in phonorecords, although this category does not exempt the owner of copyright in a sound recording;

(I) Choreographic works, pantomimes, literary, dramatic, and musical works published only as embodied in motion pictures;

(J) Published works in the form of two-dimensional games, decals, fabric patches or emblems, calendars, instructions for needle work, needle work and craft kits; and

(K) Works reproduced on three-dimensional containers such as boxes, cases, and cartons.

(ii) *Motion pictures*. In the case of published or unpublished motion pictures, the deposit of one complete copy will suffice. The deposit of a copy or copies for any published or unpublished motion picture must be accompanied by a separate description of its contents, such as a continuity, pressbook, or synopsis. In any case where the deposit copy or copies required for registration of a motion picture cannot be viewed for examining purposes on equipment in the Registration and Recordation Program of the Copyright Office, the description accompanying the deposit must comply with §202.21(h) of these regulations. The Library of Congress may, at its sole discretion, enter into an agreement permitting the return of copies of published motion pictures to the depositor under certain conditions and establishing certain rights and obligations of the Library of Congress with respect to such copies. In the event of termination of such an agreement by the Library, it shall not be subject to reinstatement, nor shall the depositor or any successor in interest of the depositor be entitled to any similar or subsequent agreement with the Library, unless at the sole discretion of the Library it would be in the best interests of the Library to reinstate the agreement or enter into a new agreement. In the case of unpublished motion pictures (including television transmission programs that have been fixed and transmitted to the public, but have not been published), the deposit of identifying material in compliance with §202.21 of these regulations may be made and will suffice in lieu of an actual copy. In the case of colorized versions of motion pictures made from pre-existing black and white motion pictures, in addition to the deposit of one complete copy of the colorized motion picture and the separate description of its contents as specified above, the deposit shall consist of one complete print of the black and white version of the motion picture from which the colorized version was prepared. If special relief from this requirement is requested and granted, the claimant shall make a good faith effort to deposit the best available, near-archival quality black and white print, as a condition of any grant of special relief.

(iii) *Holograms.* In the case of any work deposited in the form of a three-dimensional hologram, the copy or copies shall be accompanied by:

(A) Precise instructions for displaying the image fixed in the hologram; and

(B) Photographs or other identifying material complying with §202.21 of these regulations and clearly showing the displayed image.

The number of sets of instructions and identifying material shall be the same as the number of copies required. In the case of a work in the form of a two-dimensional hologram, the image of which is visible without the use of a machine or device, one actual copy of the work shall be deposited.

(iv) *Certain pictorial and graphic works.* In the case of any unpublished pictorial or graphic work, deposit of identifying material in compliance with §202.21 of these regulations may be made and will suffice in lieu of deposit of an actual copy. In the case of a published pictorial or graphic work, deposit of one complete copy, or of identifying material in compliance with §202.21 of these regulations, may be made and will suffice in lieu of deposit of two actual copies where an individual author is the owner of copyright, and either:

(A) Less than five copies of the work have been published; or

(B) The work has been published and sold or offered for sale in a limited edition consisting of no more than 300 numbered copies.

(v) *Commercial prints and labels.* In the case of prints, labels, and other advertising matter, including catalogs, published in connection with the rental, lease, lending, licensing, or sale of articles of merchandise, works of authorship, or services, the deposit of one complete copy will suffice in lieu of two copies. Where the print or label is published in a larger work, such as a newspaper or other periodical, one copy of the entire page or pages upon which it appears may be submitted in lieu of the entire larger work. In the case of prints or labels physically inseparable from a three-dimensional object, identifying material complying with §202.21 of these regulations must be submitted rather than an actual copy or copies except under the conditions of paragraph (c)(2)(xi)(B)(*4*) of this section.

(vi) *Tests.* In the case of tests, and answer material for tests, published separately from other literary works, the deposit of one complete copy will suffice in lieu of two copies. In the case of any secure test the Copyright Office will return the deposit to the applicant promptly after examination: Provided, That sufficient portions, description, or the like are retained so as to constitute a sufficient archival record of the deposit.

(vii) *Computer programs and databases embodied in machine-readable copies other than CD-ROM format.* In cases where a computer program, database, compilation, statistical compendium, or the like, if unpublished is fixed, or if published is published only in the form of machine-readable copies (such as magnetic tape or disks, punched cards, semiconductor chip products, or the like) other than a CD-ROM format, from which the work cannot ordinarily be perceived except with the aid of a machine or device, the deposit shall consist of:

(A) For published or unpublished computer programs, one copy of identifying portions of the program, reproduced in a form visually perceptible without the aid of a machine or device, either on paper or in microform. For these purposes "identifying portions" shall mean one of the following:

(*1*) The first and last 25 pages or equivalent units of the source code if reproduced on paper, or at least the first and last 25 pages or equivalent units of the source code if reproduced in microform, together with the page or equivalent unit containing the copyright notice, if any. If the program is 50 pages or less, the required deposit will be the entire source code. In the case of revised versions of computer programs, if the revisions occur throughout the entire program, the deposit of the page containing the copyright notice and the first and last 25 pages of source code will suffice; if the revisions do not occur in the first and last 25 pages, the deposit should consist of the page containing the copyright notice and any 50 pages of source code representative of the revised material; or

(*2*) Where the program contains trade secret material, the page or equivalent unit containing the copyright notice, if any, plus one of the following: the first and last 25 pages or equivalent units of source code with portions of the source code containing trade secrets blocked-out, provided that the blocked-out portions are proportionately less than the material remaining, and the deposit reveals an appreciable amount of original computer code; or the first and last 10 pages or equivalent units of source code alone with no blocked-out portions; or the first and last 25 pages of object code, together with any 10 or more consecutive pages of source code with no blocked-out portions; or for programs consisting of, or less than, 50 pages or equivalent units, entire source code with the trade secret portions blocked-out, provided that the blocked-out portions are proportionately less than the material remaining, and the remaining portion reveals an appreciable amount of original computer code. If the copyright claim is in a revision not contained in the first and last 25 pages, the deposit shall consist of either 20 pages of source code representative of the revised material with no blocked-out portions, or any 50 pages of source code representative of the revised material with portions of the source code containing trade secrets blocked-out, provided that the blocked-out portions are proportinately less than the material remaining and the deposit reveals an appreciable amount of original computer code. Whatever method is used to block out trade secret material, at least an appreciable amount of original computer code must remain visible.

(B) Where registration of a program containing trade secrets is made on the basis of an object code deposit the Copyright Office will make registration under its rule of doubt and warn that no determination has been made concerning the existence of copyrightable authorship.

(C) Where the application to claim copyright in a computer program includes a specific claim in related computer screen displays, the deposit, in addition to the identifying portions specified in paragraph (c)(2)(vii)(A) of this section, shall consist of:

(*1*) Visual reproductions of the copyrightable expression in the form of printouts, photographs, or drawings no smaller than 3×3 inches and no larger than 9×12 inches; or

(*2*) If the authorship in the work is predominantly audiovisual, a one-half inch VHS format videotape reproducing the copyrightable expression, except that printouts, photographs, or drawings no smaller than 3×3 inches and no larger than 9×12 inches must be deposited in lieu of videotape where the computer screen material simply constitutes a demonstration of the functioning of the computer program.

(D) For published and unpublished automated databases, compilations, statistical compendia, and the like, so fixed or published, one copy of identifying portions of the work, reproduced in a form visually perceptible without the aid of a machine or device, either on paper or in microform. For these purposes:

(*1*) *Identifying portions* shall generally mean either the first and last 25 pages or equivalent units of the work if reproduced on paper or in microform.

(*2*) *Datafile* and *file* shall mean a group of data records pertaining to a common subject matter regardless of their size or the number of data items in them.

(*3*) In the case of individual registration of a revised version of the works identified in paragraph (c)(2)(vii) (D) of this section, the identifying portions deposited shall contain 50 representative pages or data records which have been added or modified.

(*4*) If the work is an automated database comprising multiple separate or distinct data files, "identifying portions" shall instead consist of 50 complete data records from each data file or the entire data file, whichever is less, and the descriptive statement required by paragraph (c)(2)(vii)(D)(5) of this section.

(*5*) In the case of group registration for revised or updated versions of a database, the claimant shall deposit identifying portions that contain 50 representative pages or equivalent units, or representative data records which have been marked to disclose (or do in fact disclose solely) the new material added on one representative publication date if published, or on one representative creation date, if unpublished, and shall also deposit a brief typed or printed descriptive statement containing the notice of copyright information required under paragraphs (c)(2)(vii)(D)(6) or (7) of this section, if the work bears a notice, and;

(*i*) The title of the database;

(*ii*) A subtitle, date of creation or publication, or other information, to distinguish any separate or distinct data files for cataloging purposes;

(*iii*) The name and address of the copyright claimant;

(*iv*) For each separate file, its name and content, including its subject, the origin(s) of the data, and the approximate number of data records it contains; and

(*v*) In the case of revised or updated versions of an automated database, information as to the nature and frequency of changes in the database and some identification of the location within the database or the separate data files of the revisions.

(*6*) For a copyright notice embodied in machine-readable form, the statement shall describe exactly the visually perceptible content of the notice which appears in or with the database, and the manner and frequency with which it is displayed (e.g., at user's terminal only at sign-on, or continuously on terminal display, or on printouts, etc.).

(7) If a visually perceptible copyright notice is placed on any copies of the work (or on magnetic tape reels or containers therefor), a sample of such notice must also accompany the statement.

(viii) *Machine-readable copies of works other than computer programs, databases, and works fixed in a CD-ROM format.* Where a literary, musical, pictorial, graphic, or audiovisual work, or a sound recording, except for works fixed in a CD-ROM format and literary works which are computer programs, databases, compilations, statistical compendia or the like, if unpublished has been fixed or, if published, has been published only in machine-readable form, the deposit must consist of identifying material. The type of identifying material submitted should generally be appropriate to the type of work embodied in machine-readable form, but in all cases should be that which best represents the copyrightable content of the work. In all cases the identifying material must include the title of the work. A synopsis may also be requested in addition to the other deposit materials as appropriate in the discretion of the Copyright Office. In the case of any published work subject to this section, the identifying material must include a representation of the copyright notice, if one exists. Identifying material requirements for certain types of works are specified below. In the case of the types of works listed below, the requirements specified shall apply except that, in any case where the specific requirements are not appropriate for a given work the form of the identifying material required will be determined by the Copyright Office in consultation with the applicant, but the Copyright Office will make the final determination of the acceptability of the identifying material.

(A) For pictorial or graphic works, the deposit shall consist of identifying material in compliance with §202.21 of these regulations;

(B) For audiovisual works, the deposit shall consist of either a videotape of the work depicting representative portions of the copyrightable content, or a series of photographs or drawings, depicting representative portions of the work, plus in all cases a separate synopsis of the work;

(C) For musical compositions, the deposit shall consist of a transcription of the entire work such as a score, or a reproduction of the entire work on an audiocassette or other phonorecord;

(D) For sound recordings, the deposit shall consist of a reproduction of the entire work on an audiocassette or other phonorecord;

(E) For literary works, the deposit shall consist of a transcription of representative portions of the work including the first and last 25 pages or equivalent units, and five or more pages indicative of the remainder.

(ix) *Copies containing both visually-perceptible and machine-readable material other than a CD-ROM format.* Where a published literary work is embodied in copies containing both visually-perceptible and machine-readable material, except in the case of a CD-ROM format, the deposit shall consist of the visually-perceptible material and identifying portions of the machine-readable material.

(x) *Works reproduced in or on sheetlike materials.* In the case of any unpublished work that is fixed, or any published work that is published, only in the form of a two-dimensional reproduction on sheetlike materials such as textiles and other fabrics, wallpaper and similar commercial wall coverings, carpeting, floor tile, and similar commercial floor coverings, and wrapping paper and similar packaging material, the deposit shall consist of one copy in the form of an actual swatch or piece of such material sufficient to show all elements of the work in which copyright is claimed and the copyright notice appearing on the work, if any. If the work consists of a repeated pictorial or graphic design, the complete design and at least part of one repetition must be shown. If the sheetlike material in or on which a published work has been reproduced has been embodied in or attached to a three-dimensional object, such as furniture, or any other three-dimensional manufactured article, and the work has been published only in that form, the deposit must consist of identifying material complying with §202.21 of these regulations instead of a copy. If the sheet-like material in or on which a published work has been reproduced has been embodied in or attached to a two-dimensional object such as wearing apparel, bed linen, or a similar item, and the work has been published only in that form, the deposit must consist of identifying material complying with §202.21 of these regulations instead of a copy unless the copy can be folded for storage in a form that does not exceed four inches in thickness.

(xi) *Works reproduced in or on three-dimensional objects.* (A) In the following cases the deposit must consist of identifying material complying with §201.21 of these regulations instead of a copy or copies:

(*1*) Any three-dimensional sculptural work, including any illustration or formulation of artistic expression or information in three-dimensional form. Examples of such works include statues, carvings, ceramics, moldings, constructions, models, and maquettes; and

(*2*) Any two-dimensional or three-dimensional work that, if unpublished, has been fixed, or, if published, has been published only in or on jewelry, dolls, toys, games, except as provided in paragraph (c)(2)(xi)(B)(*3*) of this section, or any three-dimensional useful article.

(B) In the following cases the requirements of paragraph (c)(2)(xi)(A) of this section for the deposit of identifying material shall not apply:

(*1*) Three-dimensional cartographic representations of area, such as globes and relief models;

(*2*) Works that have been fixed or published in or on a useful article that comprises one of the elements of the unit of publication of an educational or instructional kit which also includes a literary or audiovisual work, a sound recording, or any combination of such works;

(*3*) Published games consisting of multiple parts that are packaged and published in a box or similar container with flat sides and with dimensions of no more than 12×24×6 inches;

(*4*) Works reproduced on three-dimensional containers or holders such as boxes, cases, and cartons, where the container or holder can be readily opened out, unfolded, slit at the corners, or in some other way made adaptable for flat storage, and the copy, when flattened, does not exceed 96 inches in any dimension; or

(*5*) Any three-dimensional sculptural work that, if unpublished, has been fixed, or, if published, has been published only in the form of jewelry cast in base metal which does not exceed four inches in any dimension.

(xii) *Soundtracks.* For separate registration of an unpublished work that is fixed, or a published work that is published, only as embodied in a soundtrack that is an integral part of a motion picture, the deposit of identifying material in compliance with §202.21 of these regulations will suffice in lieu of an actual copy of the motion picture.

(xiii) *Oversize deposits.* In any case where the deposit otherwise required by this section exceeds 96 inches in any dimension, identifying material complying with §202.21 of these regulations must be submitted instead of an actual copy or copies.

(xiv) *Pictorial advertising material.* In the case of published pictorial advertising material, except for advertising material published in connection with motion pictures, the deposit of either one copy as published or prepublication material consisting of camera-ready copy is acceptable.

(xv) *Contributions to collective works.* In the case of published contributions to collective works, the deposit of either one complete copy of the best edition of the entire collective work, the complete section containing the contribution if published in a newspaper, the entire page containing the contribution, the contribution cut from the paper in which it appeared, or a photocopy of the contribution itself as it was published in the collective work, will suffice in lieu of two complete copies of the entire collective work.

(xvi) *Phonorecords.* In any case where the deposit phonorecord or phonorecords submitted for registration of a claim to copyright is inaudible on audio playback devices in the Registration and Recordation Program of the Copyright Office, the Office will seek an appropriate deposit in accordance with paragraph (d) of this section.

(xvii) *Group registration of serials.* For group registration of related serials, as specified in §202.3(b)(6), the deposit must consist of one complete copy of the best edition of each issue included in the group registration. In addition, two complimentary subscriptions to any serial for which group registration is sought must be entered and maintained in the name of the Library of Congress, and the copies must be submitted regularly and promptly after publication.

(xviii) *Architectural works.* (A) For designs of unconstructed buildings, the deposit must consist of one complete copy of an architectural drawing or blueprint in visually perceptible form showing the overall form of the building and any interior arrangements of spaces and/or design elements in which copyright is claimed. For archival purposes, the Copyright Office prefers that the drawing submissions consist of the following in descending order of preference:

(*1*) Original format, or best quality form of reproduction, including offset or silk screen printing;

(*2*) Xerographic or photographic copies on good quality paper;

(*3*) Positive photostat or photodirect positive;

(*4*) Blue line copies (diazo or ozalid process).

The Copyright Office prefers that the deposit disclose the name(s) of the architect(s) and draftsperson(s) and the building site, if known.

(B) For designs of constructed buildings, the deposit must consist of one complete copy of an architectural drawing or blueprint in visually perceptible form showing the overall form of the building and any interior arrangement of spaces and/or design elements in which copyright is claimed. In addition, the deposit must also include identifying material in the form of photographs complying with §202.21 of these regulations, which clearly discloses the architectural works being registered. For archival purposes, the Copyright Office prefers that the drawing submissions constitute the most finished form of presentation drawings and consist of the following in descending order of preference:

(*1*) Original format, or best quality form of reproduction, including offset or silk screen printing;

(*2*) Xerographic or photographic copies on good quality paper;

(*3*) Positive photostat or photodirect positive;

(*4*) Blue line copies (diazo or ozalid process).

With respect to the accompanying photographs, the Copyright Office prefers 8×10 inches, good quality photographs, which clearly show several exterior and interior views. The Copyright Office prefers that the deposit disclose the name(s) of the architect(s) and draftsperson(s) and the building site.

(xix) *Works fixed in a CD-ROM format*

(A) Where a work is fixed in a CD-ROM format, the deposit must consist of one complete copy of the entire CD-ROM package, including a complete copy of any accompanying operating software and instructional manual, and a printed version of the work embodied in the CD-ROM, if the work is fixed in print as well as a CD-ROM. A complete copy of a published CD-ROM package includes all of the elements comprising the applicable unit of publication, including elements that if considered separately would not be copyrightable subject matter or could be the subject of a separate registration.

(B) In any case where the work fixed in a CD-ROM package cannot be viewed on equipment available in the Registration and Recordation Program of the Copyright Office, the Office will seek an appropriate deposit in accordance with paragraph (d) of this section, in addition to the deposit of the CD-ROM package.

(xx) *Photographs: group registration.* For groups of photographs registered with one application under §§202.3(b)(3)(i)(B) (unpublished collections) or 202.3(b)(9) (group registration of published photographs), photographs must be deposited in one of the following formats (listed in the Library's order of preference):

(A) Digital form on one or more CD-ROMs (including CD-RW's) or DVD-ROMs, in one of the following formats: JPEG, GIF, TIFF, or PCD;

(B) Unmounted prints measuring at least 3 inches by 3 inches (not to exceed 20 inches by 24 inches);

(C) Contact sheets;

(D) Slides, each with a single image;

(E) A format in which the photograph has been published (e.g., clippings from newspapers or magazines);

(F) A photocopy of each of the photographs included in the group, clearly depicting the photograph, provided that if registration is made pursuant to §202.3(b)(9) for group registration of photographs, the photocopy must be either a photocopy of an unmounted print measuring at least 3 inches by 3 inches (not to exceed 20 inches by 24 inches) or a photocopy of the photograph in a format in which it has been published, and if the photograph was published as a color photograph, the photocopy must be a color photocopy;

(G) Slides, each containing up to 36 images; or

(H) A videotape clearly depicting each photograph.

(d) *Special relief.*

(1) In any case the Register of Copyrights may, after consultation with other appropriate officials of the Library of Congress and upon such conditions as the Register may determine after such consultation:

(i) Permit the deposit of one copy or phonorecord, or alternative identifying material, in lieu of the one or two copies or phonorecords otherwise required by paragraph (c)(1) of this section;

(ii) Permit the deposit of incomplete copies or phonorecords, or copies or phonorecords other than those normally comprising the best edition; or

(iii) Permit the deposit of an actual copy or copies, in lieu of the identifying material otherwise required by this section; or

(iv) Permit the deposit of identifying material which does not comply with §202.21 of these regulations.

(2) Any decision as to whether to grant such special relief, and the conditions under which special relief is to be granted, shall be made by the Register of Copyrights after consultation with other appropriate officials of the Library of Congress, and shall be based upon the acquisition policies of the Library of Congress then in force and the archival and examining requirements of the Copyright Office.

(3) Requests for special relief under this paragraph may be combined with requests for special relief under §202.19(e) of these regulations. Whether so combined or made solely under this paragraph, such requests shall be made in writing to the Associate Register for Registration and Recordation Program of the Copyright Office, shall be signed by or on behalf of the person signing the

application for registration, and shall set forth specific reasons why the request should be granted.

(4) The Register of Copyrights may, after consultation with other appropriate officials of the Library of Congress, terminate any ongoing or continuous grant of special relief. Notice of termination shall be given in writing and shall be sent to the individual person or organization to whom the grant of special relief had been given, at the last address shown in the records of the Copyright Office. A notice of termination may be given at any time, but it shall state a specific date of termination that is at least 30 days later than the date the notice is mailed. Termination shall not affect the validity of any deposit or registration made earlier under the grant of special relief.

(e) *Use of copies and phonorecords deposited for the Library of Congress.* Copies and phonorecords deposited for the Library of Congress under section 407 of title 17 and §202.19 of these regulations may be used to satisfy the deposit provisions of this section if they are accompanied by an application for registration of claim to copyright in the work represented by the deposit, and either a registration fee or a deposit account number on the application.

APPENDIX 17:
MANDATORY DEPOSIT REQUIREMENTS

Section 407 of the 1976 Copyright Act:

§ 407. Deposit of copies or phonorecords for Library of Congress

(a) Except as provided by subsection (c), and subject to the provisions of subsection (e), the owner of copyright or of the exclusive right of publication in a work published in the United States shall deposit, within three months after the date of such publication—

(1) two complete copies of the best edition; or

(2) if the work is a sound recording, two complete phonorecords of the best edition, together with any printed or other visually perceptible material published with such phonorecords.

Neither the deposit requirements of this subsection nor the acquisition provisions of subsection (e) are conditions of copyright protection.

(b) The required copies or phonorecords shall be deposited in the Copyright Office for the use or disposition of the Library of Congress. The Register of Copyrights shall, when requested by the depositor and upon payment of the fee prescribed by *section 708,* issue a receipt for the deposit.

(c) The Register of Copyrights may by regulation exempt any categories of material from the deposit requirements of this section, or require deposit of only one copy or phonorecord with respect to any categories. Such regulations shall provide either for complete exemption from the deposit requirements of this section, or for alternative forms of deposit aimed at providing a satisfactory archival record of a work without imposing practical or financial hardships on the depositor, where the individual author is the owner of copyright in a pictorial, graphic, or sculptural work and (i) less than five copies of the work have been published, or (ii) the work has been published in a limited edition consisting of numbered copies, the monetary value of which would make the mandatory deposit of two copies of the best edition of the work burdensome, unfair, or unreasonable.

(d) At any time after publication of a work as provided by subsection(a), the Register of Copyrights may make written demand for the required deposit on any of the persons obligated to make the deposit under subsection (a). Unless deposit is made within three months after the demand is received, the person or persons on whom the demand was made are liable—

(1) to a fine of not more than $250 for each work; and

(2) to pay into a specially designated fund in the Library of Congress the total retail price of the copies or phonorecords demanded, or, if no retail price has been fixed, the reasonable cost to the Library of Congress of acquiring them; and

(3) to pay a fine of $2,500, in addition to any fine or liability imposed under clauses (1) and (2), if such person willfully or repeatedly fails or refuses to comply with such a demand.

(e) With respect to transmission programs that have been fixed and transmitted to the public in the United States but have not been published, the Register of Copyrights shall, after consulting with the Librarian of Congress and other interested organizations and officials, establish regulations governing the acquisition, through deposit or otherwise, of copies or phonorecords of such programs for the collections of the Library of Congress.

(1) The Librarian of Congress shall be permitted, under the standards and conditions set forth in such regulations, to make a fixation of a transmission program directly from a transmission to the public, and to reproduce one copy or phonorecord from such fixation for archival purposes.

(2) Such regulations shall also provide standards and procedures by which the Register of Copyrights may make written demand, upon the owner of the right of transmission in the United States, for the deposit of a copy or phonorecord of a specific transmission program. Such deposit may, at the option of the owner of the right of transmission in the United States, be accomplished by gift, by loan for purposes of reproduction, or by sale at a price not to exceed the cost of reproducing and supplying the copy or phonorecord. The regulations established under this clause shall provide reasonable periods of not less than three months for compliance

with a demand, and shall allow for extensions of such periods and adjustments in the scope of the demand or the methods for fulfilling it, as reasonably warranted by the circumstances. Willful failure or refusal to comply with the conditions prescribed by such regulations shall subject the owner of the right of transmission in the United States to liability for an amount, not to exceed the cost of reproducing and supplying the copy or phonorecord in question, to be paid into a specially designated fund in the Library of Congress.

(3) Nothing in this subsection shall be construed to require the making or retention, for purposes of deposit, of any copy or phonorecord of an unpublished transmission program, the transmission of which occurs before the receipt of a specific written demand as provided by clause (2).

(4) No activity undertaken in compliance with regulations prescribed under clauses (1) and (2) of this subsection shall result in liability if intended solely to assist in the acquisition of copies or phonorecords under this subsection.

Section 202.19 of title 37 of the CFR:

§ 202.19 Deposit of published copies or phonorecords for the Library of Congress.

(a) *General.* This section prescribes rules pertaining to the deposit of copies and phonorecords of published works for the Library of Congress under section 407 of title 17 of the United States Code, as amended by Pub. L. 94–553. The provisions of this section are not applicable to the deposit of copies and phonorecords for purposes of copyright registration under section 408 of title 17, except as expressly adopted in §202.20 of these regulations.

(b) *Definitions.* For the purposes of this section:

(1)

(i) The *best edition* of a work is the edition, published in the United States at any time before the date of deposit, that the Library of Congress determines to be most suitable for its purposes. The "best edition" requirement is described in detail at Appendix B to this part.

(ii) Criteria for selection of the "best edition" from among two or more published editions of the same version of the same work are set forth in the statement entitled "Best Edition of Published Copyrighted Works for the Collections of the Library of Congress" (hereafter referred to as the "Best Edition Statement") in effect at the time of deposit.

(iii) Where no specific criteria for the selection of the "best edition" are established in the Best Edition Statement, that edition which, in the judgment of the Library of Congress, represents the highest quality for its purposes shall be considered the "best edition." In such cases:

(A) When the Copyright Office is aware that two or more editions of a work have been published it will consult with other appropriate officials of the Library of Congress to obtain instructions as to the "best edition" and (except in cases for which special relief is granted) will require deposit of that edition; and

(B) When a potential depositor is uncertain which of two or more published editions comprises the "best edition," inquiry should be made to the Copyright Acquisitions Division.

(iv) Where differences between two or more "editions" of a work represent variations in copyrightable content, each edition is considered a separate version, and hence a different work, for the purpose of this section, and criteria of "best edition" based on such differences do not apply.

(2) A *complete* copy includes all elements comprising the unit of publication of the best edition of the work, including elements that, if considered separately, would not be copyrightable subject matter or would otherwise be exempt from mandatory deposit requirements under paragraph (c) of this section. In the case of sound recordings, a "complete" phonorecord includes the phonorecord, together with any printed or other visually perceptible material published with such phonorecord (such as textual or pictorial matter appearing on record sleeves or album covers, or embodied in leaflets or booklets included in a sleeve, album, or other container). In the case of a musical composition published in copies only, or in both copies and phonorecords:

(i) If the only publication of copies in the United States took place by the rental, lease, or lending of a full score and parts, a full score is a "complete" copy; and

(ii) If the only publication of copies in the United States took place by the rental, lease, or lending of a conductor's score and parts, a conductor's score is a "complete" copy.

In the case of a motion picture, a copy is "complete" if the reproduction of all of the visual and aural elements comprising the copyrightable subject matter in the work is clean, undamaged, undeteriorated, and free of splices, and if the copy itself and its physical housing are free of any defects that would interfere with the performance of the work or that would cause mechanical, visual, or audible defects or distortions.

(3) The terms *architectural works, copies, collective work, device, fixed, literary work, machine, motion picture, phonorecord, publication, sound recording, useful article*, and their variant forms, have the meanings given to them in 17 U.S.C. 101.

(c) *Exemptions from deposit requirements.* The following categories of material are exempt from the deposit requirements of section 407(a) of title 17:

(1) Diagrams and models illustrating scientific or technical works or formulating scientific or technical information in linear or three-dimensional form, such as an architectural or engineering blueprint, plan, or design, a mechanical drawing, or an anatomical model.

(2) Greeting cards, picture postcards, and stationery.

(3) Lectures, sermons, speeches, and addresses when published individually and not as a collection of the works of one or more authors.

(4) Literary, dramatic, and musical works published only as embodied in phonorecords. This category does not exempt the owner of copyright, or of the exclusive right of publication, in a sound recording resulting from the fixation of such works in a phonorecord from the applicable deposit requirements for the sound recording.

(5) Automated databases available only on-line in the United States. The exemption does not include the following: automated databases distributed in the form of machine-readable copies (such as magnetic tape or disks, CD-ROM formats, punch cards, or the like); computerized information works in the nature of statistical compendia, serials, and reference works; works published in a form requiring the use of a machine or device for purposes of optical enlargement (such as film, filmstrips, slide films and works published in any variety of microform); works published in visually perceptible form but used in connection with optical scanning devices; and works reproduced in CD-ROM formats.

(6) Three-dimensional sculptural works, and any works published only as reproduced in or on jewelry, dolls, toys, games, plaques, floor coverings, wallpaper and similar commercial wall coverings, textiles and other fabrics, packaging material, or any useful article. Globes, relief models, and similar cartographic representations of area are not within this category and are subject to the applicable deposit requirements.

(7) Prints, labels, and other advertising matter, including catalogs, published in connection with the rental lease, lending, licensing, or sale of articles of merchandise, works of authorship, or services.

(8) Tests, and answer material for tests when published separately from other literary works.

(9) Works first published as individual contributions to collective works. This category does not exempt the owner of copyright, or of the exclusive right of publication, in the collective work as a whole, from the applicable deposit requirements for the collective work.

(10) Works first published outside the United States and later published in the United States without change in copyrightable content, if:

(i) Registration for the work was made under 17 U.S.C. 408 before the work was published in the United States; or

(ii) Registration for the work was made under 17 U.S.C. 408 after the work was published in the United States but before a demand for deposit is made under 17 U.S.C. 407(d).

(11) Works published only as embodied in a soundtrack that is an integral part of a motion picture. This category does not exempt the owner of copyright, or of the exclusive right of publication, in the motion picture, from the applicable deposit requirements for the motion picture.

(12) Motion pictures that consist of television transmission programs and that have been published, if at all, only by reason of a license or other grant to a nonprofit institution of the right to make a fixation of such programs directly from a transmission to the public, with or without the right to make further uses of such fixations.

(d) *Nature of required deposit.*

(1) Subject to the provisions of paragraph (d)(2) of this section, the deposit required to satisfy the provisions of section 407(a) of title 17 shall consist of:

(i) In the case of published works other than sound recordings, two complete copies of the best edition; and

(ii) In the case of published sound recordings, two complete phonorecords of the best edition.

(2) In the case of certain published works not exempt from deposit requirements under paragraph (c) of this section, the following special provisions shall apply:

(i) In the case of published three-dimensional cartographic representations of area, such as globes and relief models, the deposit of one complete copy of the best edition of the work will suffice in lieu of the two copies required by paragraph (d)(1) of this section.

(ii) In the case of published motion pictures, the deposit of one complete copy of the best edition of the work will suffice in lieu of the two copies required by paragraph (d)(1) of this section. Any deposit of a published motion picture must be accompanied by a separate description of its contents, such as a continuity, pressbook, or synopsis. The Library of Congress may, at its sole discretion, enter into an agreement permitting the return of copies of published motion pictures to the depositor under certain conditions and establishing certain rights and obligations of the Library with respect to such copies. In the event of termination of such an agreement by the Library it shall not be subject to reinstatement, nor shall the depositor or any successor in interest of the depositor be entitled to any similar or subsequent agreement with the Library, unless at the sole discretion of the Library it would be in the best interests of the Library to reinstate the agreement or enter into a new agreement.

(iii) In the case of any published work deposited in the form of a hologram, the deposit shall be accompanied by:

(A) Two sets of precise instructions for displaying the image fixed in the hologram; and

(B) Two sets of identifying material in compliance with §202.21 of these regulations and clearly showing the displayed image.

(iv) In any case where an individual author is the owner of copyright in a published pictorial or graphic work and (A) less than five copies of the work have been published, or (B) the work has been published and sold or offered for sale in a limited edition consisting of no more than three hundred numbered copies, the deposit of one complete copy of the best edition of the work or, alternatively, the deposit of photographs or other identifying material in compliance with §202.21 of these regulations, will suffice in lieu of the two copies required by paragraph (d)(1) of this section.

(v) In the case of a musical composition published in copies only, or in both copies and phonorecords, if the only publication of copies in the United States took place by rental, lease, or lending, the deposit of one complete copy of the best edition will suffice in lieu of the two copies required by paragraph (d)(1) of this section.

(vi) In the case of published multimedia kits, that include literary works, audiovisual works, sound recordings, or any combination of such works, the deposit of one complete copy of the best edition will suffice in lieu of the two copies required by paragraph (d)(1) of this section.

(vii) In the case of published computer programs and published computerized information works, such as statistical compendia, serials, and reference works that are not copy-protected, the deposit of one complete copy of the best edition as specified in the current Library of Congress Best Edition Statement will suffice in lieu of the two copies required by paragraph (d)(1) of this section. If the works are copy-protected, two copies of the best edition are required.

(viii) In the case of published architectural works, the deposit shall consist of the most finished form of presentation drawings in the following descending order of preference:

(A) Original format, or best quality form of reproduction, including offset or silk screen printing;

(B) Xerographic or photographic copies on good quality paper;

(C) Positive photostat or photodirect positive;

(D) Blue line copies (diazo or ozalid process). If photographs are submitted, they should be 8×10 inches and should clearly show several exterior and interior views. The deposit should disclose the name(s) of the architect(s) and draftsperson(s) and the building site.

(e) *Special relief.*

(1) In the case of any published work not exempt from deposit under paragraph (c) of this section, the Register of Copyrights may, after consultation with other appropriate officials of the Library of Congress and upon such conditions as the Register may determine after such consultation:

(i) Grant an exemption from the deposit requirements of section 407(a) of title 17 on an individual basis for single works or series or groups of works; or

(ii) Permit the deposit of one copy or phonorecord, or alternative identifying material, in lieu of the two copies or phonorecords required by paragraph (d)(1) of this section; or

(iii) Permit the deposit of incomplete copies or phonorecords, or copies or phonorecords other than those normally comprising the best edition; or

(iv) Permit the deposit of identifying material which does not comply with §202.21 of these regulations.

(2) Any decision as to whether to grant such special relief, and the conditions under which special relief is to be granted, shall be made by the Register of Copyrights after consultation with other appropriate officials of the Library of Congress, and shall be based upon the acquisition policies of the Library of Congress then in force.

(3) Requests for special relief under this paragraph shall be made in writing to the Associate Register for Registration and Recordation Program, shall be signed by or on behalf of the owner of copyright or of the exclusive right of publication in the work, and shall set forth specific reasons why the request should be granted.

(4) The Register of Copyrights may, after consultation with other appropriate officials of the Library of Congress, terminate any ongoing or continuous grant of special relief. Notice of termination shall be given in writing and shall be sent to the individual person or organization to whom the grant of special relief had been given, at the last address shown in the records of the Copyright Office. A notice of termination may be given at any time, but it shall state a specific date of termination that is at least 30 days later than the date the notice is mailed. Termination shall not affect the validity of any deposit made earlier under the grant of special relief.

(f) *Submission and receipt of copies and phonorecords.*

(1) All copies and phonorecords deposited in the Copyright Office will be considered to be deposited only in compliance with section 407 of title 17 unless they are accompanied by an application for registration of a claim to copyright in the work represented by the deposit, and either a registration fee or a deposit account number on the application. Copies or phonorecords deposited without such an accompanying application and either a fee or a deposit account notation will not be connected with or held for receipt of separate applications, and will not satisfy the deposit provisions of section 408 of title 17 or §202.20 of these regulations.

(2) All copies and phonorecords deposited in the Copyright Office under section 407 of title 17, unless accompanied by written instructions to the contrary, will be considered to be deposited by the person or persons named in the copyright notice on the work.

(3) Upon request by the depositor made at the time of the deposit, the Copyright Office will issue a certificate of receipt for the deposit of copies or phonorecords of a work under this section. Certificates of receipt will be issued in response to requests made after the date of deposit only if the requesting party is identified in the records of the Copyright Office as having made the deposit. In either case, requests for a certificate of receipt must be in writing and accompanied by the appropriate fee, as required in §201.3(c). A certificate of receipt will include identification of the depositor, the work deposited, and the nature and format of the copy or phonorecord deposited, together with the date of receipt.

APPENDIX 18:
PRE-REGISTRATION

Excerpt from section 408 of the 1976 Act:

§ 408. Copyright registration in general

(f) PREREGISTRATION OF WORKS BEING PREPARED FOR COMMERCIAL DISTRIBUTION.—

(1) RULEMAKING.—Not later than 180 days after the date of enactment of this subsection, the Register of Copyrights shall issue regulations to establish procedures for preregistration of a work that is being prepared for commercial distribution and has not been published.

(2) CLASS OF WORKS.—The regulations established under paragraph (1) shall permit preregistration for any work that is in a class of works that the Register determines has had a history of infringement prior to authorized commercial distribution.

(3) APPLICATION FOR REGISTRATION.—Not later than 3 months after the first publication of a work preregistered under this subsection, the applicant shall submit to the Copyright Office–

(A) an application for registration of the work;

(B) a deposit; and

(C) the applicable fee.

(4) EFFECT OF UNTIMELY APPLICATION.—An action under this chapter for infringement of a work preregistered under this subsection, in a case in which the infringement commenced no later than 2 months after the first publication of the work, shall be dismissed if the items described in paragraph (3) are not submitted to the Copyright Office in proper form within the earlier of—

(A) 3 months after the first publication of the work; or

(B) 1 month after the copyright owner has learned of the infringement.

Section 202.16 of title 37 of the CFR:

§ 202.16 Preregistration of copyrights.

(a) *General.* This section prescribes rules pertaining to the preregistration of copyright claims in works eligible for preregistration under Section 408(f) of 17 U.S.C.

(b) *Definitions.* For the purposes of this section—

(1) A work is in a *class of works that the Register of Copyrights has determined has had a history of infringement prior to authorized commercial release* if it falls within one of the following classes of works:

(i) Motion pictures;

(ii) Sound recordings;

(iii) Musical compositions;

(iv) Literary works being prepared for publication in book form;

(v) Computer programs (including videogames); or

(vi) Advertising or marketing photographs.

(2) A work is *being prepared for commercial distribution* if:

(i) The claimant, in a statement certified by the authorized preregistering party, has a reasonable expectation that the work will be commercially distributed to the public; and

(ii) Preparation of the work has commenced and at least some portion of the work has been fixed in a tangible medium of expression, as follows:

(A) For a motion picture, filming of the motion picture must have commenced;

(B) For a sound recording, recording of the sounds must have commenced;

(C) For a musical composition, at least some of the musical composition must have been fixed either in the form of musical notation or in a copy or phonorecord embodying a performance of some or all of the work;

(D) For a literary work being prepared for publication in book form, the actual writing of the text of the work must have commenced;

(E) For a computer program, at least some of the computer code (either source code or object code) must have been fixed; and

(F) For an advertising or marketing photograph, the photograph (or, in the case of a group of photographs intended for simultaneous publication, at least one of the photographs) must have been taken.

(3) A work *eligible for preregistration* is a work that is:

(i) Unpublished;

(ii) Being prepared for commercial distribution; and

(iii) In a class of works that the Register of Copyrights has determined has had a history of infringement prior to authorized commercial release.

(c) *Preregistration—*

(1) *General.* A work eligible for preregistration may be preregistered by submitting an application and fee to the Copyright Office pursuant to the requirements set forth in this section.

(2) *Works excluded.* Works that are not copyrightable subject matter under title 17 of the U.S. Code may not be preregistered in the Copyright Office.

(3) *Application form.* An application for preregistration is made using Electronic Form PRE. The application must be submitted electronically on the Copyright Office website at: *http://www. copyright.gov.*

(4) *Preregistration as a single work.* For the purpose of preregistration on a single application and upon payment of a single preregistration fee, all copyrightable elements that are otherwise recognizable as self-contained works, that are to be included and first published in a single unit of publication, and in which the copyright claimant is the same, shall be considered a single work eligible for preregistration.

(5) *Fee—*

(i) *Amount.* The filing fee for preregistration is prescribed in §201.3(c).

(ii) *Method of payment*

(A) Copyright Office deposit account. The Copyright Office maintains a system of Deposit Accounts for the convenience of those who frequently use its services and for those who file applications electronically. The system allows an individual or firm to establish a Deposit Account in the Copyright Office and to make advance deposits in that account. Deposit Account holders can charge preregistration fees against the balance in their accounts instead of using credit cards for each request of service. For information on Deposit Accounts, please download a copy of Circular 5, "How to Open and Maintain a Deposit Account in the Copyright Office," or write the Register of Copyrights, Copyright Office, Library of Congress, Washington, D.C. 20559.

(B) Credit cards, debit cards and electronic funds transfer. The online preregistration filing system will provide options for payment by means of credit or debit cards and by means of electronic funds transfers. Applicants will be redirected to the Department of Treasury's Pay.gov website to make payments with credit or debit cards, or directly from their bank accounts by means of ACH debit transactions.

(C) No refunds. The preregistration filing fee is not refundable.

(6) *Description.* No deposit of the work being preregistered should be submitted with an application for preregistration. The preregistration applicant should submit a detailed description, of not more than 2,000 characters (approximately 330 words), of the work as part of the application. The description should be based on information available at the time of the application sufficient to reasonably identify the work. Generally, the Copyright Office will not review descriptions for adequacy, but in an action for infringement of a preregistered work, the court may evaluate the adequacy of the description to determine whether the preregistration actually describes the work that is alleged to be infringed, taking into account the information available to the applicant at the time of preregistration and taking into account the legitimate interest of the applicant in protecting confidential information.

(i) For motion pictures, such a description should include the following information to the extent known at the time of filing: the subject matter, a summary or outline, the director, the primary actors, the principal location of filming, and any other information that would assist in identifying the particular work being preregistered.

(ii) For sound recordings, the identifying description should include the following information to the extent known at the time of filing: the subject matter of the work or works recorded, the performer or performing group, the genre of the work recorded (e.g., classical, pop, musical comedy, soft rock, heavy metal, gospel, rap, hip-hop, blues, jazz), the titles of the musical compositions being recorded, the principal recording location, the composer(s) of the recorded musical compositions embodied on the sound recording, and any other information that would assist in identifying the particular work being preregistered.

(iii) For musical compositions, the identifying description should include the following information to the extent known at the time of filing: the subject matter of the lyrics, if any, the genre of the work (for example, classical, pop, musical comedy, soft rock, heavy metal, gospel, rap, hip-hop, blues, jazz), the performer, principal recording location, record label, motion picture, or other information relating to any sound recordings or motion pictures that are being prepared for commercial distribution and will include the musical composition, and any other detail or characteristic that may assist in identifying the particular musical composition.

(iv) For literary works in book form, the identifying description should include to the extent known at the time of filing: the genre of the book, e.g., biography, novel, history, etc., and should include a brief summary of the work including, the subject matter (e.g., a biography of President Bush, a history of the war in Iraq, a fantasy novel); a description (where applicable) of the plot, primary characters, events, or other key elements of the content of the work; and any other salient characteristics of the book, e.g., whether it is a later edition or revision of a previous work, as well as any other detail which may assist in identifying the literary work in book form.

(v) For computer programs (including videogames), the identifying description should include to the extent known at the time of filing, the nature, purpose and function of the computer program, including the programming language in which it is written, any particular organization or structure in which the program has been created; the form in which it is expected to be published, e.g. as an online-only product; whether there have been previous versions (and identification of such previous versions); the identities of persons involved in the creation of the computer program; and, if the work is a videogame, also describe the subject matter of the videogame and the overall object, goal or purpose of the game, its characters, if any, and the general setting and surrounding found in the game.

(vi) For advertising or marketing photographs, the description should include the subject matter depicted in the photograph or photographs, including information such as the particular product, event, public figure, or other item or occurrence which the photograph is intended to advertise or market. To the extent possible and applicable, the description for photographs should give additional details which will assist in identifying the particular photographs, such as the party for whom such advertising photographs are taken; the approximate time periods during which the photographs are taken; the approximate number of photos which may be included in the grouping; any events associated with the photographs; and the location and physical setting or surrounding depicted in the photographs. The description may also explain the general presentation, e.g., the lighting, background scenery, positioning of elements of the subject matter as it is seen in the photographs, and should provide any locations and events, if applicable, associated with the photographs.

(7) *Review of preregistration information.* The Copyright Office will conduct a limited review of applications for preregistration, in order to ascertain whether the application describes a work that is in a class of works that the Register of Copyrights has determined has had a history of infringement prior to authorized commercial release. However, a work will not be preregistered unless an applicant has provided all of the information requested on the application and has certified that all of the information provided on the application is correct to the best of the applicant's knowledge.

(8) *Certification.* The person submitting an application for preregistration must certify on the application that he or she is the author, copyright claimant, or owner of exclusive rights, or the authorized agent of the author, copyright claimant, or owner of exclusive rights, of the work submitted for this preregistration; that the information given in this application is correct to the best of his or her knowledge; that the work is being prepared for commercial distribution; and that he or she has a reasonable expectation that the work will be commercially distributed to the public.

(9) *Effective date of preregistration*. The effective date of a preregistration is the day on which an application and fee for preregistration of a work, which the Copyright Office later notifies the claimant has been preregistered or which a court of competent jurisdiction has concluded was acceptable for preregistration, have been received in the Copyright Office.

(10) *Notification of preregistration*. Upon completion of the preregistration, the Copyright Office will provide the claimant official notification by email of the preregistration.

(11) *Certification of preregistation*. A certified copy of the official notification may be obtained in physical form from the Records Research and Certification Section of the Information and Records Division at the address stated in §201.1(a)(3) of this chapter.

(12) *Public record of preregistration*. The preregistration record will also be available to the public on the Copyright Office website, *http://www.copyright.gov*.

(13) *Effect of preregistration*. Preregistration of a work offers certain advantages to a copyright owner pursuant to 17 U.S.C. 408(f), 411 and 412. However, preregistration of a work does not constitute prima facie evidence of the validity of the copyright or of the facts stated in the application for preregistration or in the preregistration record. The fact that a work has been preregistered does not create any presumption that the Copyright Office will register the work upon submission of an application for registration.

(14) *Petition for recognition of a new class of works*. At any time an interested party may petition the Register of Copyrights for a determination as to whether a particular class of works has had a history of copyright infringement prior to authorized release that would justify inclusion of that class of works among the classes of works eligible for preregistration.

APPENDIX 19:
DEFINITIONS RELATED TO
LITERARY WORKS

Excerpt from section 101 of the 1976 Act:

"Literary works" are works, other than audiovisual works, expressed in words, numbers, or other verbal or numerical symbols or indicia, regardless of the nature of the material objects, such as books, periodicals, manuscripts, phonorecords, film, tapes, disks, or cards, in which they are embodied.

A "computer program" is a set of statements or instructions to be used directly or indirectly in a computer in order to bring about a certain result.

APPENDIX 20:
DEFINITIONS RELATED TO VISUAL ART

Excerpt from section 101 of the 1976 Act:

"Pictorial, graphic, and sculptural works" include two-dimensional and three-dimensional works of fine, graphic, and applied art, photographs, prints and art reproductions, maps, globes, charts, diagrams, models, and technical drawings, including architectural plans. Such works shall include works of artistic craftsmanship insofar as their form but not their mechanical or utilitarian aspects are concerned; the design of a useful article, as defined in this section, shall be considered a pictorial, graphic, or sculptural work only if, and only to the extent that, such design incorporates pictorial, graphic, or sculptural features that can be identified separately from, and are capable of existing independently of, the utilitarian aspects of the article.

A "useful article" is an article having an intrinsic utilitarian function that is not merely to portray the appearance of the article or to convey information. An article that is normally a part of a useful article is considered a "useful article."

A "work of visual art" is—

(1) a painting, drawing, print or sculpture, existing in a single copy, in a limited edition of 200 copies or fewer that are signed and consecutively numbered by the author, or, in the case of a sculpture, in multiple cast, carved, or fabricated sculptures of 200 or fewer that are consecutively numbered by the author and bear the signature or other identifying mark of the author; or

(2) a still photographic image produced for exhibition purposes only, existing in a single copy that is signed by the author, or in a limited edition of 200 copies or fewer that are signed and consecutively numbered by the author.

A work of visual art does not include—

(A)(i) any poster, map, globe, chart, technical drawing, diagram, model, applied art, motion picture or other audiovisual work, book, magazine, newspaper, periodical, data base, electronic information service, electronic publication, or similar publication;

(ii) any merchandising item or advertising, promotional, descriptive, covering, or packaging material or container;

(iii) any portion or part of any item described in clause (i) or (ii);

(B) any work made for hire; or

(C) any work not subject to copyright protection under this title.

APPENDIX 21:
VISUAL ARTISTS RIGHTS ACT OF 1990

As set forth in section 106A of the 1976 Act:

§ 106A. Rights of certain authors to attribution and integrity

(a) RIGHTS OF ATTRIBUTION AND INTEGRITY.—Subject to section 107 and independent of the exclusive rights provided in section 106, the author of a work of visual art—

(1) shall have the right—

(A) to claim authorship of that work, and

(B) to prevent the use of his or her name as the author of any work of visual art which he or she did not create;

(2) shall have the right to prevent the use of his or her name as the author of the work of visual art in the event of a distortion, mutilation, or other modification of the work which would be prejudicial to his or her honor or reputation; and

(3) subject to the limitations set forth in section 113(d), shall have the right—

(A) to prevent any intentional distortion, mutilation, or other modification of that work which would be prejudicial to his or her honor or reputation, and any intentional distortion, mutilation, or modification of that work is a violation of that right, and

(B) to prevent any destruction of a work of recognized stature, and any intentional or grossly negligent destruction of that work is a violation of that right.

(b) SCOPE AND EXERCISE OF RIGHTS.—Only the author of a work of visual art has the rights conferred by subsection (a) in that work, whether or not the author is the copyright owner. The authors of a joint work of visual art are coowners of the rights conferred by subsection (a) in that work.

(c) Exceptions.—(1) The modification of a work of visual art which is the result of the passage of time or the inherent nature of the materials is not a distortion, mutilation, or other modification described in subsection (a)(3)(A).

(2) The modification of a work of visual art which is the result of conservation, or of the public presentation, including lighting and placement, of the work is not a destruction, distortion, mutilation, or other modification described in subsection (a)(3) unless the modification is caused by gross negligence.

(3) The rights described in paragraphs (1) and (2) of subsection (a) shall not apply to any reproduction, depiction, portrayal, or other use of a work in, upon, or in any connection with any item described in subparagraph (A) or (B) of the definition of "work of visual art" in section 101, and any such reproduction, depiction, portrayal, or other use of a work is not a destruction, distortion, mutilation, or other modification described in paragraph (3) of subsection (a).

(d) Duration of Rights.—(1) With respect to works of visual art created on or after the effective date set forth in section 610(a) of the Visual Artists Rights Act of 1990, the rights conferred by subsection (a) shall endure for a term consisting of the life of the author.

(2) With respect to works of visual art created before the effective date set forth in section 610(a) of the Visual Artists Rights Act of 1990, but title to which has not, as of such effective date, been transferred from the author, the rights conferred by subsection (a) shall be coextensive with, and shall expire at the same time as, the rights conferred by section 106.

(3) In the case of a joint work prepared by two or more authors, the rights conferred by subsection (a) shall endure for a term consisting of the life of the last surviving author.

(4) All terms of the rights conferred by subsection (a) run to the end of the calendar year in which they would otherwise expire.

(e) Transfer and Waiver.—(1) The rights conferred by subsection (a) may not be transferred, but those rights may be waived if the author expressly agrees to such waiver in a written instrument signed by the author. Such instrument shall specifically identify the work, and uses of that work, to which the waiver applies, and the waiver shall apply only to the work and uses so identified. In the case of a joint work prepared by two or more authors, a waiver of rights under this paragraph made by one such author waives such rights for all such authors.

(2) Ownership of the rights conferred by subsection (a) with respect to a work of visual art is distinct from ownership of any copy of that work, or of a copyright or any exclusive right under a copyright in that work. Transfer of ownership of any copy of a work of visual art, or of a copyright or any exclusive right under a copyright, shall not constitute a waiver of the rights conferred by subsection (a). Except as may otherwise be agreed by the author in a written instrument signed by the author, a waiver of the rights conferred by subsection (a) with respect to a work of visual art shall not constitute a transfer of ownership of any copy of that work, or of ownership of a copyright or of any exclusive right under a copyright in that work.

APPENDIX 22:
DEFINITIONS RELATED TO SOUND
RECORDINGS

Excerpt from section 101 of the 1976 Act:

"Sound recordings" are works that result from the fixation of a series of musical, spoken, or other sounds, but not including the sounds accompanying a motion picture or other audiovisual work, regardless of the nature of the material objects, such as disks, tapes, or other phonorecords, in which they are embodied.

"Phonorecords" are material objects in which sounds, other than those accompanying a motion picture or other audiovisual work, are fixed by any method now known or later developed, and from which the sounds can be perceived, reproduced, or otherwise communicated, either directly or with the aid of a machine or device. The term "phonorecords" includes the material object in which the sounds are first fixed.

APPENDIX 23:
REFUSAL OF REGISTRATION

Excerpt from section 410 of the 1976 Act:

§ 410. **Registration of claim and issuance of certificate**

(b) In any case in which the Register of Copyrights determines that, in accordance with the provisions of this title, the material deposited does not constitute copyrightable subject matter or that the claim is invalid for any other reason, the Register shall refuse registration and shall notify the applicant in writing of the reasons for such refusal.

Section 202.5 of title 37 of the CFR:

§ 202.5 **Reconsideration Procedure for Refusals to Register.**

(a) *General.* This section prescribes rules pertaining to procedures for administrative review of the Copyright Office's refusal to register a claim to copyright, a mask work, or a vessel hull design upon a finding by the Office that the application for registration does not satisfy the legal requirements of title 17 of the United States Code. If an applicant's initial claim is refused, the applicant is entitled to request that the initial refusal to register be reconsidered.

(b) *First reconsideration.* Upon receiving a written notification from the Registration and Recordation Program explaining the reasons for a refusal to register, an applicant may request that the Registration and Recordation Program reconsider its initial decision to refuse registration, subject to the following requirements:

(1) An applicant must request in writing that the Registration and Recordation Program reconsider its decision. A request for reconsideration must include the reasons the applicant believes registration was improperly refused, including any legal arguments in

support of those reasons and any supplementary information. The Registration and Recordation Program will base its decision on the applicant's written submissions.

(2) The fee set forth in §201.3(d)(3)(i) of this chapter must accompany the first request for reconsideration.

(3) The first request for reconsideration and the applicable fee must be received by the Copyright Office no later than three months from the date that appears in the Registration and Recordation Program written notice of its initial decision to refuse registration. When the ending date for the three-month time period falls on a weekend or a Federal holiday, the ending day of the three-month period shall be extended to the next Federal work day.

(4) If the Registration and Recordation Program decides to register an applicant's work in response to the first request for reconsideration, it will notify the applicant in writing of the decision and the work will be registered. However, if the Registration and Recordation Program again refuses to register the work, it will send the applicant a written notification stating the reasons for refusal within four months of the date on which the first request for reconsideration is received by the Registration and Recordation Program. When the ending date for the four-month time period falls on a weekend or a Federal holiday, the ending day of the four-month period shall be extended to the next Federal work day. Failure by the Registration and Recordation Program to send the written notification within the four-month period shall not result in registration of the applicant's work.

(c) *Second reconsideration.* Upon receiving written notification of the Registration and Recordation Program's decision to refuse registration in response to the first request for reconsideration, an applicant may request that the Review Board reconsider the Registration and Recordation Program's refusal to register, subject to the following requirements:

(1) An applicant must request in writing that the Review Board reconsider the Registration and Recordation Program's decision to refuse registration. The second request for reconsideration must include the reasons the applicant believes registration was improperly refused, including any legal arguments in support of those reasons and any supplementary information, and must address the reasons stated by the Registration and Recordation Program for refusing registration upon first reconsideration. The Board will base its decision on the applicant's written submissions.

(2) The fee set forth in §201.3(d)(3)(ii) of this chapter must accompany the second request for reconsideration.

(3) The second request for reconsideration and the applicable fee must be received in the Copyright Office no later than three months from the date that appears in the Registration and Recordation Program's written notice of its decision to refuse registration after the first request for reconsideration. When the ending date for the three-month time period falls on a weekend or a Federal holiday, the ending day of the three-month period shall be extended to the next Federal work day.

(4) If the Review Board decides to register an applicant's work in response to a second request for reconsideration, it will notify the applicant in writing of the decision and the work will be registered. If the Review Board upholds the refusal to register the work, it will send the applicant a written notification stating the reasons for refusal.

(d) *Submission of reconsiderations.*

(1) All mail, including any that is hand delivered, should be addressed as follows: RECONSIDERATION, Copyright RAC Division, P.O. Box 71380, Washington, DC 20024–1380. If hand delivered by a commercial, non-government courier or messenger, a request for reconsideration must be delivered between 8:30 a.m. and 4 p.m. to: Congressional Courier Acceptance Site, located at Second and D Streets, NE., Washington, DC. If hand delivered by a private party, a request for reconsideration must be delivered between 8:30 a.m. and 5 p.m. to: Room 401 of the James Madison Memorial Building, located at 101 Independence Avenue, SE., Washington, DC.

(2) The first page of the written request must contain the Copyright Office control number and clearly indicate either "FIRST RECONSIDERATION" or "SECOND RECONSIDERATION," as appropriate, on the subject line.

(e) *Suspension or wavier of time requirements.* For any particular request for reconsideration, the provisions relating to the time requirements for submitting a request under this section may be suspended or waived, in whole or in part, by the Register of Copyrights upon a showing of good cause. Such suspension or waiver shall apply only to the request at issue and shall not be relevant with respect to any other request for reconsideration from that applicant or any other applicant.

(f) *Composition of the Review Board.* The Review Board shall consist of three members; the first two members are the Register of Copyrights and the General Counsel or their respective designees. The third member will be designated by the Register.

(g) *Final agency action.* A decision by the Review Board in response to a second request for reconsideration constitutes final agency action.

APPENDIX 24:
FORM CA FOR THE CORRECTION OF
A REGISTRATION

 Form CA

Detach and read these instructions before completing this form.
Make sure all applicable spaces have been filled in before you return this form.

BASIC INFORMATION

Use Form CA When:
- An earlier registration has been completed in the Copyright Office; and
- Some of the facts given in that registration are incorrect or incomplete; and
- You want to place the correct or complete facts on record.

Purpose of Supplementary Copyright Registration: As a rule, only one basic copyright registration can be made for the same work. To take care of cases where information in the basic registration turns out to be incorrect or incomplete, section 408(d) of the copyright law provides for "the filing of an application for supplementary registration, to correct an error in a copyright registration or to amplify the information given in a registration."

Who May File: Once basic registration has been made for a work, any author or other copyright claimant or owner of any exclusive right in the work or the duly authorized agent of any such author, other claimant, or owner who wishes to correct or amplify the information given in the basic registration may submit Form CA.

Please Note: Do not use Form CA to correct errors in statements on the copies or phonorecords of the work in question or to reflect changes in the content of the work. If the work has been changed substantially, filing a form CA is not appropriate and you should consider making an entirely new registration for the revised version to cover the additions or revisions. Do not use Form CA as a substitute for renewal registration. Renewal of copyright cannot be accomplished by using Form CA. For information on renewal of copyright, request Circular 15, *Renewal of Copyright*, from the Copyright Office. Do not use Form CA to correct an error regarding publication when the work was registered as an unpublished work.

Do not use Form CA as a substitute for recording a transfer of copyright or other document pertaining to rights under a copyright. Recording a document under section 205 of the statute gives all persons

Third: Complete all applicable spaces on the form following the line-by-line instructions on the back of this page. Use a typewriter or print the information in black ink.

Fourth: Detach this sheet and send your completed Form CA along with a *photocopy* of the front and back of the certificate of registration being amended to:

> *Library of Congress*
> *Copyright Office*
> *101 Independence Avenue SE*
> *Washington, DC 20559-6000*

Do not send copies, phonorecords, or supporting documents other than the photocopied certificate with your application. They cannot be made part of the record of a supplementary registration.

Fee: Unless you have a deposit account in the Copyright Office, your application must be accompanied by a nonrefundable filing fee in the form of a check or money order payable to *Register of Copyrights*. If you use a deposit account, give the account name and number on the form.

*Note: Copyright Office fees are subject to change. For current fees, check the Copyright Office website at *www.copyright.gov*, write the Copyright Office, or call (202) 707-3000.

What Happens When a Supplementary Registration Is Made? When a supplementary registration is completed, the Copyright Office will assign it a new registration number in the appropriate registration category and will issue a certificate of supplementary registration under that number. The basic registration will not be cancelled. The two registrations will stand in the Copyright Office records. The supplementary registration will have the effect of calling the public's attention to a possible error or omission in the basic registration and of placing the correct facts or the additional information on official record.

constructive notice of the facts stated in the document and may have other important consequences in cases of infringement or conflicting transfers. Supplementary registration does not have that legal effect. For information on recording a document, request Circular 12, *Recordation of Transfers and Other Documents*, from the Copyright Office. To record a document in the Copyright Office, request the Document Cover Sheet.

How to Apply for Supplementary Registration

First: Study the information on this page to make sure that filing an application on Form CA is the best procedure to follow in your case.

Second: Read the back of this page for specific instructions on filling out Form CA. Before starting to complete the form, make sure that you have all the necessary detailed information from the certificate of the basic registration.

For Further Information

- **Internet:** Circulars, application forms, announcements, and other related materials are available at *www.copyright.gov*

- **Telephone:** For general information about copyright, call the Public Information Office at (202) 707-3000 (TTY (202) 707-6737). Staff members are on duty from 8:30 a.m through 5:00 p.m., eastern time, Monday through Friday, except federal holidays. Recorded information is available 24 hours a day. If you know which application forms and circulars you want, call the Forms and Publications Hotline at (202) 707-9100 24 hours a day.

- **Regular Mail:** Write to:
  Library of Congress
  Copyright Office
  Public Information Office
  101 Independence Avenue SE
  Washington, DC 20559-6000

LINE-BY-LINE INSTRUCTIONS

Please type or print neatly using black ink. The certificate of registration is created by copying your CA application form.

SPACE A: Identification of Basic Registration

General Instructions: The information in this part identifies the basic registration that will be corrected or amplified. Even if the purpose of filing Form CA is to change one of these items, each item must agree exactly with the information as it already appears in the basic registration, that is, as it appears in the registration you wish to correct. Do not give any new information in this part.

Title of Work: Give the title as it appears in the basic registration.

Registration Number: Give the registration number (the series of numbers preceded by one or more letters) that appears in the upper right-hand corner of the certificate of registration. Give only one basic registration number since one CA form may correct or amend only one basic registration.

Registration Date: Give the year when the basic registration was completed.

Name(s) of Author(s) and Copyright Claimant(s): Give all the names as they appear in the basic registration.

SPACE B: Correction

General Instructions: Complete this part *only* if information in the basic registration *was incorrect at the time that basic registration was made.* Leave this part blank and complete Part C instead if your purpose is to add, update, or clarify information rather than to rectify an actual error.

Location and Nature of Incorrect Information: Give the line number and the heading or description of the space in the basic registration where the error occurs. Example: Line number 2...Citizenship of author.

Incorrect Information as It Appears in Basic Registration: Transcribe the incorrect statement exactly as it appears in the basic registration, even if you have already given this information in Part A.

Corrected Information: Give the statement as it should have appeared in the application of the basic registration.

Explanation of Correction: You may need to add an explanation to clarify this correction.

SPACE C: Amplification

General Instructions: Complete this part if you want to provide any of the following: (1) information that was omitted at the time of basic registration; (2) changes in facts other than ownership but including changes such as title or address of claimant that have occurred since the basic registration; or (3) explanations clarifying information in the basic registration.

Location and Nature of Information to Be Amplified: Give the line number and the heading or description of the space in the basic registration where the information to be amplified appears.

Amplified Information: Give a statement of the additional, updated, or explanatory information as clearly and succinctly as possible. You should add an explanation of the amplification if it is necessary.

SPACES D,E,F,G: Continuation, Fee, Certification, Return Address

Continuation (Part D): Use this space if you do not have enough room in Parts B or C.

Deposit Account and Mailing Instructions (Part E): If you maintain a Deposit Account in the Copyright Office, identify it in Part E. Otherwise, send the nonrefundable filing fee with your form. The space headed "Correspondence" should contain the name, address, telephone number with area code, and fax and email numbers, if available, of the person to be consulted if correspondence about the form becomes necessary.

Certification (Part F): The application is not acceptable unless it bears the handwritten signature of the author, or other copyright claimant, or of the owner of exclusive right(s), or of the duly authorized agent of such author, claimant, or owner.

Address for Return of Certificate (Part G): The address box must be completed legibly, since a reproduced image of that space will appear in the window of the mailing envelope.

Copyright Office fees are subject to change. For current fees, check the Copyright Office website at www.copyright.gov, write the Copyright Office, or call (202) 707-3000.

Form CA
For Supplementary Registration
UNITED STATES COPYRIGHT OFFICE

REGISTRATION NUMBER

TX	TXU	PA	PAU	VA	VAU	SR	SRU	RE

EFFECTIVE DATE OF SUPPLEMENTARY REGISTRATION

Month   Day   Year

DO NOT WRITE ABOVE THIS LINE. IF YOU NEED MORE SPACE, USE A SEPARATE CONTINUATION SHEET.

A

Title of Work ▼

Registration Number of the Basic Registration ▼

Year of Basic Registration ▼

Name(s) of Author(s) ▼

Name(s) of Copyright Claimant(s) ▼

B

Location and Nature of Incorrect Information in Basic Registration ▼

Line Number _____ Line Heading or Description _____

Incorrect Information as It Appears in Basic Registration ▼

Corrected Information ▼

Explanation of Correction ▼

C

Location and Nature of Information in Basic Registration to be Amplified ▼

Line Number _____ Line Heading or Description _____

Amplified Information and Explanation of Information ▼

MORE ON BACK ▶   · Complete all applicable spaces (D-G) on the reverse side of this page.
· See detailed instructions.   · Sign the form at Space F.

DO NOT WRITE HERE

Page 1 of _____ pages

FORM CA RECEIVED	FORM CA
FUNDS RECEIVED DATE	
EXAMINED BY	FOR COPYRIGHT OFFICE USE ONLY
CORRESPONDENCE ❏	
REFERENCE TO THIS REGISTRATION ADDED TO BASIC REGISTRATION ❏ YES ❏ NO	

DO NOT WRITE ABOVE THIS LINE. IF YOU NEED MORE SPACE, USE A SEPARATE CONTINUATION SHEET.

Continuation of: ❏ Part B *or* ❏ Part C

Correspondence: Give name and address to which correspondence about this application should be sent.

Phone (_____) _____ Fax (_____) _____ Email _____

Deposit Account: If the registration fee is to be charged to a Deposit Account established in the Copyright Office, give name and number of Account.

Name _____

Account Number _____

Certification* I, the undersigned, hereby certify that I am the: (Check only one)

❏ author　　❏ owner of exclusive right(s)

❏ other copyright claimant　❏ duly authorized agent of _____

　　　　　　　　　　　　　Name of author or other copyright claimant, or owner of exclusive right(s) ▲

of the work identified in this application and that the statements made by me in this application are correct to the best of my knowledge.

Typed or printed name ▼ _____　　Date ▼ _____

Handwritten signature (X) ▼

Certificate will be mailed in window envelope to this address:	Name ▼	YOU MUST: • Complete all necessary spaces • Sign your application in Space F
	Number/Street/Apt ▼	SEND ALL ELEMENTS IN THE SAME PACKAGE: 1. Application form 2. Nonrefundable filing fee in check or money order payable to *Register of Copyrights*
	City/State/ZIP ▼	MAIL TO: Library of Congress Copyright Office 101 Independence Avenue SE Washington, DC 20559-6000

* 17 *USC* §506(e): Any person who knowingly makes a false representation of a material fact in the application for copyright registration provided for by section 409, or in any written statement filed in connection with the application, shall be fined not more than $2,500.

Form CA–Full　Rev: 07/2006　Print: 07/2006—··,000　Printed on recycled paper　　　　　U.S. Government Printing Office: 2006·······/··.···

APPENDIX 25:
RENEWAL TERMS

Excerpt from section 304 of the 1976 Act:

§ 304. Duration of copyright: Subsisting copyrights

(a) COPYRIGHTS IN THEIR FIRST TERM ON JANUARY 1, 1978.—

(1)(A) Any copyright, in the first term of which is subsisting on January 1, 1978, shall endure for 28 years from the date it was originally secured.

(B) In the case of—

(i) any posthumous work or of any periodical, cyclopedic, or other composite work upon which the copyright was originally secured by the proprietor thereof, or

(ii) any work copyrighted by a corporate body (otherwise than as assignee or licensee of the individual author) or by an employer for whom such work is made for hire,

the proprietor of such copyright shall be entitled to a renewal and extension of the copyright in such work for the further term of 67 years.

(C) In the case of any other copyrighted work, including a contribution by an individual author to a periodical or to a cyclopedic or other composite work—

(i) the author of such work, if the author is still living,

(ii) the widow, widower, or children of the author, if the author is not living,

(iii) the author's executors, if such author, widow, widower, or children are not living, or

(iv) the author's next of kin, in the absence of a will of the author, shall be entitled to a renewal and extension of the copyright in such work for a further term of 67 years.

(2)(A) At the expiration of the original term of copyright in a work specified in paragraph (1)(B) of this subsection, the copyright shall endure for a renewed and extended further term of 67 years, which—

(i) if an application to register a claim to such further term has been made to the Copyright Office within 1 year before the expiration of the original term of copyright, and the claim is registered, shall vest, upon the beginning of such further term, in the proprietor of the copyright who is entitled to claim the renewal of copyright at the time the application is made; or

(ii) if no such application is made or the claim pursuant to such application is not registered, shall vest, upon the beginning of such further term, in the person or entity that was the proprietor of the copyright as of the last day of the original term of copyright.

(B) At the expiration of the original term of copyright in a work specified in paragraph (1)(C) of this subsection, the copyright shall endure for a renewed and extended further term of 67 years, which—

(i) if an application to register a claim to such further term has been made to the Copyright Office within 1 year before the expiration of the original term of copyright, and the claim is registered, shall vest, upon the beginning of such further term, in any person who is entitled under paragraph (1)(C) to the renewal and extension of the copyright at the time the application is made; or

(ii) if no such application is made or the claim pursuant to such application is not registered, shall vest, upon the beginning of such further term, in any person entitled under paragraph (1)(C), as of the last day of the original term of copyright, to the renewal and extension of the copyright.

(3)(A) An application to register a claim to the renewed and extended term of copyright in a work may be made to the Copyright Office—

(i) within 1 year before the expiration of the original term of copyright by any person entitled under paragraph (1)(B) or (C) to such further term of 67 years; and

(ii) at any time during the renewed and extended term by any person in whom such further term vested, under paragraph (2)(A) or (B), or by any successor or assign of such person, if the application is made in the name of such person.

(B) Such an application is not a condition of the renewal and extension of the copyright in a work for a further term of 67 years.

(4)(A) If an application to register a claim to the renewed and extended term of copyright in a work is not made within 1 year before the expiration of the original term of copyright in a work, or if the claim pursuant to such application is not registered, then a derivative work prepared under authority of a grant of a transfer or license of the copyright that is made before the expiration of the original term of copyright may continue to be used under the terms of the grant during the renewed and extended term of copyright without infringing the copyright, except that such use does not extend to the preparation during such renewed and extended term of other derivative works based upon the copyrighted work covered by such grant.

(B) If an application to register a claim to the renewed and extended term of copyright in a work is made within 1 year before its expiration, and the claim is registered, the certificate of such registration shall constitute prima facie evidence as to the validity of the copyright during its renewed and extended term and of the facts stated in the certificate. The evidentiary weight to be accorded the certificates of a registration of a renewed and extended term of copyright made after the end of that 1-year period shall be within the discretion of the court.

APPENDIX 26:
FORM RE FOR THE RENEWAL OF COPYRIGHT

Instructions for Form RE

Read these instructions before completing the application.

- ► **Use this form** for works published or registered from January 1, 1964, through December 31, 1977.
- ► **Do not use this form** for works published or registered before January 1, 1964, or after December 31, 1977.

    See circular 15, *Renewal of Copyright*, and Code of Federal Regulations (37 CFR 202.17), *Registration of Claims to Copyright—Renewals*, for more detailed information.

    All Copyright Office forms and circulars are available at *www.copyright.gov*.

How to complete this form

Use a black pen or type information.

Leave blank any question that does not apply to your copyright claim.

Use *Continuation Form RE/CON* to add the names of authors or statutory claimants if there are more than four, or if you need additional space for titles.

Complete a *Form RE/Addendum* in addition to a Form RE if the work, or the collective work in which it was first published, was not registered during the original term of copyright.

To obtain additional forms

Visit the Copyright Office website at *www.copyright.gov* and click on Forms under Publications. Scroll down to Renewals and select the appropriate forms. Or call the Copyright Office Forms Hotline at (202) 707-9100 and request Form RE and instructions. Also, request Form RE/CON and/or Form RE/Addendum, if necessary.

What to send

1 · **Forms** · Form RE (completed and signed) and Form RE/CON (if any) if the work was registered during the original term. If the work, or the collective work in which it was first published, was not registered during the original term, send Form RE and Form RE/Addendum.

2 · **Filing fee(s)** · Each Form RE (including RE/CON) requires a fee of $75. The Form RE/Addendum requires a separate fee of $220. If you send a Form RE and a Form RE/Addendum, the combined fee for both forms is $295. Send a check or money order made payable

to Register of Copyrights for the entire amount. If you are filing from outside the United States your check or money order must be redeemable in U.S. dollars without a service or exchange fee. If you are sending multiple renewal claims together, you may send a single check or money order for the entire amount due. Or, if you have a deposit account with the Copyright Office, give the account number in Section 5.

3 · **Deposit** · A deposit copy must accompany a Form RE/Addendum. For deposit copy requirements, see instructions for Form RE/Addendum. EXCEPTION: *A deposit copy is not required when the sole purpose of the Form RE/Addendum is to establish eligibility of a contribution to a work that was registered during its original term.*

Where to send your application

Mail the signed application, fee(s), and deposit copy (if any) in the same package to:

Library of Congress
U.S. Copyright Office-RE
101 Independence Avenue SE
Washington, DC 20559-6239

If your package includes a deposit copy that is electronic in nature, use a box rather than an envelope for mailing to the Copyright Office to avoid damage from Library security measures.

Questions about completing the application?

The instructions will guide you; however, copyright specialists are available in the Public Information Office between 8:00 AM and

FORM RE FOR THE RENEWAL OF COPYRIGHT

5:00 PM Monday–Friday, eastern time, except federal holidays, and can be reached by phone at (202) 707-5959. You may also send an email message directly from the website at www.copyright.gov.

Line-by-Line Instructions

Section 1 · Title and Original Term Information

1a · Title of work as first published or registered · Give the title (or an identifying phrase that could serve as a title) as it was given in the original registration (or in the published edition, if the work was never registered). If the complete title will not fit, give the remainder in space B on Form RE/CON. If the work is a periodical, give the volume, number, issue date, and ISSN, if any. If the work is a contribution to a periodical or other collective work, give the title of the contribution. If the work is an episode in a series, give the episode title and complete line c to give title information about the series.

1b · Alternative title · Complete line 1b only if the work was published under a different title than the one given in the original registration. Do not include contents titles here.

1c · If first published as a contribution to a periodical or other collective work · If the work was first published as a contribution to a periodical or other collective work, give the title of the periodical or other collective work on this line and the volume, number, issue date, and ISSN, if any. NOTE: *If the claim is in a contribution by a U.S. author to an English-language periodical or literary work first published abroad, a Form RE/Addendum is required to establish eligibility for registration of the contribution.*

1d · Has this work (or the work in which it was first published, if a contribution) ever been registered? · If the work (or the work in which the contribution or material was first published) was registered during its original term of copyright, check "yes," and give the registration number. If the work (or the work in which the contribution or material was first published) was not registered, check "no" and complete a Form RE/Addendum to provide information about the original copyright term and eligibility for registration. NOTE: *If you do not know whether the work (or the work in which the contribution or material was first registered, you may either conduct a search of our records here at the Copyright Office in Washington, DC, or request the Copyright Office to do the search for you. Information about requesting a search can be found in Circular 22. See also note in 1c above.*

1e · Publication or registration date · Give the complete date of first publication (month/day/year). Or, if the work was registered prior to its publication as an unpublished work, give the date of registration. If the work was registered as an unpublished work, give the latest date stamped in the lower left corner of the second page of the original certificate of registration. NOTE: *Under the 1909 Copyright Law, statutory copyright protection was secured on the date of first publication, provided the work was published with the required copyright notice, or on the date of registration, if the work was registered prior to its publication.*

1f · Year given in copyright notice, if earlier than publication · If the year in the copyright notice in the published edition is earlier than the year of publication, give the earlier year in the notice. If there are multiple years in the copyright notice, list all of them.

NOTE: *Generally, the original and renewal copyright terms are calculated from the year in the copyright notice, if it is earlier than the year of publication. If an International Standard Book Number was assigned to the work, give the number.*

1g · Original copyright claimant(s) · Give the name(s) of the copyright claimant(s) as identified in the original registration or in the copyright notice on the published edition, if the work was not registered during the original term. If there were multiple claimants, separate the names with commas. If you need more space, use space C of Form RE/CON.

1h · If the work was originally registered in Class Ai or Bi, was a U.S. edition registered? · Answer this question only if the renewal claim is based on an *ad interim* registration (Ai or Bi classes). NOTE: *Ad interim copyright was a short-term U.S. copyright available to nondramatic English-language books and periodicals that were manufactured and first published abroad prior to 1978. It was secured by registration within six months of first publication abroad and lasted for a maximum of five years from publication. If a U.S. edition was manufactured and published in the U.S. with the required copyright notice before the ad interim copyright expired, full-term protection was secured. If ad interim copyright was incapable of subsisting on December 31, 1977, the work may be eligible for renewal registration even if copies were not manufactured and published in the U.S. within five years of publication abroad. Also, if a work was manufactured and published in the U.S. within five years of publication abroad, but the U.S. edition was not registered, renewal registration may be possible for both editions. For more information about ad interim copyright, see Circular 15.*

1i · If the original registration record was corrected or amplified by supplementary registration on Form CA · Complete this line only if a supplementary registration was made during the original term of copyright to correct or amplify the information in the original registration record. Give the registration number and effective date of the supplementary registration.

Section 2 · Work or Material Claimed and Author Information

2a · Copyright for the renewal term is claimed in · Check only one option. Check option 1 if the renewal claim covers the entire work as originally registered or first published. Check option 2 if the claim is in a contribution first published in a periodical or other collective work. Check option 3 if the claim covers only the revisions in a previously registered or published edition of the work (such as a new musical arrangement or revised text), or option 4 if the claim is limited to a separate element of authorship created by an author (such as illustrations or photographs in a literary work). NOTE: *Option 4 does not apply to joint works (such as songs) or to works incorporating elements of authorship that are integral to the work as a whole (such as motion pictures).* Or check option 5 if the renewal claim is based on the first publication of a work that was registered as an unpublished work (such as a song or other musical or dramatic work).

2b · The following author(s) contributed to the material claimed · Name only the author(s) who contributed to the work or the material claimed in line 2a. Examples: If you checked option 1, name all authors identified in the original registration or in the published edition. If the original registration did not name an author (as in

Understanding Copyright Law: A Beginner's Guide

the case of periodicals), give the name of the author at the time of creation. If you checked option 2, name the author(s) of the contribution. If you checked options 3 or 4, name only the author(s) of the material added to the derivative work or the separate element of authorship. If you checked option 5, name the author(s) of the original work; do not name the author(s) of any material added to the published work. If there are more than 4 authors, use space D of Form RE/CON.

Name · If the author is an individual, give the name as it appears in the original registration, or in the published edition, as well as the pseudonym, if given in the original registration or published edition. If the author is an organization, give the name as it appeared in the original registration or the complete legal name of the organization at the time the work was created, if the work was not registered during the original term.

This author created · Complete this line if the original registration gave an authorship statement for the author, or if the work was not registered during the original term. NOTE: *Do not give terms that are not subject to copyright protection, such as idea, process, concept, title, or name.*

Date of death · Give the date of death for any author who is deceased. If you do not know the complete date of death, you may give a partial date such as the month and year, or only the year.

Section 3 · Renewal Term Ownership Information

Please read the following paragraphs before attempting to complete this section of the application.

Information about who is entitled by law to claim copyright for the renewal term. Section 304 of the current law states that, if a renewal registration is not made in the Copyright Office before the expiration of the original term of copyright, copyright for the renewal term vests automatically in the person or entity entitled to claim that right on the last day of the original term of copyright, that is, on December 31st of the 28th year following publication or registration as an unpublished work. Generally, the individual author is so entitled, if still alive on that date. When the author dies during the original term, the law prescribes that the following persons are entitled to claim copyright for the renewal term in this order:

1 the *widow(er)* and/or surviving *child(ren)*;

2 the *executor* named in the author's will, if there is no widow(er) or surviving child;

3 a person recognized by state law as the *next of kin of the author*, provided there was no widow(er) or surviving child, and the author died intestate.

NOTE: *Based on case law, if the author's will failed to name an executor, or if the executor died or was no longer acting in that capacity at the time of registration, a court-appointed administrator may claim on behalf of the legatees.*

For certain types of works, such as composite and posthumous works and works made for hire, the law provides that *the copyright proprietor* on the last day of the original term of copyright may claim copyright for the renewal term.

All of these parties—the author, the deceased author's heirs, the proprietor—are known as *statutory claimants*. NOTE: *Copyright cannot vest in a deceased person or a defunct organization. To be named as a statutory claimant, an individual must be alive or, in the case of an organization, still be in existence at the time of registration.*

The law also states that an *assignee* or a *successor* of a statutory claimant in whom the renewal copyright vested may submit an application for the renewal term, *provided* a claim has not been registered already in the name of the statutory claimant. For example, if the statutory claimant assigned the copyright for the renewal term, but did not register a claim to copyright for the renewal term, the assignee may submit the application. Likewise, if a statutory claimant dies before registering a renewal claim, the successor under the will of the statutory claimant in whom the renewal copyright vested may submit an application. NOTE: *Such registrations must identify the statutory claimant in whom the renewal copyright vested, as well as the assignee or successor. For more information about who may submit an application for the renewal copyright, see 37 CFR 202.17.*

3a · *Name the party or parties* · Name the party or parties so entitled. Do not include any statutory claimants you do not represent, or on whose behalf renewal claims have already been registered. Use space E of Form RE/CON if there are more than four statutory claimants. NOTE: *To calculate when the original term ended, add 28 years to the year of publication or registration from space 1e. Or, if the work was published with an earlier year date in the copyright notice, add 28 years to the year given in space 1f.*

As the · Give the basis of the claim for each statutory claimant. For example, if the individual author created the work in his or her personal capacity, the statutory claimant may claim as the "author," the "widow(er) or child of the deceased author," the "executor of the deceased author" or the "next of kin of the deceased author, there being no will." (If a court-appointed administrator was acting in the capacity of an executor on that date, the administrator may claim as the "administrator c.t.a. (or d.b.n.c.t.a.) of the deceased author.") If more than one author is named in section 2, specify which author is deceased; for example, "widow of the deceased author, Benjamin Bracket." If the work is a posthumous or composite work, or if it was created as a "work made for hire," the statutory claimant may claim as "proprietor of copyright in a work made for hire (or in a posthumous or composite work.)" NOTE: *For a work to be "posthumous" for renewal registration purposes, it had to be unpublished at the time of the author's death, with no assignment of copyright or other exploitation having occurred during the author's lifetime. A separate written statement to this effect must accompany a renewal claim in a posthumous work.*

Address · Give the current and complete address of each statutory claimant, or give the year of death, if the statutory claimant is an individual who died after the renewal copyright vested. If the address is an "in care of" address, include the name of the addressee (representative). If you do not know the address of a claimant, do not name that claimant.

3b · *This application is submitted by or on behalf of the* · Check only one option. If the party submitting the application is, or represents, the statutory claimant(s) named in line 3a, check option 1 and go on to section 4. Or, if the party submitting the application is, or represents, the assignee or successor of the statutory claimant named in line 3a check option 2. In this case, complete 3c.

3c · *Information about the assignee/successor* · Give the name and address of the assignee or successor and designate the means of transfer. NOTE: *An assignee or successor may submit an application only if a claim in the name of the statutory claimant has not already been registered.*

Section 4 · Certification

The applicant must certify that he or she is, or represents, the statutory claimant(s) or the assignee/successor, and that the information given on the application is accurate.

Section 5 · Payment, Correspondence, and Mailing Information

By completing the deposit account information, the applicant authorizes the Copyright Office to deduct the required fee(s) from the deposit account. Otherwise, a check or money order must accompany the application (and deposit copy, if any). Give contact information for correspondence regarding registration issues and a complete mailing address for mailing the certificate. That address, as given, will appear in the window of the envelope.

☾ Form RE

For Renewal Registration · United States Copyright Office

REGISTRATION NUMBER

EFFECTIVE DATE OF RENEWAL REGISTRATION

ANSWER ONLY THE QUESTIONS THAT APPLY TO YOUR CLAIM.

DO NOT WRITE ABOVE THIS LINE.
IF YOU NEED MORE SPACE, USE FORM RE/CON.

MM ___ DD ___ YYYY

1 TITLE AND ORIGINAL TERM INFORMATION

A Title of work as first published or registered: _____

IF YOU NEED MORE SPACE, USE SPACE B ON FORM RE/CON

If periodical, give: Volume: _____ Number: _____ Issue date: _____ ISSN: _____

B Alternative title: _____

IF YOU NEED MORE SPACE, USE B ON FORM RE/CON

C If first published as a contribution to a periodical or other collective work, give title of larger work:

_____

IF YOU NEED MORE SPACE, USE SPACE B ON FORM RE/CON

If periodical, give: Volume: _____ Number: _____ Issue date: _____ ISSN: _____

D Has this work (or the work in which it was first published, if a contribution) ever been registered?
Yes ☐ *Give registration number:* _____ ◄ OR ► No ☐ *(Complete Form RE/Addendum.)*

E Publication date: _____ ◄ OR ► Registration date, if registered as unpublished work: _____
(MM/DD/YYYY) (MM/DD/YYYY)

F Year date(s) in copyright notice, if earlier than actual publication year date: 19 _____ ISBN: _____

G Original copyright claimant(s): _____

IF YOU NEED MORE SPACE, USE B ON FORM RE/CON

H If the work was originally registered in Class Ai or Bi, was a U.S. edition registered?
Yes ☐ *Give registration number:* _____ ◄ OR ► No ☐

I If the original registration record was corrected or amplified by supplementary registration on Form CA, give the registration
number and effective date of the supplementary registration: Number: _____ Date: _____

2 WORK OR MATERIAL CLAIMED AND AUTHOR INFORMATION

A Copyright for the renewal term is claimed in: *(Check only one.)*

1 ☐ the entire work.

2 ☐ a contribution first published in a periodical or other collective work.

3 ☐ revisions in previously published or registered work. *Describe revisions:* _____

4 ☐ separate element(s) of authorship in a larger work. *Specify element(s):* _____

OR ►

5 ☐ The renewal claim is based on the first publication of a work previously
registered as an unpublished work under registration number: _____

B The following author(s) contributed to the work or material claimed:

Name: _____ This author created: _____

Date of death, if applicable: _____
(MM/DD/YYYY)

Name: _____ This author created: _____

Date of death, if applicable: _____
(MM/DD/YYYY)

Name: _____ This author created: _____

Date of death, if applicable: _____
(MM/DD/YYYY)

Name: _____ This author created: _____

Date of death, if applicable: _____
(MM/DD/YYYY)

IF THERE ARE ADDITIONAL AUTHORS, USE SPACE D ON FORM RE/CON.

APPLICATION RECEIVED:

CORRESPONDENCE: ☐ YES

EXAMINED BY:

FUNDS RECEIVED:

DO NOT WRITE ABOVE THIS LINE.
IF YOU NEED MORE SPACE, USE FORM RE/CON.

3

RENEWAL TERM OWNERSHIP INFORMATION

A Name the party or parties entitled by law to claim the renewal copyright on the last day of the original 28-year term of copyright. For each statutory claimant named, give the basis of the claim, and provide a *current* address. *Read instructions.*

Name: _____ as the: _____
Address: _____ ◄ OR ► Year of death: _____

Name: _____ as the: _____
Address: _____ ◄ OR ► Year of death: _____

Name: _____ as the: _____
Address: _____ ◄ OR ► Year of death: _____

Name: _____ as the: _____
Address: _____ ◄ OR ► Year of death: _____

IF THERE ARE ADDITIONAL STATUTORY CLAIMANTS, USE SPACE E ON FORM RE/CON.

B This application is submitted by or on behalf of the: *(Check only one.)*
☐ Statutory claimant(s) named above. *(Go on to section 4.)*
OR ►
☐ Assignee/successor of the statutory claimant(s) named above. *(Complete space C below.)*

C _____ by _____
ASSIGNEE/SUCCESSOR   MEANS OF TRANSFER
Current address: _____

4

CERTIFICATION

I, the undersigned, hereby certify that I am the statutory claimant, the assignee/successor, or the duly authorized agent of the statutory claimant or assignee/successor, and that the statements made by me in this application are correct.

Typed or printed name: _____ Date: _____

Handwritten signature: _____

5

PAYMENT, CORRESPONDENCE, AND MAILING INFORMATION

Deposit account number: _____ Account name: _____
Contact information for correspondence, including name and mailing address: _____

Phone: (____) _____ Fax: (____) _____ Email: _____

MAILING ADDRESS FOR CERTIFICATE:

NAME

NUMBER/STREET   APT/SUITE

CITY/TOWN   STATE/PROVINCE   ZIP/POSTAL CODE   COUNTRY

17 USC §506(e): Any person who knowingly makes a false representation of a material fact in the application for copyright registration provided for by section 409, or in any written statement filed in connection with the application, shall be fined not more than $2,500.

FORM RE REV: 10/2007 PRINT: 10/2007—XX,000 Printed on recycled paper

U.S. GOVERNMENT PRINTING OFFICE: 2007-330-945/60,XXX

APPENDIX 27:
CANCELLATION OF REGISTRATION

Section 201.7 of title 37 of the CFR:

§ 201.7 Cancellation of completed registrations.

(a) *Definition.* Cancellation is an action taken by the Copyright Office whereby either the registration is eliminated on the ground that the registration is invalid under the applicable law and regulations, or the registration number is eliminated and a new registration is made under a different class and number.

(b) *General policy.* The Copyright Office will cancel a completed registration only in those cases where:

(1) It is clear that no registration should have been made because the work does not constitute copyrightable subject matter or fails to satisfy the other legal and formal requirements for obtaining copyright;

(2) Registration may be authorized but the application, deposit material, or fee does not meet the requirements of the law and Copyright Office regulations, and the Office is unable to get the defect corrected; or

(3) An existing registration in the wrong class is to be replaced by a new registration in the correct class.

(c) *Circumstances under which a registration will be cancelled.*

(1) Where the Copyright Office becomes aware after registration that a work is not copyrightable, either because the authorship is *de minimis* or the work does not contain authorship subject to copyright, the registration will be cancelled. The copyright claimant will be notified by correspondence of the proposed cancellation and the reasons therefor, and be given 30 days, from the date the

Copyright Office letter is mailed, to show cause in writing why the cancellation should not be made. If the claimant fails to respond within the 30 day period, or if the Office after considering the response, determines that the registration was made in error and not in accordance with title 17 U.S.C., Chapters 1 through 8, the registration will be cancelled.

(2) When a check received in payment of a registration fee is returned to the Copyright Office marked "insufficient funds" or is otherwise uncollectible the Copyright Office will immediately cancel any registration(s) for which the dishonored check was submitted and will notify the remitter the registration has been cancelled because the check was returned as uncollectible.

(3) Where registration is made in the wrong class, the Copyright Office will cancel the first registration, replace it with a new registration in the correct class, and issue a corrected certificate.

(4) Where registration has been made for a work which appears to be copyrightable but after registration the Copyright Office becomes aware that, on the administrative record before the Office, the statutory requirements have apparently not been satisfied, or that information essential to registration has been omitted entirely from the application or is questionable, or correct deposit material has not been deposited, the Office will correspond with the copyright claimant in an attempt to secure the required information or deposit material or to clarify the information previously given on the application. If the Copyright Office receives no reply to its correspondence within 30 days of the date the letter is mailed, or the response does not resolve the substantive defect, the registration will be cancelled. The correspondence will include the reason for the cancellation. The following are instances where a completed registration will be cancelled unless the substantive defect in the registration can be cured:

(i) Eligibility for registration has not been established;

(ii) A work published before March 1, 1989, was registered more than 5 years after the date of first publication and the deposit copy or phonorecord does not contain a statutory copyright notice;

(iii) The deposit copies or phonorecords of a work published before January 1, 1978 do not contain a copyright notice or the notice is defective;

(iv) A renewal claim was registered after the statutory time limits for registration had apparently expired;

(v) The application and copy(s) or phonorecord(s) do not match each other and the Office cannot locate a copy or phonorecord as described in the application elsewhere in the Copyright Office or the Library of Congress;

(vi) The application for registration does not identify a copyright claimant or it appears from the transfer statement on the application or elsewhere that the "claimant" named in the application does not have the right to claim copyright;

(vii) A claim to copyright is based on material added to a pre-existing work and a reading of the application in its totality indicates that there is no copyrightable new material on which to base a claim;

(viii) A work subject to the manufacturing provisions of the Act of 1909 was apparently published in violation of those provisions;

(ix) For a work published after January 1, 1978, the only claimant given on the application was deceased on the date the application was certified;

(x) A work is not anonymous or pseudonymous and statements on the application and/or copy vary so much that the author cannot be identified; and

(xi) Statements on the application conflict or are so unclear that the claimant cannot be adequately identified.

(d) *Minor substantive errors.* Where a registration includes minor substantive errors or omissions which would generally have been rectified before registration, the Copyright Office will attempt to rectify the error through correspondence with the remitter. Except in those cases enumerated in paragraph (c) of this section, if the Office is unable for any reason to obtain the correct information or deposit copy, the registration record will be annotated to state the nature of the informality and show that the Copyright Office attempted to correct the registration.

APPENDIX 28:
CONTRACTING PARTIES TO TREATIES

Berne Convention (Total Contracting Parties: 164)

CONTRACTING PARTY	STATUS	ENTRY INTO FORCE
Albania	In Force	March 6, 1994
Algeria	In Force	April 19, 1998
Andorra	In Force	June 2, 2004
Antigua and Barbuda	In Force	March 17, 2000
Argentina	In Force	June 10, 1967
Armenia	In Force	October 19, 2000
Australia	In Force	April 14, 1928
Austria	In Force	October 1, 1920
Azerbaijan	In Force	June 4, 1999
Bahamas	In Force	July 10, 1973
Bahrain	In Force	March 2, 1997
Bangladesh	In Force	May 4, 1999
Barbados	In Force	July 30, 1983
Belarus	In Force	December 12, 1997
Belgium	In Force	December 5, 1887
Belize	In Force	June 17, 2000
Benin	In Force	January 3, 1961
Bhutan	In Force	November 25, 2004
Bolivia	In Force	November 4, 1993
Bosnia and Herzegovina	In Force	March 1, 1992
Botswana	In Force	April 15, 1998
Brazil	In Force	February 9, 1922

CONTRACTING PARTY	STATUS	ENTRY INTO FORCE
Brunei Darussalam	In Force	August 30, 2006
Bulgaria	In Force	December 5, 1921
Burkina Faso	In Force	August 19, 1963
Cameroon	In Force	September 21, 1964
Canada	In Force	April 10, 1928
Cape Verde	In Force	July 7, 1997
Central African Republic	In Force	September 3, 1977
Chad	In Force	November 25, 1971
Chile	In Force	June 5, 1970
China	In Force	October 15, 1992
Colombia	In Force	March 7, 1988
Comoros	In Force	April 17, 2005
Congo	In Force	May 8, 1962
Costa Rica	In Force	June 10, 1978
Côte d'Ivoire	In Force	January 1, 1962
Croatia	In Force	October 8, 1991
Cuba	In Force	February 20, 1997
Cyprus	In Force	February 24, 1964
Czech Republic	In Force	January 1, 1993
Democratic People's Republic of Korea	In Force	April 28, 2003
Democratic Republic of the Congo	In Force	October 8, 1963
Denmark	In Force	July 1, 1903
Djibouti	In Force	May 13, 2002
Dominica	In Force	August 7, 1999
Dominican Republic	In Force	December 24, 1997
Ecuador	In Force	October 9, 1991
Egypt	In Force	June 7, 1977
El Salvador	In Force	February 19, 1994
Equatorial Guinea	In Force	June 26, 1997
Estonia	In Force	October 26, 1994
Fiji	In Force	December 1, 1971
Finland	In Force	April 1, 1928
France	In Force	December 5, 1887
Gabon	In Force	March 26, 1962

Understanding Copyright Law: A Beginner's Guide

CONTRACTING PARTY	STATUS	ENTRY INTO FORCE
Gambia	In Force	March 7, 1993
Georgia	In Force	May 16, 1995
Germany	In Force	December 5, 1887
Ghana	In Force	October 11, 1991
Greece	In Force	November 9, 1920
Grenada	In Force	September 22, 1998
Guatemala	In Force	July 28, 1997
Guinea	In Force	November 20, 1980
Guinea-Bissau	In Force	July 22, 1991
Guyana	In Force	October 25, 1994
Haiti	In Force	January 11, 1996
Holy See	In Force	September 12, 1935
Honduras	In Force	January 25, 1990
Hungary	In Force	February 14, 1922
Iceland	In Force	September 7, 1947
India	In Force	April 1, 1928
Indonesia	In Force	September 5, 1997
Ireland	In Force	October 5, 1927
Israel	In Force	March 24, 1950
Italy	In Force	December 5, 1887
Jamaica	In Force	January 1, 1994
Japan	In Force	July 15, 1899
Jordan	In Force	July 28, 1999
Kazakhstan	In Force	April 12, 1999
Kenya	In Force	June 11, 1993
Kyrgyzstan	In Force	July 8, 1999
Latvia	In Force	August 11, 1995
Lebanon	In Force	September 30, 1947
Lesotho	In Force	September 28, 1989
Liberia	In Force	March 8, 1989
Libyan Arab Jamahiriya	In Force	September 28, 1976
Liechtenstein	In Force	July 30, 1931
Lithuania	In Force	December 14, 1994
Luxembourg	In Force	June 20, 1888

CONTRACTING PARTY	STATUS	ENTRY INTO FORCE
Madagascar	In Force	January 1, 1966
Malawi	In Force	October 12, 1991
Malaysia	In Force	October 1, 1990
Mali	In Force	March 19, 1962
Malta	In Force	September 21, 1964
Mauritania	In Force	February 6, 1973
Mauritius	In Force	May 10, 1989
Mexico	In Force	June 11, 1967
Micronesia (Federated States of)	In Force	October 7, 2003
Monaco	In Force	May 30, 1889
Mongolia	In Force	March 12, 1998
Montenegro	In Force	June 3, 2006
Morocco	In Force	June 16, 1917
Namibia	In Force	March 21, 1990
Nepal	In Force	January 11, 2006
Netherlands	In Force	November 1, 1912
New Zealand	In Force	April 24, 1928
Nicaragua	In Force	August 23, 2000
Niger	In Force	May 2, 1962
Nigeria	In Force	September 14, 1993
Norway	In Force	April 13, 1896
Oman	In Force	July 14, 1999
Pakistan	In Force	July 5, 1948
Panama	In Force	June 8, 1996
Paraguay	In Force	January 2, 1992
Peru	In Force	August 20, 1988
Philippines	In Force	August 1, 1951
Poland	In Force	January 28, 1920
Portugal	In Force	March 29, 1911
Qatar	In Force	July 5, 2000
Republic of Korea	In Force	August 21, 1996
Republic of Moldova	In Force	November 2, 1995
Romania	In Force	January 1, 1927
Russian Federation	In Force	March 13, 1995
Rwanda	In Force	March 1, 1984

CONTRACTING PARTY	STATUS	ENTRY INTO FORCE
Saint Kitts and Nevis	In Force	April 9, 1995
Saint Lucia	In Force	August 24, 1993
Saint Vincent and the Grenadines	In Force	August 29, 1995
Samoa	In Force	July 21, 2006
Saudi Arabia	In Force	March 11, 2004
Senegal	In Force	August 25, 1962
Serbia	In Force	April 27, 1992
Singapore	In Force	December 21, 1998
Slovakia	In Force	January 1, 1993
Slovenia	In Force	June 25, 1991
South Africa	In Force	October 3, 1928
Spain	In Force	December 5, 1887
Sri Lanka	In Force	July 20, 1959
Sudan	In Force	December 28, 2000
Suriname	In Force	February 23, 1977
Swaziland	In Force	December 14, 1998
Sweden	In Force	August 1, 1904
Switzerland	In Force	December 5, 1887
Syrian Arab Republic	In Force	June 11, 2004
Tajikistan	In Force	March 9, 2000
Thailand	In Force	July 17, 1931
The former Yugoslav Republic of Macedonia	In Force	September 8, 1991
Togo	In Force	April 30, 1975
Tonga	In Force	June 14, 2001
Trinidad and Tobago	In Force	August 16, 1988
Tunisia	In Force	December 5, 1887
Turkey	In Force	January 1, 1952
Ukraine	In Force	October 25, 1995
United Arab Emirates	In Force	July 14, 2004
United Kingdom	In Force	December 5, 1887
United Republic of Tanzania	In Force	July 25, 1994
United States of America	In Force	March 1, 1989
Uruguay	In Force	July 10, 1967
Uzbekistan	In Force	April 19, 2005

CONTRACTING PARTY	STATUS	ENTRY INTO FORCE
Venezuela (Bolivarian Republic of)	In Force	December 30, 1982
Viet Nam	In Force	October 26, 2004
Yemen	In Force	July 14, 2008
Zambia	In Force	January 2, 1992
Zimbabwe	In Force	April 18, 1980
Source: http://www.wipo.int		

WIPO Copyright Treaty (WCT) (Total Contracting Parties: 70)

CONTRACTING PARTY	STATUS	ENTRY INTO FORCE
Albania	In Force	August 6, 2005
Argentina	In Force	March 6, 2002
Armenia	In Force	March 6, 2005
Australia	In Force	July 26, 2007
Austria	Signature	
Azerbaijan	In Force	April 11, 2006
Bahrain	In Force	December 15, 2005
Belarus	In Force	March 6, 2002
Belgium	In Force	August 30, 2006
Benin	In Force	April 16, 2006
Bolivia	Signature	
Botswana	In Force	January 27, 2005
Bulgaria	In Force	March 6, 2002
Burkina Faso	In Force	March 6, 2002
Canada	Signature	
Chile	In Force	March 6, 2002
China	In Force	June 9, 2007
Colombia	In Force	March 6, 2002
Costa Rica	In Force	March 6, 2002
Croatia	In Force	March 6, 2002
Cyprus	In Force	November 4, 2003
Czech Republic	In Force	March 6, 2002
Denmark	Signature	
Dominican Republic	In Force	January 10, 2006
Ecuador	In Force	March 6, 2002

CONTRACTING PARTY	STATUS	ENTRY INTO FORCE
El Salvador	In Force	March 6, 2002
Estonia	Signature	
European Community	Signature	
Finland	Signature	
France	Signature	
Gabon	In Force	March 6, 2002
Georgia	In Force	March 6, 2002
Germany	Signature	
Ghana	In Force	November 18, 2006
Greece	Signature	
Guatemala	In Force	February 4, 2003
Guinea	In Force	May 25, 2002
Honduras	In Force	May 20, 2002
Hungary	In Force	March 6, 2002
Indonesia	In Force	March 6, 2002
Ireland	Signature	
Israel	Signature	
Italy	Signature	
Jamaica	In Force	June 12, 2002
Japan	In Force	March 6, 2002
Jordan	In Force	April 27, 2004
Kazakhstan	In Force	November 12, 2004
Kenya	Signature	
Kyrgyzstan	In Force	March 6, 2002
Latvia	In Force	March 6, 2002
Liechtenstein	In Force	April 30, 2007
Lithuania	In Force	March 6, 2002
Luxembourg	Signature	
Mali	In Force	April 24, 2002
Mexico	In Force	March 6, 2002
Monaco	Signature	
Mongolia	In Force	October 25, 2002
Montenegro	In Force	June 3, 2006
Namibia	Signature	

CONTRACTING PARTY	STATUS	ENTRY INTO FORCE
Netherlands	Signature	
Nicaragua	In Force	March 6, 2003
Nigeria	Signature	
Oman	In Force	September 20, 2005
Panama	In Force	March 6, 2002
Paraguay	In Force	March 6, 2002
Peru	In Force	March 6, 2002
Philippines	In Force	October 4, 2002
Poland	In Force	March 23, 2004
Portugal	Signature	
Qatar	In Force	October 28, 2005
Republic of Korea	In Force	June 24, 2004
Republic of Moldova	In Force	March 6, 2002
Romania	In Force	March 6, 2002
Russian Federation	In Force	February 5, 2009
Saint Lucia	In Force	March 6, 2002
Senegal	In Force	May 18, 2002
Serbia	In Force	June 13, 2003
Singapore	In Force	April 17, 2005
Slovakia	In Force	March 6, 2002
Slovenia	In Force	March 6, 2002
South Africa	Signature	
Spain	Signature	
Sweden	Signature	
Switzerland	In Force	July 1, 2008
Tajikistan	In Force	April 5, 2009
The former Yugoslav Republic of Macedonia	In Force	February 4, 2004
Togo	In Force	May 21, 2003
Trinidad and Tobago	In Force	November 28, 2008
Turkey	In Force	November 28, 2008
Ukraine	In Force	March 6, 2002
United Arab Emirates	In Force	July 14, 2004
United Kingdom	Signature	
United States of America	In Force	March 6, 2002

CONTRACTING PARTY	STATUS	ENTRY INTO FORCE
Uruguay	In Force	June 5, 2009
Venezuela (Bolivarian Republic of)	Signature	
Source: http://www.wipo.int		

WIPO Performances and Phonograms Treaty (WPPT) (Total Contracting Parties: 68)

CONTRACTING PARTY	STATUS	ENTRY INTO FORCE
Albania	In Force	May 20, 2002
Argentina	In Force	May 20, 2002
Armenia	In Force	March 6, 2005
Australia	In Force	July 26, 2007
Austria	Signature	
Azerbaijan	In Force	April 11, 2006
Bahrain	In Force	December 15, 2005
Belarus	In Force	May 20, 2002
Belgium	In Force	August 30, 2006
Benin	In Force	April 16, 2006
Bolivia	Signature	
Botswana	In Force	January 27, 2005
Bulgaria	In Force	May 20, 2002
Burkina Faso	In Force	May 20, 2002
Canada	Signature	
Chile	In Force	May 20, 2002
China	In Force	June 9, 2007
Colombia	In Force	May 20, 2002
Costa Rica	In Force	May 20, 2002
Croatia	In Force	May 20, 2002
Cyprus	In Force	December 2, 2005
Czech Republic	In Force	May 20, 2002
Denmark	Signature	
Dominican Republic	In Force	January 10, 2006
Ecuador	In Force	May 20, 2002
El Salvador	In Force	May 20, 2002
Estonia	Signature	

CONTRACTING PARTY	STATUS	ENTRY INTO FORCE
European Community	Signature	
Finland	Signature	
France	Signature	
Gabon	In Force	May 20, 2002
Georgia	In Force	May 20, 2002
Germany	Signature	
Ghana	Signature	
Greece	Signature	
Guatemala	In Force	January 8, 2003
Guinea	In Force	May 25, 2002
Honduras	In Force	May 20, 2002
Hungary	In Force	May 20, 2002
Indonesia	In Force	February 15, 2005
Ireland	Signature	
Israel	Signature	
Italy	Signature	
Jamaica	In Force	June 12, 2002
Japan	In Force	October 9, 2002
Jordan	In Force	May 24, 2004
Kazakhstan	In Force	November 12, 2004
Kenya	Signature	
Kyrgyzstan	In Force	August 15, 2002
Latvia	In Force	May 20, 2002
Liechtenstein	In Force	April 30, 2007
Lithuania	In Force	May 20, 2002
Luxembourg	Signature	
Mali	In Force	May 20, 2002
Mexico	In Force	May 20, 2002
Monaco	Signature	
Mongolia	In Force	October 25, 2002
Montenegro	In Force	June 3, 2006
Namibia	Signature	
Netherlands	Signature	
Nicaragua	In Force	March 6, 2003
Nigeria	Signature	

CONTRACTING PARTY	STATUS	ENTRY INTO FORCE
Oman	In Force	September 20, 2005
Panama	In Force	May 20, 2002
Paraguay	In Force	May 20, 2002
Peru	In Force	July 18, 2002
Philippines	In Force	October 4, 2002
Poland	In Force	October 21, 2003
Portugal	Signature	
Qatar	In Force	October 28, 2005
Republic of Korea	In Force	March 18, 2009
Republic of Moldova	In Force	May 20, 2002
Romania	In Force	May 20, 2002
Russian Federation	In Force	February 5, 2009
Saint Lucia	In Force	May 20, 2002
Senegal	In Force	May 20, 2002
Serbia	In Force	June 13, 2003
Singapore	In Force	April 17, 2005
Slovakia	In Force	May 20, 2002
Slovenia	In Force	May 20, 2002
South Africa	Signature	
Spain	Signature	
Sweden	Signature	
Switzerland	In Force	July 1, 2008
The former Yugoslav Republic of Macedonia	In Force	March 20, 2005
Togo	In Force	May 21, 2003
Trinidad and Tobago	In Force	November 28, 2008
Turkey	In Force	November 28, 2008
Ukraine	In Force	May 20, 2002
United Arab Emirates	In Force	June 9, 2005
United Kingdom	Signature	
United States of America	In Force	May 20, 2002
Uruguay	In Force	August 28, 2008
Venezuela (Bolivarian Republic of)	Signature	
Source: http://www.wipo.int		

Trade-Related Aspects of Intellectual Property Rights (TRIPS) Treaty (Total Contracting Parties: 153)

Albania	8 September 2000
Angola	23 November 1996
Antigua and Barbuda	1 January 1995
Argentina	1 January 1995
Armenia	5 February 2003
Australia	1 January 1995
Austria	1 January 1995
Bahrain, Kingdom of	1 January 1995
Bangladesh	1 January 1995
Barbados	1 January 1995
Belgium	1 January 1995
Belize	1 January 1995
Benin	22 February 1996
Bolivia	12 September 1995
Botswana	31 May 1995
Brazil	1 January 1995
Brunei Darussalam	1 January 1995
Bulgaria	1 December 1996
Burkina Faso	3 June 1995
Burundi	23 July 1995
Cambodia	13 October 2004
Cameroon	13 December 1995
Canada	1 January 1995
Cape Verde	23 July 2008
Central African Republic	31 May 1995
Chad	19 October 1996
Chile	1 January 1995
China	11 December 2001
Colombia	30 April 1995
Congo	27 March 1997
Costa Rica	1 January 1995
Côte d'Ivoire	1 January 1995
Croatia	30 November 2000

Cuba	20 April 1995
Cyprus	30 July 1995
Czech Republic	1 January 1995
Democratic Republic of the Congo	1 January 1997
Denmark	1 January 1995
Djibouti	31 May 1995
Dominica	1 January 1995
Dominican Republic	9 March 1995
Ecuador	21 January 1996
Egypt	30 June 1995
El Salvador	7 May 1995
Estonia	13 November 1999
European Communities	1 January 1995
Fiji	14 January 1996
Finland	1 January 1995
Former Yugoslav Republic of Macedonia (FYROM)	4 April 2003
France	1 January 1995
Gabon	1 January 1995
The Gambia	23 October 1996
Georgia	14 June 2000
Germany	1 January 1995
Ghana	1 January 1995
Greece	1 January 1995
Grenada	22 February 1996
Guatemala	21 July 1995
Guinea	25 October 1995
Guinea Bissau	31 May 1995
Guyana	1 January 1995
Haiti	30 January 1996
Honduras	1 January 1995
Hong Kong, China	1 January 1995
Hungary	1 January 1995
Iceland	1 January 1995
India	1 January 1995
Indonesia	1 January 1995

Ireland	1 January 1995
Israel	21 April 1995
Italy	1 January 1995
Jamaica	9 March 1995
Japan	1 January 1995
Jordan	11 April 2000
Kenya	1 January 1995
Korea, Republic of	1 January 1995
Kuwait	1 January 1995
Kyrgyz Republic	20 December 1998
Latvia	10 February 1999
Lesotho	31 May 1995
Liechtenstein	1 September 1995
Lithuania	31 May 2001
Luxembourg	1 January 1995
Macao, China	1 January 1995
Madagascar	17 November 1995
Malawi	31 May 1995
Malaysia	1 January 1995
Maldives	31 May 1995
Mali	31 May 1995
Malta	1 January 1995
Mauritania	31 May 1995
Mauritius	1 January 1995
Mexico	1 January 1995
Moldova	26 July 2001
Mongolia	29 January 1997
Morocco	1 January 1995
Mozambique	26 August 1995
Myanmar	1 January 1995
Namibia	1 January 1995
Nepal	23 April 2004
Netherlands—For the Kingdom in Europe	1 January 1995
Netherlands Antilles	1 January 1995
New Zealand	1 January 1995

Nicaragua	3 September 1995
Niger	13 December 1996
Nigeria	1 January 1995
Norway	1 January 1995
Oman	9 November 2000
Pakistan	1 January 1995
Panama	6 September 1997
Papua New Guinea	9 June 1996
Paraguay	1 January 1995
Peru	1 January 1995
Philippines	1 January 1995
Poland	1 July 1995
Portugal	1 January 1995
Qatar	13 January 1996
Romania	1 January 1995
Rwanda	22 May 1996
Saint Kitts and Nevis	21 February 1996
Saint Lucia	1 January 1995
Saint Vincent & the Grenadines	1 January 1995
Saudi Arabia	11 December 2005
Senegal	1 January 1995
Sierra Leone	23 July 1995
Singapore	1 January 1995
Slovak Republic	1 January 1995
Slovenia	30 July 1995
Solomon Islands	26 July 1996
South Africa	1 January 1995
Spain	1 January 1995
Sri Lanka	1 January 1995
Suriname	1 January 1995
Swaziland	1 January 1995
Sweden	1 January 1995
Switzerland	1 July 1995
Chinese Taipei	1 January 2002
Tanzania	1 January 1995

Thailand	1 January 1995
Togo	31 May 1995
Tonga	27 July 2007
Trinidad and Tobago	1 March 1995
Tunisia	29 March 1995
Turkey	26 March 1995
Uganda	1 January 1995
Ukraine	16 May 2008
United Arab Emirates	10 April 1996
United Kingdom	1 January 1995
United States of America	1 January 1995
Uruguay	1 January 1995
Venezuela (Bolivarian Republic of)	1 January 1995
Viet Nam	11 January 2007
Zambia	1 January 1995
Zimbabwe	5 March 1995
Source: http://www.wto.org	

APPENDIX 29:
TRANSFERS AND RECORDAL

Excerpt from section 101 of the 1976 Act:

A "transfer of copyright ownership" is an assignment, mortgage, exclusive license, or any other conveyance, alienation, or hypothecation of a copyright or of any of the exclusive rights comprised in a copyright, whether or not it is limited in time or place of effect, but not including a nonexclusive license.

Excerpt from section 201 of the 1976 Act:

§ 201. Ownership of copyright

(d) TRANSFER OF OWNERSHIP.—

(1) The ownership of a copyright may be transferred in whole or in part by any means of conveyance or by operation of law, and may be bequeathed by will or pass as personal property by the applicable laws of intestate succession.

(2) Any of the exclusive rights comprised in a copyright, including any subdivision of any of the rights specified by section 106, may be transferred as provided by clause (1) and owned separately. The owner of any particular exclusive right is entitled, to the extent of that right, to all of the protection and remedies accorded to the copyright owner by this title.

Sections 202, 204 and 205 of the 1976 Act:

§ 202. Ownership of copyright as distinct from ownership of material object

Ownership of a copyright, or of any of the exclusive rights under a copyright, is distinct from ownership of any material object in which the work is embodied. Transfer of ownership of any material object, including the copy or phonorecord in which the work is first fixed, does not of itself convey any rights in the copyrighted work embodied in the object; nor, in the absence of an agreement, does transfer of ownership of a copyright or of any exclusive rights under a copyright convey property rights in any material object.

§ 204. Execution of transfers of copyright ownership

(a) A transfer of copyright ownership, other than by operation of law, is not valid unless an instrument of conveyance, or a note or memorandum of the transfer, is in writing and signed by the owner of the rights conveyed or such owner's duly authorized agent.

(b) A certificate of acknowledgment is not required for the validity of a transfer, but is prima facie evidence of the execution of the transfer if—

(1) in the case of a transfer executed in the United States, the certificate is issued by a person authorized to administer oaths within the United States; or

(2) in the case of a transfer executed in a foreign country, the certificate is issued by a diplomatic or consular officer of the United States, or by a person authorized to administer oaths whose authority is proved by a certificate of such an officer.

§ 205. Recordation of transfers and other documents

(a) Conditions for Recordation.—Any transfer of copyright ownership or other document pertaining to a copyright may be recorded in the Copyright Office if the document filed for recordation bears the actual signature of the person who executed it, or if it is accompanied by a sworn or official certification that it is a true copy of the original, signed document.

(b) Certificate of Recordation.—The Register of Copyrights shall, upon receipt of a document as provided by subsection (a) and of the fee provided by section 708, record the document and return it with a certificate of recordation.

(c) Recordation as Constructive Notice.—Recordation of a document in the Copyright Office gives all persons constructive notice of the facts stated in the recorded document, but only if—

(1) the document, or material attached to it, specifically identifies the work to which it pertains so that, after the document is indexed by the Register of Copyrights, it would be revealed by a reasonable search under the title or registration number of the work; and

(2) registration has been made for the work.

(d) PRIORITY BETWEEN CONFLICTING TRANSFERS.—As between two conflicting transfers, the one executed first prevails if it is recorded, in the manner required to give constructive notice under subsection (c), within one month after its execution in the United States or within two months after its execution outside the United States, or at any time before recordation in such manner of the later transfer. Otherwise the later transfer prevails if recorded first in such manner, and if taken in good faith, for valuable consideration or on the basis of a binding promise to pay royalties, and without notice of the earlier transfer.

(e) PRIORITY BETWEEN CONFLICTING TRANSFER OF OWNERSHIP AND NONEXCLUSIVE LICENSE.—A nonexclusive license, whether recorded or not, prevails over a conflicting transfer of copyright ownership if the license is evidenced by a written instrument signed by the owner of the rights licensed or such owner's duly authorized agent, and if

(1) the license was taken before execution of the transfer; or

(2) the license was taken in good faith before recordation of the transfer and without notice of it.

APPENDIX 30:
DOCUMENT COVER SHEET FOR
RECORDAL

 Document Cover Sheet · Basic Information

Read all of the instructions below before completing this form.
Use of the Document Cover Sheet is optional but encouraged.

When to use this form Use the Document Cover Sheet when you are submitting a document for recordation in the U.S. Copyright Office.

Mailing requirements It is important to send the original cover sheet and one copy of the cover sheet for each document that is being submitted for recordation. The two copies of the Document Cover Sheet, the document, and the fee must be sent together in the same envelope or package. The Copyright Office cannot process them unless they are received together. Send to: *Library of Congress, Copyright Office, Documents Recordation Section, 101 Independence Avenue SE, Washington, DC 20559-6000*

Cover sheets should be typed or printed and should contain the information requested so that the Copyright Office can process the document and return it. Be sure to complete space 8 so that the recorded document can be returned. The Copyright Office will process the document based on the information in the document or an attachment that is part of the document. Information for indexing will not be taken from the Document Cover Sheet or attachments that were *not* part of the document when it was executed (signed). To be recorded, the document must satisfy the recordation requirements of the copyright law and Copyright Office regulations.

The person submitting a document with a cover sheet is solely responsible for verifying the correctness of the cover sheet and the sufficiency of the document. Recording a document submitted with or without a cover sheet does not constitute a determination by the Copyright Office of the document's validity or effect. Only a court may make such a determination.

When a Document Cover Sheet is submitted, it will be imaged with the document as part of the public record.

PRIVACY ACT ADVISORY STATEMENT *(Required by the Privacy Act of 1974 (P.L. 93-579))*: The authority for requesting this information is title 17 USC, sec. 205. Furnishing the requested information is voluntary. But if the information is not provided, it may be necessary to delay recordation.

The principal uses of the requested information are the establishment and maintenance of a public record and the evaluation for compliance with the recordation requirements of section 205 of the copyright code. Other routine uses include public inspection and copying, preparation of public indexes, preparation of public catalogs of copyright recordations, and preparation of search reports upon request.

NOTE: No other advisory statement will be given in connection with this application. Please keep this statement and refer to it if we communicate with you regarding this cover sheet.

Space-by-Space Instructions

Space 1: First party given in the document This information is only used to connect the Document Cover Sheet and the document if they become separated. No information is entered in the catalog record from this space.

Space 2: First title given in the document This information is only used to connect the Document Cover Sheet and the document if they become separated. No information is entered in the catalog record from this space.

Space 3: Total number of titles in the document The total number of titles (including a.k.a. and other variant titles of a work) determines the recordation fee. In the case of multiple title documents, titles that are repeated in documents are counted as a single title, except where the document lists different issues, volumes, episode numbers, etc. following each title. Each such entry is regarded as a separate title and will be indexed separately and counted separately when computing the fee for recording the document. The Copyright Office verifies title counts.

Space 4: Amount of fee calculated There is a basic fee for recording a document containing one title. There is an additional charge for each group of up to 10 additional titles. "Alternative" titles, "formerly-known-as" titles, and "also-known-as" titles are considered to be extra titles. Titles are counted by groups. If there are fewer than 10 titles in a group, the fee for a group still applies. Copyright Office fees are subject to change. For current fees, check the Copyright Office website at *www.copyright.gov*, write the Copyright Office, or call (202) 707-3000. Please remember that the fee is based on the number of titles in a document, not the number of works.

Space 5: Fee enclosed Check the appropriate box. If a Copyright Office deposit account is to be charged, give the Copyright Office

deposit account number and name. The Office only accepts domestic money orders and checks payable through a U.S. bank with American Bankers Association routing numbers. International and postal money orders are not accepted.

Space 6: Completeness of document Check the appropriate box. Please read the "Important note"if checking "Record 'as is.'" All documents recorded under §205 of the Copyright Act must be complete by their own terms to be recorded. Notices of termination recorded under §203, §304(c), and §304(d) must be complete and exact duplicates of the notices as served. Please refer to Copyright Office regulations in Chapter 37 CFR §201.4 and §201.10 and Circular 12, *Recordation of Transfers and Other Documents*, for more information.

Space 7: Certification of photocopied documents Complete this section only if submitting a photocopied document in lieu of a document bearing the actual original signature. If a photocopy of the original signed document is submitted, it must be accompanied by a sworn certification. A sworn certification signed by at least one of the parties to the document or that party's authorized representative (who is identified as such at space 7) will satisfy that requirement. The date entered in the date field should be the date you sign the Document Cover Sheet. Copies of documents on file in a federal, state, or local government office must be accompanied by an original official certification.

Space 8: Return to Give the name and address of the person to whom the recorded document should be returned. The Copyright Office does not maintain paper files of recorded documents. The documents are imaged and returned to the person or firm designated in this space. Please include telephone number, fax number, and email address in case we need to contact you.

Document Cover Sheet
UNITED STATES COPYRIGHT OFFICE

Copyright Office fees are subject to change.
For current fees check the Copyright Office website at
www.copyright.gov, write to the Copyright Office,
or call (202) 707-3000.

For Recordation of Documents

Volume _____ Document _____

Volume _____ Document _____

Date of recordation M _____ D _____ Y _____
(ASSIGNED BY THE COPYRIGHT OFFICE)

Funds received _____

DO NOT WRITE ABOVE THIS LINE · SEE INSTRUCTIONS ON REVERSE

To the Register of Copyrights: *Please record the accompanying original document or properly certified copy thereof.*

1 First party name given in the document _____
(IMPORTANT: *Please read instruction for this and other spaces.*)

2 First title given in the document _____

3 Total number of titles in the document _____

4 Amount of fee calculated _____

5 Fee enclosed
☐ Check ☐ Money order
☐ Fee authorized to be charged to Copyright Office deposit account

Deposit account number _____

Deposit account name _____

6 Completeness of document
☐ Document is complete by its own terms ☐ Document is not complete. Record "as is."

IMPORTANT NOTE: *A request to record a document "as is" under 37 CFR §201.4(c)(2) is an assertion that: (a) the attachment is completely unavailable for recordation; (b) the attachment is not essential to the identification of the subject matter of the document; and (c) it would be impossible or wholly impracticable to have the parties to the document sign or initial a deletion of the reference to the attachment.*

7 Certification of Photocopied Document Complete this certification if a photocopy of the original signed document is substituted for a document bearing the actual original signature.
NOTE: *This space may not be used for documents that require an official certification.*

I declare under penalty of perjury that the accompanying document is a true and correct copy of the original document.

Signature _____ Date _____

Duly authorized agent of _____

8 Return to:

Name _____

Number/street _____ Apt/suite _____

City _____ State _____ Zip _____

Phone number _____ Fax number _____

Email _____

SEND TO: *Library of Congress, Copyright Office, Documents Recordation Section, 101 Independence Avenue SE, Washington, DC 20559-6000*
INCLUDE ALL THESE TOGETHER: (1) Two copies of this form; (2) payment from a deposit account or by check/money order payable to *Register of Copyrights;* and (3) your document.

FORM DCS REV: 09/2007 PRINT: 09/2007 — ••,000 Printed on recycled paper   U.S. Government Printing Office: 2007-330-945/60,•••

Understanding Copyright Law: A Beginner's Guide

APPENDIX 31:
TERMINATION OF TRANSFER

Section 203 of the 1976 Act:

§ 203. Termination of transfers and licenses granted by the author

(a) CONDITIONS FOR TERMINATION.—In the case of any work other than a work made for hire, the exclusive or nonexclusive grant of a transfer or license of copyright or of any right under a copyright, executed by the author on or after January 1, 1978, otherwise than by will, is subject to termination under the following conditions:

(1) In the case of a grant executed by one author, termination of the grant may be effected by that author or, if the author is dead, by the person or persons who, under clause (2) of this subsection, own and are entitled to exercise a total of more than one-half of that author's termination interest. In the case of a grant executed by two or more authors of a joint work, termination of the grant may be effected by a majority of the authors who executed it; if any of such authors is dead, the termination interest of any such author may be exercised as a unit by the person or persons who, under clause (2) of this subsection, own and are entitled to exercise a total of more than one-half of that author's interest.

(2) Where an author is dead, his or her termination interest is owned, and may be exercised, as follows:

(A) The widow or widower owns the author's entire termination interest unless there are any surviving children or grandchildren of the author, in which case the widow or widower owns one-half of the author's interest.

(B) The author's surviving children, and the surviving children of any dead child of the author, own the author's entire termination interest unless there is a widow or widower, in which case the ownership of one-half of the author's interest is divided among them.

(C) The rights of the author's children and grandchildren are in all cases divided among them and exercised on a per stirpes basis according to the number of such author's children represented; the share of the children of a dead child in a termination interest can be exercised only by the action of a majority of them.

(D) In the event that the author's widow or widower, children, and grandchildren are not living, the author's executor, administrator, personal representative, or trustee shall own the author's entire termination interest.

(3) Termination of the grant may be effected at any time during a period of five years beginning at the end of thirty-five years from the date of execution of the grant; or, if the grant covers the right of publication of the work, the period begins at the end of thirty-five years from the date of publication of the work under the grant or at the end of forty years from the date of execution of the grant, whichever term ends earlier.

(4) The termination shall be effected by serving an advance notice in writing, signed by the number and proportion of owners of termination interests required under clauses (1) and (2) of this subsection, or by their duly authorized agents, upon the grantee or the grantee's successor in title.

(A) The notice shall state the effective date of the termination, which shall fall within the five-year period specified by clause (3) of this subsection, and the notice shall be served not less than two or more than ten years before that date. A copy of the notice shall be recorded in the Copyright Office before the effective date of termination, as a condition to its taking effect.

(B) The notice shall comply, in form, content, and manner of service, with requirements that the Register of Copyrights shall prescribe by regulation.

(5) Termination of the grant may be effected notwithstanding any agreement to the contrary, including an agreement to make a will or to make any future grant.

(b) Effect of Termination.—Upon the effective date of termination, all rights under this title that were covered by the terminated grants revert to the author, authors, and other persons owning termination interests under clauses (1) and (2) of subsection (a), including those owners who did not join in signing the notice of termination under clause (4) of subsection (a), but with the following limitations:

(1) A derivative work prepared under authority of the grant before its termination may continue to be utilized under the terms of the grant after its termination, but this privilege does not extend to the preparation after the termination of other derivative works based upon the copyrighted work covered by the terminated grant.

(2) The future rights that will revert upon termination of the grant become vested on the date the notice of termination has been served as provided by clause (4) of subsection (a). The rights vest in the author, authors, and other persons named in, and in the proportionate shares provided by, clauses (1) and (2) of subsection (a).

(3) Subject to the provisions of clause (4) of this subsection, a further grant, or agreement to make a further grant, of any right covered by a terminated grant is valid only if it is signed by the same number and proportion of the owners, in whom the right has vested under clause (2) of this subsection, as are required to terminate the grant under clauses (1) and (2) of subsection (a). Such further grant or agreement is effective with respect to all of the persons in whom the right it covers has vested under clause (2) of this subsection, including those who did not join in signing it. If any person dies after rights under a terminated grant have vested in him or her, that person's legal representatives, legatees, or heirs at law represent him or her for purposes of this clause.

(4) A further grant, or agreement to make a further grant, of any right covered by a terminated grant is valid only if it is made after the effective date of the termination. As an exception, however, an agreement for such a further grant may be made between the persons provided by clause (3) of this subsection and the original grantee or such grantee's successor in title, after the notice of termination has been served as provided by clause (4) of subsection (a).

(5) Termination of a grant under this section affects only those rights covered by the grants that arise under this title, and in no way affects rights arising under any other Federal, State, or foreign laws.

(6) Unless and until termination is effected under this section, the grant, if it does not provide otherwise, continues in effect for the term of copyright provided by this title.

Excerpt from section 304 of the 1976 Act:

§ 304. Duration of copyright: Subsisting copyrights

(c) TERMINATION OF TRANSFERS AND LICENSES COVERING EXTENDED RENEWAL TERM.—In the case of any copyright subsisting in either its first or renewal term on January 1, 1978, other than a copyright in a work made for hire, the exclusive or nonexclusive grant of a transfer or license of the renewal copyright or any right under it, executed before January 1, 1978, by any of the persons designated by subsection (a) (1)(C) of this section, otherwise than by will, is subject to termination under the following conditions:

(1) In the case of a grant executed by a person or persons other than the author, termination of the grant may be effected by the surviving person or persons who executed it. In the case of a grant executed by one or more of the authors of the work, termination of the grant may be effected, to the extent of a particular author's share in the ownership of the renewal copyright, by the author who executed it or, if such author is dead, by the person or persons who, under clause (2) of this subsection, own and are entitled to exercise a total of more than one-half of that author's termination interest.

(2) Where an author is dead, his or her termination interest is owned, and may be exercised, as follows:

(A) The widow or widower owns the author's entire termination interest unless there are any surviving children or grandchildren of the author, in which case the widow or widower owns one-half of the author's interest.

(B) The author's surviving children, and the surviving children of any dead child of the author, own the author's entire termination interest unless there is a widow or widower, in which case the ownership of one-half of the author's interest is divided among them.

(C) The rights of the author's children and grandchildren are in all cases divided among them and exercised on a per stirpes basis according to the number of such author's children represented; the share of the children of a dead child in a termination interest can be exercised only by the action of a majority of them.

(D) In the event that the author's widow or widower, children, and grandchildren are not living, the author's executor, administrator, personal representative, or trustee shall own the author's entire termination interest.

(3) Termination of the grant may be effected at any time during a period of five years beginning at the end of fifty-six years from the date copyright was originally secured, or beginning on January 1, 1978, whichever is later.

(4) The termination shall be effected by serving an advance notice in writing upon the grantee or the grantee's successor in title. In the case of a grant executed by a person or persons other than the author, the notice shall be signed by all of those entitled to terminate the grant under clause (1) of this subsection, or by their duly authorized agents. In the case of a grant executed by one or more of the authors of the work, the notice as to any one author's share shall be signed by that author or his or her duly authorized agent or, if that author is dead, by the number and proportion of the owners of his or her termination interest required under clauses (1) and (2) of this subsection, or by their duly authorized agents.

(A) The notice shall state the effective date of the termination, which shall fall within the five-year period specified by clause (3) of this subsection, or, in the case of a termination under subsection (d), within the five-year period specified by subsection (d)(2), and the notice shall be served not less than two or more than ten years before that date. A copy of the notice shall be recorded in the Copyright Office before the effective date of termination, as a condition to its taking effect.

(B) The notice shall comply, in form, content, and manner of service, with requirements that the Register of Copyrights shall prescribe by regulation.

(5) Termination of the grant may be effected notwithstanding any agreement to the contrary, including an agreement to make a will or to make any future grant.

(6) In the case of a grant executed by a person or persons other than the author, all rights under this title that were covered by the terminated grant revert, upon the effective date of termination, to all of those entitled to terminate the grant under clause (1) of this subsection. In the case of a grant executed by one or more of the authors of the work, all of a particular author's rights under this title that were covered by the terminated grant revert, upon the effective date of termination, to that author or, if that author is dead, to the persons owning his or her termination interest under

clause (2) of this subsection, including those owners who did not join in signing the notice of termination under clause (4) of this subsection. In all cases the reversion of rights is subject to the following limitations:

(A) A derivative work prepared under authority of the grant before its termination may continue to be utilized under the terms of the grant after its termination, but this privilege does not extend to the preparation after the termination of other derivative works based upon the copyrighted work covered by the terminated grant.

(B) The future rights that will revert upon termination of the grant become vested on the date the notice of termination has been served as provided by clause (4) of this subsection.

(C) Where the author's rights revert to two or more persons under clause (2) of this subsection, they shall vest in those persons in the proportionate shares provided by that clause. In such a case, and subject to the provisions of subclause (D) of this clause, a further grant, or agreement to make a further grant, of a particular author's share with respect to any right covered by a terminated grant is valid only if it is signed by the same number and proportion of the owners, in whom the right has vested under this clause, as are required to terminate the grant under clause (2) of this subsection. Such further grant or agreement is effective with respect to all of the persons in whom the right it covers has vested under this subclause, including those who did not join in signing it. If any person dies after rights under a terminated grant have vested in him or her, that person's legal representatives, legatees, or heirs at law represent him or her for purposes of this subclause.

(D) A further grant, or agreement to make a further grant, of any right covered by a terminated grant is valid only if it is made after the effective date of the termination. As an exception, however, an agreement for such a further grant may be made between the author or any of the persons provided by the first sentence of clause (6) of this subsection, or between the persons provided by subclause (C) of this clause, and the original grantee or such grantee's successor in title, after the notice of termination has been served as provided by clause (4) of this subsection.

(E) Termination of a grant under this subsection affects only those rights covered by the grant that arise under this title, and in no way affects rights arising under any other Federal, State, or foreign laws.

(F) Unless and until termination is effected under this subsection, the grant, if it does not provide otherwise, continues in effect for the remainder of the extended renewal term.

(d) TERMINATION RIGHTS PROVIDED IN SUBSECTION (c) WHICH HAVE EXPIRED ON OR BEFORE THE EFFECTIVE DATE OF THE SONNY BONO COPYRIGHT TERM EXTENSION ACT.—In the case of any copyright other than a work made for hire, subsisting in its renewal term on the effective date of the Sonny Bono Copyright Term Extension Act[2] for which the termination right provided in subsection (c) has expired by such date, where the author or owner of the termination right has not previously exercised such termination right, the exclusive or nonexclusive grant of a transfer or license of the renewal copyright or any right under it, executed before January 1, 1978, by any of the persons designated in subsection (a)(1)(C) of this section, other than by will, is subject to termination under the following conditions:

(1) The conditions specified in subsections (c) (1), (2), (4), (5), and (6) of this section apply to terminations of the last 20 years of copyright term as provided by the amendments made by the Sonny Bono Copyright Term Extension Act.

(2) Termination of the grant may be effected at any time during a period of 5 years beginning at the end of 75 years from the date copyright was originally secured.

Section 201.10 of title 37 of the CFR:

§ 201.10 Notices of termination of transfers and licenses.

This section covers notices of termination of transfers and licenses under sections 203, 304(c) and 304(d) of title 17, of the United States Code. A termination under section 304(d) is possible only if no termination was made under section 304(c), and federal copyright was originally secured on or between January 1, 1923, and October 26, 1939.

(a) *Form.* The Copyright Office does not provide printed forms for the use of persons serving notices of termination.

b) *Contents.*

(1) A notice of termination covering the extended renewal term under sections 304(c) and 304(d) of title 17, U.S.C., must include a clear identification of each of the following:

(i) Whether the termination is made under section 304(c) or under section 304(d);

(ii) The name of each grantee whose rights are being terminated, or the grantee's successor in title, and each address at which service of the notice is being made;

(iii) The title and the name of at least one author of, and the date copyright was originally secured in, each work to which the notice of termination applies; and, if possible and practicable, the original copyright registration number;

(iv) A brief statement reasonably identifying the grant to which the notice of termination applies;

(v) The effective date of termination;

(vi) If termination is made under section 304(d), a statement that termination of renewal term rights under section 304(c) has not been previously exercised; and

(vii) In the case of a termination of a grant executed by a person or persons other than the author, a listing of the surviving person or persons who executed the grant. In the case of a termination of a grant executed by one or more of the authors of the work where the termination is exercised by the successors of a deceased author, a listing of the names and relationships to that deceased author of all of the following, together with specific indication of the person or persons executing the notice who constitute more than one-half of that author's termination interest: That author's surviving widow or widower; and all of that author's surviving children; and, where any of that author's children are dead, all of the surviving children of any such deceased child of that author; however, instead of the information required by this paragraph (vii), the notice may contain both of the following:

> (A) A statement of as much of such information as is currently available to the person or persons signing the notice, with a brief explanation of the reasons why full information is or may be lacking; together with

> (B) A statement that, to the best knowledge and belief of the person or persons signing the notice, the notice has been signed by all persons whose signature is necessary to terminate the grant under section 304 of title 17, U.S.C., or by their duly authorized agents.

(2) A notice of termination of an exclusive or nonexclusive grant of a transfer or license of copyright or of any right under a copyright, executed by the author on or after January 1, 1978, under

section 203 of title 17, U.S.C., must include a clear identification of each of the following:

(i) A statement that the termination is made under section 203;

(ii) The name of each grantee whose rights are being terminated, or the grantee's successor in title, and each address at which service of the notice is being made;

(iii) The date of execution of the grant being terminated and, if the grant covered the right of publication of a work, the date of publication of the work under the grant;

(iv) For each work to which the notice of termination applies, the title of the work and the name of the author or, in the case of a joint work, the authors who executed the grant being terminated; and, if possible and practicable, the original copyright registration number;

(v) A brief statement reasonably identifying the grant to which the notice of termination applies;

(vi) The effective date of termination; and

(vii) In the case of a termination of a grant executed by one or more of the authors of the work where the termination is exercised by the successors of a deceased author, a listing of the names and relationships to that deceased author of all of the following, together with specific indication of the person or persons executing the notice who constitute more than one-half of that author's termination interest: That author's surviving widow or widower; and all of that author's surviving children; and, where any of that author's children are dead, all of the surviving children of any such deceased child of that author; however, instead of the information required by this paragraph (b)(2)(vii), the notice may contain both of the following:

(A) A statement of as much of such information as is currently available to the person or persons signing the notice, with a brief explanation of the reasons why full information is or may be lacking; together with

(B) A statement that, to the best knowledge and belief of the person or persons signing the notice, the notice has been signed by all persons whose signature is necessary to terminate the grant under section 203 of title 17, U.S.C., or by their duly authorized agents.

(3) Clear identification of the information specified by paragraphs (b)(1) and (b)(2) of this section requires a complete and unambiguous statement of facts in the notice itself, without incorporation by reference of information in other documents or records.

(c) *Signature.*

(1) In the case of a termination of a grant under section 304(c) or section 304(d) executed by a person or persons other than the author, the notice shall be signed by all of the surviving person or persons who executed the grant, or by their duly authorized agents.

(2) In the case of a termination of a grant under section 304(c) or section 304(d) executed by one or more of the authors of the work, the notice as to any one author's share shall be signed by that author or by his or her duly authorized agent. If that author is dead, the notice shall be signed by the number and proportion of the owners of that author's termination interest required under section 304(c) or section 304(d), whichever applies, of title 17, U.S.C., or by their duly authorized agents, and shall contain a brief statement of their relationship or relationships to that author.

(3) In the case of a termination of a grant under section 203 executed by one or more of the authors of the work, the notice shall be signed by each author who is terminating the grant or by his or her duly authorized agent. If that author is dead, the notice shall be signed by the number and proportion of the owners of that author's termination interest required under section 203 of title 17, U.S.C., or by their duly authorized agents, and shall contain a brief statement of their relationship or relationships to that author.

(4) Where a signature is by a duly authorized agent, it shall clearly identify the person or persons on whose behalf the agent is acting.

(5) The handwritten signature of each person effecting the termination shall either be accompanied by a statement of the full name and address of that person, typewritten or printed legibly by hand, or shall clearly correspond to such a statement elswhere in the notice.

(d) *Service.*

(1) The notice of termination shall be served upon each grantee whose rights are being terminated, or the grantee's successor in

title, by personal service, or by first-class mail sent to an address which, after a reasonable investigation, is found to be the last known address of the grantee or successor in title.

(2) The service provision of section 203, section 304(c) or section 304(d) of title 17, U.S.C., whichever applies, will be satisfied if, before the notice of termination is served, a reasonable investigation is made by the person or persons executing the notice as to the current ownership of the rights being terminated, and based on such investigation:

(i) If there is no reason to believe that such rights have been transferred by the grantee to a successor in title, the notice is served on the grantee; or

(ii) If there is reason to believe that such rights have been transferred by the grantee to a particular successor in title, the notice is served on such successor in title.

(3) For purposes of paragraph (d)(2) of this section, a *reasonable investigation* includes, but is not limited to, a search of the records in the Copyright Office; in the case of a musical composition with respect to which performing rights are licensed by a performing rights society, a "reasonable investigation" also includes a report from that performing rights society identifying the person or persons claiming current ownership of the rights being terminated.

(4) Compliance with the provisions of paragraphs (d)(2) and (d)(3) of this section will satisfy the service requirements of section 203, section 304(c), or section 304(d) of title 17, U.S.C., whichever applies. However, as long as the statutory requirements have been met, the failure to comply with the regulatory provisions of paragraph (d)(2) or (d)(3) of this section will not affect the validity of the service.

(e) *Harmless errors.*

(1) Harmless errors in a notice that do not materially affect the adequacy of the information required to serve the purposes of section 203, section 304(c), or section 304(d) of title 17, U.S.C., whichever applies, shall not render the notice invalid.

(2) Without prejudice to the general rule provided by paragraph (e)(1) of this section, errors made in giving the date or registration number referred to in paragraph (b)(1)(iii), (b)(2)(iii), or (b)(2)(iv) of this section, or in complying with the provisions of paragraph (b)(1)(vii) or (b)(2)(vii) of this section, or in describing the precise relationships under paragraph (c)(2) or (c)(3) of this

section, shall not affect the validity of the notice if the errors were made in good faith and without any intention to deceive, mislead, or conceal relevant information.

(f) *Recordation.*

(1) A copy of the notice of termination will be recorded in the Copyright Office upon payment of the fee prescribed by paragraph (2) of this paragraph (f) and upon compliance with the following provisions:

(i) The copy submitted for recordation shall be a complete and exact duplicate of the notice of termination as served and shall include the actual signature or signatures, or a reproduction of the actual signature or signatures, appearing on the notice; where separate copies of the same notice were served on more than one grantee or successor in title, only one copy need be submitted for recordation; and

(ii) The copy submitted for recordation shall be accompanied by a statement setting forth the date on which the notice was served and the manner of service, unless such information is contained in the notice. In instances where service is made by first-class mail, the date of service shall be the day the notice of termination was deposited with the United States Postal Service.

(iii) The copy submitted for recordation must be legible per the requirements of §201.4(c)(3).

(2) The fee for recordation of a document is prescribed in §201.3(c).

(3) The date of recordation is the date when all of the elements required for recordation, including the prescribed fee and, if required, the statement referred to in paragraph (f)(1)(ii) of this section, have been received in the Copyright Office. After recordation, the document, including any accompanying statement, is returned to the sender with a certificate of record.

(4) Notwithstanding anything to the contrary in this section, the Copyright Office reserves the right to refuse recordation of a notice of termination if, in the judgment of the Copyright Office, such notice of termination is untimely. If a document is submitted as a notice of termination after the statutory deadline has expired, the Office will offer to record the document as a "document pertaining to copyright" pursuant to §201.4(c)(3), but the Office will not index the document as a notice of termination. Whether a document so

recorded is sufficient in any instance to effect termination as a matter of law shall be determined by a court of competent jurisdiction.

(5) A copy of the notice of termination shall be recorded in the Copyright Office before the effective date of termination, as a condition to its taking effect. However, the fact that the Office has recorded the notice does not mean that it is otherwise sufficient under the law. Recordation of a notice of termination by the Copyright Office is without prejudice to any party claiming that the legal and formal requirements for issuing a valid notice have not been met.

(6) Notices of termination should be submitted to the address specified in §201.1(b)(2).

APPENDIX 32:
PROVISIONS OF THE DIGITAL
MILLENIUM COPYRIGHT ACT

Excerpts from chapter 12 of the 1976 Act:

§ 1201. Circumvention of copyright protection systems

(a) Violations Regarding Circumvention of Technological Measures.—
(1)(A) No person shall circumvent a technological measure that effectively controls access to a work protected under this title. The prohibition contained in the preceding sentence shall take effect at the end of the 2-year period beginning on the date of the enactment of this chapter.

(B) The prohibition contained in subparagraph (A) shall not apply to persons who are users of a copyrighted work which is in a particular class of works, if such persons are, or are likely to be in the succeeding 3-year period, adversely affected by virtue of such prohibition in their ability to make noninfringing uses of that particular class of works under this title, as determined under subparagraph (C).

(C) During the 2-year period described in subparagraph (A), and during each succeeding 3-year period, the Librarian of Congress, upon the recommendation of the Register of Copyrights, who shall consult with the Assistant Secretary for Communications and Information of the Department of Commerce and report and comment on his or her views in making such recommendation, shall make the determination in a rulemaking proceeding for purposes of subparagraph (B) of whether persons who are users of a copyrighted work are, or are likely to be in the succeeding 3-year period, adversely affected by the prohibition under subparagraph (A) in their ability to make noninfringing uses under this title of a particular class of copyrighted works. In conducting such rulemaking, the Librarian shall examine—

(i) the availability for use of copyrighted works;

(ii) the availability for use of works for nonprofit archival, preservation, and educational purposes;

(iii) the impact that the prohibition on the circumvention of technological measures applied to copyrighted works has on criticism, comment, news reporting, teaching, scholarship, or research;

(iv) the effect of circumvention of technological measures on the market for or value of copyrighted works; and

(v) such other factors as the Librarian considers appropriate.

(D) The Librarian shall publish any class of copyrighted works for which the Librarian has determined, pursuant to the rulemaking conducted under subparagraph (C), that noninfringing uses by persons who are users of a copyrighted work are, or are likely to be, adversely affected, and the prohibition contained in subparagraph (A) shall not apply to such users with respect to such class of works for the ensuing 3-year period.

(E) Neither the exception under subparagraph (B) from the applicability of the prohibition contained in subparagraph (A), nor any determination made in a rulemaking conducted under subparagraph (C), may be used as a defense in any action to enforce any provision of this title other than this paragraph.

(2) No person shall manufacture, import, offer to the public, provide, or otherwise traffic in any technology, product, service, device, component, or part thereof, that—

(A) is primarily designed or produced for the purpose of circumventing a technological measure that effectively controls access to a work protected under this title;

(B) has only limited commercially significant purpose or use other than to circumvent a technological measure that effectively controls access to a work protected under this title; or

(C) is marketed by that person or another acting in concert with that person with that person's knowledge for use in circumventing a technological measure that effectively controls access to a work protected under this title.

(3) As used in this subsection—

(A) to "circumvent a technological measure" means to descramble a scrambled work, to decrypt an encrypted work, or otherwise to avoid, bypass, remove, deactivate, or impair a technological measure, without the authority of the copyright owner; and

(B) a technological measure "effectively controls access to a work" if the measure, in the ordinary course of its operation, requires the application of information, or a process or a treatment, with the authority of the copyright owner, to gain access to the work.

(b) ADDITIONAL VIOLATIONS.—(1) No person shall manufacture, import, offer to the public, provide, or otherwise traffic in any technology, product, service, device, component, or part thereof, that—

(A) is primarily designed or produced for the purpose of circumventing protection afforded by a technological measure that effectively protects a right of a copyright owner under this title in a work or a portion thereof;

(B) has only limited commercially significant purpose or use other than to circumvent protection afforded by a technological measure that effectively protects a right of a copyright owner under this title in a work or a portion thereof; or

(C) is marketed by that person or another acting in concert with that person with that person's knowledge for use in circumventing protection afforded by a technological measure that effectively protects a right of a copyright owner under this title in a work or a portion thereof.

(2) As used in this subsection—

(A) to "circumvent protection afforded by a technological measure" means avoiding, bypassing, removing, deactivating, or otherwise impairing a technological measure; and

(B) a technological measure "effectively protects a right of a copyright owner under this title" if the measure, in the ordinary course of its operation, prevents, restricts, or otherwise limits the exercise of a right of a copyright owner under this title.

(c) OTHER RIGHTS, ETC., NOT AFFECTED.—(1) Nothing in this section shall affect rights, remedies, limitations, or defenses to copyright infringement, including fair use, under this title.

(2) Nothing in this section shall enlarge or diminish vicarious or contributory liability for copyright infringement in connection with any technology, product, service, device, component, or part thereof.

(3) Nothing in this section shall require that the design of, or design and selection of parts and components for, a consumer electronics, telecommunications, or computing product provide for a response to any particular technological measure, so long as such part or component, or the product in which such part or component is integrated, does not otherwise fall within the prohibitions of subsection (a)(2) or (b)(1).

(4) Nothing in this section shall enlarge or diminish any rights of free speech or the press for activities using consumer electronics, telecommunications, or computing products.

(d) EXEMPTION FOR NONPROFIT LIBRARIES, ARCHIVES, AND EDUCATIONAL INSTITUTIONS.—(1) A nonprofit library, archives, or educational institution which gains access to a commercially exploited copyrighted work solely in order to make a good faith determination of whether to acquire a copy of that work for the sole purpose of engaging in conduct permitted under this title shall not be in violation of subsection (a)(1)(A). A copy of a work to which access has been gained under this paragraph—

(A) may not be retained longer than necessary to make such good faith determination; and

(B) may not be used for any other purpose.

(2) The exemption made available under paragraph (1) shall only apply with respect to a work when an identical copy of that work is not reasonably available in another form.

(3) A nonprofit library, archives, or educational institution that willfully for the purpose of commercial advantage or financial gain violates paragraph (1)—

(A) shall, for the first offense, be subject to the civil remedies under section 1203; and

(B) shall, for repeated or subsequent offenses, in addition to the civil remedies under section 1203, forfeit the exemption provided under paragraph (1).

(4) This subsection may not be used as a defense to a claim under subsection (a)(2) or (b), nor may this subsection permit a nonprofit library, archives, or educational institution to manufacture,

import, offer to the public, provide, or otherwise traffic in any technology, product, service, component, or part thereof, which circumvents a technological measure.

(5) In order for a library or archives to qualify for the exemption under this subsection, the collections of that library or archives shall be—

(A) open to the public; or

(B) available not only to researchers affiliated with the library or archives or with the institution of which it is a part, but also to other persons doing research in a specialized field.

(e) LAW ENFORCEMENT, INTELLIGENCE, AND OTHER GOVERNMENT ACTIVITIES.—This section does not prohibit any lawfully authorized investigative, protective, information security, or intelligence activity of an officer, agent, or employee of the United States, a State, or a political subdivision of a State, or a person acting pursuant to a contract with the United States, a State, or a political subdivision of a State. For purposes of this subsection, the term "information security" means activities carried out in order to identify and address the vulnerabilities of a government computer, computer system, or computer network.

(f) REVERSE ENGINEERING.—(1) Notwithstanding the provisions of subsection (a)(1)(A), a person who has lawfully obtained the right to use a copy of a computer program may circumvent a technological measure that effectively controls access to a particular portion of that program for the sole purpose of identifying and analyzing those elements of the program that are necessary to achieve interoperability of an independently created computer program with other programs, and that have not previously been readily available to the person engaging in the circumvention, to the extent any such acts of identification and analysis do not constitute infringement under this title.

(2) Notwithstanding the provisions of subsections (a)(2) and (b), a person may develop and employ technological means to circumvent a technological measure, or to circumvent protection afforded by a technological measure, in order to enable the identification and analysis under paragraph (1), or for the purpose of enabling interoperability of an independently created computer program with other programs, if such means are necessary to achieve such interoperability, to the extent that doing so does not constitute infringement under this title.

(3) The information acquired through the acts permitted under paragraph (1), and the means permitted under paragraph (2), may

be made available to others if the person referred to in paragraph (1) or (2), as the case may be, provides such information or means solely for the purpose of enabling interoperability of an independently created computer program with other programs, and to the extent that doing so does not constitute infringement under this title or violate applicable law other than this section.

(4) For purposes of this subsection, the term "interoperability" means the ability of computer programs to exchange information, and of such programs mutually to use the information which has been exchanged.

(g) ENCRYPTION RESEARCH.—

(1) DEFINITIONS.—For purposes of this subsection—

(A) the term "encryption research" means activities necessary to identify and analyze flaws and vulnerabilities of encryption technologies applied to copyrighted works, if these activities are conducted to advance the state of knowledge in the field of encryption technology or to assist in the development of encryption products; and

(B) the term "encryption technology" means the scrambling and descrambling of information using mathematical formulas or algorithms.

(2) PERMISSIBLE ACTS OF ENCRYPTION RESEARCH.—Notwithstanding the provisions of subsection (a)(1)(A), it is not a violation of that subsection for a person to circumvent a technological measure as applied to a copy, phonorecord, performance, or display of a published work in the course of an act of good faith encryption research if—

(A) the person lawfully obtained the encrypted copy, phonorecord, performance, or display of the published work;

(B) such act is necessary to conduct such encryption research;

(C) the person made a good faith effort to obtain authorization before the circumvention; and

(D) such act does not constitute infringement under this title or a violation of applicable law other than this section, including section 1030 of title 18 and those provisions of title 18 amended by the Computer Fraud and Abuse Act of 1986.

(3) FACTORS IN DETERMINING EXEMPTION.—In determining whether a person qualifies for the exemption under paragraph (2), the factors to be considered shall include—

(A) whether the information derived from the encryption research was disseminated, and if so, whether it was disseminated in a manner reasonably calculated to advance the state of knowledge or development of encryption technology, versus whether it was disseminated in a manner that facilitates infringement under this title or a violation of applicable law other than this section, including a violation of privacy or breach of security;

(B) whether the person is engaged in a legitimate course of study, is employed, or is appropriately trained or experienced, in the field of encryption technology; and

(C) whether the person provides the copyright owner of the work to which the technological measure is applied with notice of the findings and documentation of the research, and the time when such notice is provided.

(4) USE OF TECHNOLOGICAL MEANS FOR RESEARCH ACTIVITIES.—Notwithstanding the provisions of subsection (a)(2), it is not a violation of that subsection for a person to—

(A) develop and employ technological means to circumvent a technological measure for the sole purpose of that person performing the acts of good faith encryption research described in paragraph (2); and

(B) provide the technological means to another person with whom he or she is working collaboratively for the purpose of conducting the acts of good faith encryption research described in paragraph (2) or for the purpose of having that other person verify his or her acts of good faith encryption research described in paragraph (2).

(5) REPORT TO CONGRESS.—Not later than 1 year after the date of the enactment of this chapter, the Register of Copyrights and the Assistant Secretary for Communications and Information of the Department of Commerce shall jointly report to the Congress on the effect this subsection has had on—

(A) encryption research and the development of encryption technology;

(B) the adequacy and effectiveness of technological measures designed to protect copyrighted works; and

(C) protection of copyright owners against the unauthorized access to their encrypted copyrighted works.

The report shall include legislative recommendations, if any.

(h) Exceptions Regarding Minors.—In applying subsection (a) to a component or part, the court may consider the necessity for its intended and actual incorporation in a technology, product, service, or device, which—

(1) does not itself violate the provisions of this title; and

(2) has the sole purpose to prevent the access of minors to material on the Internet.

(i) Protection of Personally Identifying Information.—

(1) Circumvention permitted.—Notwithstanding the provisions of subsection (a)(1)(A), it is not a violation of that subsection for a person to circumvent a technological measure that effectively controls access to a work protected under this title, if—

(A) the technological measure, or the work it protects, contains the capability of collecting or disseminating personally identifying information reflecting the online activities of a natural person who seeks to gain access to the work protected;

(B) in the normal course of its operation, the technological measure, or the work it protects, collects or disseminates personally identifying information about the person who seeks to gain access to the work protected, without providing conspicuous notice of such collection or dissemination to such person, and without providing such person with the capability to prevent or restrict such collection or dissemination;

(C) the act of circumvention has the sole effect of identifying and disabling the capability described in subparagraph (A), and has no other effect on the ability of any person to gain access to any work; and

(D) the act of circumvention is carried out solely for the purpose of preventing the collection or dissemination of personally identifying information about a natural person who seeks to gain access to the work protected, and is not in violation of any other law.

(2) Inapplicability to certain technological measures.—

This subsection does not apply to a technological measure, or a work it protects, that does not collect or disseminate personally identifying information and that is disclosed to a user as not having or using such capability.

(j) SECURITY TESTING.—

(1) DEFINITION.—For purposes of this subsection, the term "security testing" means accessing a computer, computer system, or computer network, solely for the purpose of good faith testing, investigating, or correcting, a security flaw or vulnerability, with the authorization of the owner or operator of such computer, computer system, or computer network.

(2) PERMISSIBLE ACTS OF SECURITY TESTING.—Notwithstanding the provisions of subsection (a)(1)(A), it is not a violation of that subsection for a person to engage in an act of security testing, if such act does not constitute infringement under this title or a violation of applicable law other than this section, including section 1030 of title 18 and those provisions of title 18 amended by the Computer Fraud and Abuse Act of 1986.

(3) FACTORS IN DETERMINING EXEMPTION.—In determining whether a person qualifies for the exemption under paragraph (2), the factors to be considered shall include—

(A) whether the information derived from the security testing was used solely to promote the security of the owner or operator of such computer, computer system or computer network, or shared directly with the developer of such computer, computer system, or computer network; and

(B) whether the information derived from the security testing was used or maintained in a manner that does not facilitate infringement under this title or a violation of applicable law other than this section, including a violation of privacy or breach of security.

(4) USE OF TECHNOLOGICAL MEANS FOR SECURITY TESTING.—Notwithstanding the provisions of subsection (a)(2), it is not a violation of that subsection for a person to develop, produce, distribute or employ technological means for the sole purpose of performing the acts of security testing described in subsection (2), provided such technological means does not otherwise violate section (a)(2).

§ 1203. Civil remedies

(a) CIVIL ACTIONS.—Any person injured by a violation of section 1201 or 1202 may bring a civil action in an appropriate United States district court for such violation.

(b) POWERS OF THE COURT.—In an action brought under subsection (a), the court—

(1) may grant temporary and permanent injunctions on such terms as it deems reasonable to prevent or restrain a violation, but in no event shall impose a prior restraint on free speech or the press protected under the 1st amendment to the Constitution;

(2) at any time while an action is pending, may order the impounding, on such terms as it deems reasonable, of any device or product that is in the custody or control of the alleged violator and that the court has reasonable cause to believe was involved in a violation;

(3) may award damages under subsection (c);

(4) in its discretion may allow the recovery of costs by or against any party other than the United States or an officer thereof;

(5) in its discretion may award reasonable attorney's fees to the prevailing party; and

(6) may, as part of a final judgment or decree finding a violation, order the remedial modification or the destruction of any device or product involved in the violation that is in the custody or control of the violator or has been impounded under paragraph (2).

(c) Award of Damages.—

(1) In general.—Except as otherwise provided in this title, a person committing a violation of section 1201 or 1202 is liable for either—

(A) the actual damages and any additional profits of the violator, as provided in paragraph (2), or

(B) statutory damages, as provided in paragraph (3).

(2) Actual damages.—The court shall award to the complaining party the actual damages suffered by the party as a result of the violation, and any profits of the violator that are attributable to the violation and are not taken into account in computing the actual damages, if the complaining party elects such damages at any time before final judgment is entered.

(3) Statutory damages.—(A) At any time before final judgment is entered, a complaining party may elect to recover an award of statutory damages for each violation of section 1201 in the sum of not less than $200 or more than $2,500 per act of circumvention, device, product, component, offer, or performance of service, as the court considers just.

(B) At any time before final judgment is entered, a complaining party may elect to recover an award of statutory damages for each violation of section 1202 in the sum of not less than $2,500 or more than $25,000.

(4) Repeated violations.—In any case in which the injured party sustains the burden of proving, and the court finds, that a person has violated section 1201 or 1202 within three years after a final judgment was entered against the person for another such violation, the court may increase the award of damages up to triple the amount that would otherwise be awarded, as the court considers just.

(5) Innocent violations.—

(A) In general.—The court in its discretion may reduce or remit the total award of damages in any case in which the violator sustains the burden of proving, and the court finds, that the violator was not aware and had no reason to believe that its acts constituted a violation.

(B) Nonprofit library, archives, educational institutions, or public broadcasting entities.—

(i) Definition.—In this subparagraph, the term "public broadcasting entity" has the meaning given such term under section 118(g).

(ii) In general.—In the case of a nonprofit library, archives, educational institution, or public broadcasting entity, the court shall remit damages in any case in which the library, archives, educational institution, or public broadcasting entity sustains the burden of proving, and the court finds, that the library, archives, educational institution, or public broadcasting entity was not aware and had no reason to believe that its acts constituted a violation.

§ 1204. Criminal offenses and penalties

(a) In General.—Any person who violates section 1201 or 1202 willfully and for purposes of commercial advantage or private financial gain—

(1) shall be fined not more than $500,000 or imprisoned for not more than 5 years, or both, for the first offense; and

(2) shall be fined not more than $1,000,000 or imprisoned for not more than 10 years, or both, for any subsequent offense.

(b) Limitation for Nonprofit Library, Archives, Educational Institution, or Public Broadcasting Entity.—Subsection (a) shall not apply to a nonprofit library, archives, educational institution, or public broadcasting entity (as defined under section 118(g)).

(c) STATUTE OF LIMITATIONS.—No criminal proceeding shall be brought under this section unless such proceeding is commenced within five years after the cause of action arose.

Excerpts from section 512 related to safe harbors and takedown provisions:

§ 512. Limitations on liability relating to material online

(a) TRANSITORY DIGITAL NETWORK COMMUNICATIONS.—A service provider shall not be liable for monetary relief, or, except as provided in subsection (j), for injunctive or other equitable relief, for infringement of copyright by reason of the provider's transmitting, routing, or providing connections for, material through a system or network controlled or operated by or for the service provider, or by reason of the intermediate and transient storage of that material in the course of such transmitting, routing, or providing connections, if—

(1) the transmission of the material was initiated by or at the direction of a person other than the service provider;

(2) the transmission, routing, provision of connections, or storage is carried out through an automatic technical process without selection of the material by the service provider;

(3) the service provider does not select the recipients of the material except as an automatic response to the request of another person;

(4) no copy of the material made by the service provider in the course of such intermediate or transient storage is maintained on the system or network in a manner ordinarily accessible to anyone other than anticipated recipients, and no such copy is maintained on the system or network in a manner ordinarily accessible to such anticipated recipients for a longer period than is reasonably necessary for the transmission, routing, or provision of connections; and

(5) the material is transmitted through the system or network without modification of its content.

(b) SYSTEM CACHING.—

(1) LIMITATION ON LIABILITY.—A service provider shall not be liable for monetary relief, or, except as provided in subsection (j), for injunctive or other equitable relief, for infringement of copyright by reason

of the intermediate and temporary storage of material on a system or network controlled or operated by or for the service provider in a case in which—

(A) the material is made available online by a person other than the service provider;

(B) the material is transmitted from the person described in subparagraph (A) through the system or network to a person other than the person described in subparagraph (A) at the direction of that other person; and

(C) the storage is carried out through an automatic technical process for the purpose of making the material available to users of the system or network who, after the material is transmitted as described in subparagraph (B), request access to the material from the person described in subparagraph (A), if the conditions set forth in paragraph (2) are met.

(2) CONDITIONS.—The conditions referred to in paragraph (1) are that—

(A) the material described in paragraph (1) is transmitted to the subsequent users described in paragraph (1)(C) without modification to its content from the manner in which the material was transmitted from the person described in paragraph (1)(A);

(B) the service provider described in paragraph (1) complies with rules concerning the refreshing, reloading, or other updating of the material when specified by the person making the material available online in accordance with a generally accepted industry standard data communications protocol for the system or network through which that person makes the material available, except that this subparagraph applies only if those rules are not used by the person described in paragraph (1)(A) to prevent or unreasonably impair the intermediate storage to which this subsection applies;

(C) the service provider does not interfere with the ability of technology associated with the material to return to the person described in paragraph (1)(A) the information that would have been available to that person if the material had been obtained by the subsequent users described in paragraph (1)(C) directly from that person, except that this subparagraph applies only if that technology -

(i) does not significantly interfere with the performance of the provider's system or network or with the intermediate storage of the material;

(ii) is consistent with generally accepted industry standard communications protocols; and

(iii) does not extract information from the provider's system or network other than the information that would have been available to the person described in paragraph (1)(A) if the subsequent users had gained access to the material directly from that person;

(D) if the person described in paragraph (1)(A) has in effect a condition that a person must meet prior to having access to the material, such as a condition based on payment of a fee or provision of a password or other information, the service provider permits access to the stored material in significant part only to users of its system or network that have met those conditions and only in accordance with those conditions; and

(E) if the person described in paragraph (1)(A) makes that material available online without the authorization of the copyright owner of the material, the service provider responds expeditiously to remove, or disable access to, the material that is claimed to be infringing upon notification of claimed infringement as described in subsection (c)(3), except that this subparagraph applies only if—

(i) the material has previously been removed from the originating site or access to it has been disabled, or a court has ordered that the material be removed from the originating site or that access to the material on the originating site be disabled; and

(ii) the party giving the notification includes in the notification a statement confirming that the material has been removed from the originating site or access to it has been disabled or that a court has ordered that the material be removed from the originating site or that access to the material on the originating site be disabled.

(c) Information Residing on Systems or Networks at Direction of Users.—

(1) In general.—A service provider shall not be liable for monetary relief, or, except as provided in subsection (j), for injunctive or other equitable relief, for infringement of copyright by reason of

the storage at the direction of a user of material that resides on a system or network controlled or operated by or for the service provider, if the service provider -

(A)(i) does not have actual knowledge that the material or an activity using the material on the system or network is infringing;

(ii) in the absence of such actual knowledge, is not aware of facts or circumstances from which infringing activity is apparent; or

(iii) upon obtaining such knowledge or awareness, acts expeditiously to remove, or disable access to, the material;

(B) does not receive a financial benefit directly attributable to the infringing activity, in a case in which the service provider has the right and ability to control such activity; and

(C) upon notification of claimed infringement as described in paragraph (3), responds expeditiously to remove, or disable access to, the material that is claimed to be infringing or to be the subject of infringing activity.

(2) DESIGNATED AGENT.—The limitations on liability established in this subsection apply to a service provider only if the service provider has designated an agent to receive notifications of claimed infringement described in paragraph (3), by making available through its service, including on its website in a location accessible to the public, and by providing to the Copyright Office, substantially the following information:

(A) the name, address, phone number, and electronic mail address of the agent.

(B) other contact information which the Register of Copyrights may deem appropriate.

The Register of Copyrights shall maintain a current directory of agents available to the public for inspection, including through the Internet, in both electronic and hard copy formats, and may require payment of a fee by service providers to cover the costs of maintaining the directory.

(3) ELEMENTS OF NOTIFICATION.—

(A) To be effective under this subsection, a notification of claimed infringement must be a written communication provided to the designated agent of a service provider that includes substantially the following:

(i) A physical or electronic signature of a person authorized to act on behalf of the owner of an exclusive right that is allegedly infringed.

(ii) Identification of the copyrighted work claimed to have been infringed, or, if multiple copyrighted works at a single online site are covered by a single notification, a representative list of such works at that site.

(iii) Identification of the material that is claimed to be infringing or to be the subject of infringing activity and that is to be removed or access to which is to be disabled, and information reasonably sufficient to permit the service provider to locate the material.

(iv) Information reasonably sufficient to permit the service provider to contact the complaining party, such as an address, telephone number, and, if available, an electronic mail address at which the complaining party may be contacted.

(v) A statement that the complaining party has a good faith belief that use of the material in the manner complained of is not authorized by the copyright owner, its agent, or the law.

(vi) A statement that the information in the notification is accurate, and under penalty of perjury, that the complaining party is authorized to act on behalf of the owner of an exclusive right that is allegedly infringed.

(B)(i) Subject to clause (ii), a notification from a copyright owner or from a person authorized to act on behalf of the copyright owner that fails to comply substantially with the provisions of subparagraph (A) shall not be considered under paragraph (1)(A) in determining whether a service provider has actual knowledge or is aware of facts or circumstances from which infringing activity is apparent.

(ii) In a case in which the notification that is provided to the service provider's designated agent fails to comply substantially with all the provisions of subparagraph (A) but substantially complies with clauses (ii), (iii), and (iv) of subparagraph (A), clause (i) of this subparagraph applies only if the service provider promptly attempts to contact the person making the notification or takes other reasonable steps to assist in the receipt of notification that substantially complies with all the provisions of subparagraph (A).

(d) INFORMATION LOCATION TOOLS.—A service provider shall not be liable for monetary relief, or, except as provided in subsection (j), for injunctive or other equitable relief, for infringement of copyright by reason of the provider referring or linking users to an online location containing infringing material or infringing activity, by using information location tools, including a directory, index, reference, pointer, or hypertext link, if the service provider—

(1)(A) does not have actual knowledge that the material or activity is infringing;

(B) in the absence of such actual knowledge, is not aware of facts or circumstances from which infringing activity is apparent; or

(C) upon obtaining such knowledge or awareness, acts expeditiously to remove, or disable access to, the material;

(2) does not receive a financial benefit directly attributable to the infringing activity, in a case in which the service provider has the right and ability to control such activity; and

(3) upon notification of claimed infringement as described in subsection (c)(3), responds expeditiously to remove, or disable access to, the material that is claimed to be infringing or to be the subject of infringing activity, except that, for purposes of this paragraph, the information described in subsection (c)(3)(A)(iii) shall be identification of the reference or link, to material or activity claimed to be infringing, that is to be removed or access to which is to be disabled, and information reasonably sufficient to permit the service provider to locate that reference or link.

APPENDIX 33:
DESIGNATION OF AGENT FORMS

**Interim Designation of Agent to Receive Notification
of Claimed Infringement**

Full Legal Name of Service Provider: _____

**Alternative Name(s) of Service Provider (including all names under which the service
provider is doing business):** _____
_____
_____

Address of Service Provider: _____

**Name of Agent Designated to Receive
Notification of Claimed Infringement:** _____

Full Address of Designated Agent to which Notification Should be Sent (a P.O. Box
or similar designation is not acceptable except where it is the only address that can be used in the geographic
location):
_____
_____

Telephone Number of Designated Agent: _____

Facsimile Number of Designated Agent: _____

Email Address of Designated Agent: _____

Signature of Officer or Representative of the Designating Service Provider:
_____ Date: _____

Typed or Printed Name and Title: _____
_____

**Note: This Interim Designation Must be Accompanied by a $80 Filing Fee
Made Payable to the Register of Copyrights.**

Amended Interim Designation of Agent to Receive Notification of Claimed Infringement

Full Legal Name of Service Provider: _____

_____

Alternative Name(s) of Service Provider (including all names under which the service provider is doing business): _____

_____

_____

Address of Service Provider: _____

Name of Agent Designated to Receive
Notification of Claimed Infringement: _____

Full Address of Designated Agent to which Notification Should be Sent (a P.O. Box or similar designation is not acceptable except where it is the only address that can be used in the geographic location):

_____

_____

Telephone Number of Designated Agent: _____

Facsimile Number of Designated Agent: _____

Email Address of Designated Agent: _____

Identify the Interim Designation to be Amended, by Service Provider Name and Filing Date, so that it may be Readily Located in the Directory Maintained by the Copyright Office: _____

Signature of Officer or Representative of the Designating Service Provider:
_____ Date: _____

Typed or Printed Name and Title: _____

_____

Note: This Amended Interim Designation Must be Accompanied by a $80 Filing Fee Made Payable to the Register of Copyrights.

GLOSSARY

Audiovisual work—a sequence of images (such as motion pictures) commonly shown via projectors, viewers, or other equipment.

Author—the creator of a work in most instances. See also **Work made for hire**.

Automated database—an organized collection of facts, data, or other information for computer use. In some cases, a frequently updated online work may qualify as an automated database.

Berne Convention—the oldest international treaty related to copyright, joined by the United States as a result of passage of the Berne Convention Implementation Act of 1988.

Berne Convention Implementation Act of 1988—legislation rendering notice of copyright optional to comport with practice in other countries, providing a means, among other things, for the United States to join the Berne Convention.

Best edition—the highest quality of a work to be deposited with the Copyright Office.

Buenos Aires Convention—copyright treaty among Latin American nations and others, largely superseded by the Berne Convention. A popular notice arising from the convention and still used today is the warning "All Rights Reserved."

Bundle of rights—common term used to describe the copyright holder's exclusive rights under section 106 of the Copyright Act of 1976.

CFR—Code of Federal Regulations, title 37 of which includes the rules of practice governing copyrights.

Claimant—for purposes of copyright registration, the author or other person or entity claiming copyright ownership.

Compulsory license—a license applicable to non-dramatic musical recordings, requiring that the copyright owner grant a license to a third party desiring to record and release a version of the musical work.

Computer program—a set of instructions used in a computer to bring about a certain result.

Contributory infringement—liability resulting from a knowing participation in an infringing activity.

Copy—the material object in which a work, other than a phonorecord, is fixed and from which it can be communicated.

Copyright Act of 1909—a predecessor to the Copyright Act of 1976 and under which many subsisting copyrights were governed.

Copyright Act of 1976—the law of copyright set forth in title 17 of the United States Code, effective as of January 1, 1978.

Copyright infringement—an illegal copying of a copyrighted work as evidenced by the substantial similarity of another work based on a reasonable possibility of access to the copyrighted work.

Copyright Office—an independent department of the Library of Congress that administers a national copyright system and is solely responsible for accepting applications and issuing registrations.

Derivative work—a work derived, or adapted from, another work.

Digital Millennium Copyright Act—also referred to as DMCA, a landmark addition to the 1976 Copyright Act addressing the effects of Internet commerce on copyrights, among other things.

Digital Performance Right in Sound Recordings Act—created an exclusive right of limited public performance regarding digital audio transmissions to the copyright owners of sound recordings.

eCO—the Copyright Office's online filing system for copyright applications and other documents related to the application and registration of a copyright.

Fair use—a common defense in copyright infringement litigation involving section 107 of the 1976 Copyright Act.

First sale doctrine—a principle set forth in section 109(a) of the Copyright Act of 1976, giving the owner of a physical object embodying a copyright the right to dispose of it following the first sale or transfer by the copyright owner.

Fixed—refers to a work's capability to be perceived or reproduced in more than a transitory way in a tangible medium of expression.

Form CA—a form used to make supplemental registration of an existing work to correct or amplify information given in the basic registration.

Form CO—a bar-coded application for copyright registration available from the eCO portal that can be downloaded and mailed to the Copyright Office. See also **eCO**.

Form PA—a form for the registration of copyright in performing arts.

Form RE—a form used to renew an existing copyright.

Form SR—a form for the registration of copyright in sound recordings.

Form TX—a form for the registration of copyright in literary works.

Form VA—a form for the registration of copyright in visual arts.

Interim designation of agent—a form suggested by the Copyright Office for an online service provider to designate an agent authorized to receive notices from copyright owners claiming infringing material is being stored by the provider.

Library of Congress—the national library of the United States, serving as the research arm of Congress.

Literary works—works (excluding audiovisual works) displayed in words, numbers or other symbols, including books, periodicals, catalogs, compilations, and computer programs.

Mandatory deposit—also referred to as the mandatory deposit rule, a requirement that all works published in the United States be deposited with the Library of Congress to enrich the national archives.

Office action—a written communication from an examiner at the Copyright Office concerning a procedural or substantive issue related to an application for registration.

Online work—a work accessible over the Internet, such as via file transfer protocol.

Orphan work—a work for which a copyright owner cannot be located despite a diligent search.

Perform—to perform a work means to render it some way, visually or aurally. See also **Public performance**.

Performing arts—for purposes of copyright registration, generally includes musical works, choreography, pantomime and audiovisual works.

Performing rights society—an entity such as ASCAP, BMI, and SESAC (for songwriters and publishers) and Sound Exchange (for sound recording copyright owners) engaged in the administration of licenses and collection and distribution of revenues for eligible public performances of copyrighted works.

Phonorecord—the material object in which sounds are fixed and from which the sounds can be communicated. A phonorecord is not a sound recording. See **Sound recording**.

Pre-registration—a pre-release registration process for works in danger of being infringed prior to distribution, available through eCO using Form PRE.

Public display—a showing of a work in public or among the public at large.

Public domain—also referred to as *p.d.*, means a work that is not protected by copyright typically because the copyright term has expired, or the work is not subject to copyright protection, or the work has lost copyright protection.

Public performance—an action taking place in public or among the public at large. See also **Perform**.

Publication—the distribution of copies or phonorecords to the public by an act of transfer of title or by rental, lease, or lending.

Register of Copyrights—the head of the U.S. Copyright Office.

Safe harbor—popular term for the limitation on liability of an online service provider for certain digital transmissions under DMCA.

Service provider—as it relates to section 512 of DMCA, means the provider of online services or network access or any operator of facilities for those purposes.

Sonny Bono Copyright Term Extension Act—also referred to as CTEA, an act of 1998 amending the 1976 Copyright Act to add a term of 20 years to subsisting copyrights.

Sound recording—a work arising from the fixation of sounds. A sound recording is not a phonorecord. See **Phonorecord**.

Statutory damages—a range of money damages set forth in section 504 of the 1976 Copyright Act.

Supplemental registration—a registration made by an author, claimant, or exclusive licensee of a work to correct or amplify information given in an underlying registration.

Takedown notice—a copyright holder's notice to an agent of an online service provider seeking removal of infringing material being stored by the provider at the request of one of its users.

TRIPS—acronym for the Agreement on Trade-Related Aspects of Intellectual Property, a treaty designed to bring global harmonization to copyright issues in international trade.

VARA–acronym for the Visual Artists Rights Act of 1990.

Vicarious liability—a form of liability for copyright infringement arising from supervision of infringing conduct and an economic interest in its outcome.

Visual arts—for purposes of copyright registration, generally includes paintings, drawings, sculptures, fine and applied art, technical drawings, architectural plans, and other works of artistic craftsmanship. For purposes of the Visual Artists Rights Act, a work of visual art is specifically defined; see **Work of Visual Art.**

WIPO—acronym for the World Intellectual Property Organization.

WIPO Copyright Treaty (WCT)—an international treaty for the specific protection of copyright in transmissions over the Internet.

WIPO Performances and Phonograms Treaty (WPPT)—an international treaty for the specific protection of copyright in digitized works of musicians and the recording industry.

Work made for hire—also referred to as a work for hire, or WFH, is a work made at the instance of another or one that falls within nine statutory classes of works made for hire under section 101 of the 1976 Copyright Act. The commissioner of a WFH is the author for copyright purposes.

Work of visual art—paintings, drawings, prints, sculpture, and photographs in numbered limited editions.

BIBLIOGRAPHY AND RECOMMENDED READING

The United States Copyright Office, http://www.copyright.gov

The World Intellectual Property Organization, http://www.wipo.int

The World Trade Organization, http://www.wto.org

The European Union Online, http://europa.eu

Nimmer, David, *Nimmer on Copyright* (11 volume treatise) (Matthew Bender, 1978–)

Printed in the USA/Agawam, MA
May 3, 2010

541088.005